Endorsements for
The Workforce Scorecard

"Building on *The HR Scorecard,* the authors have achieved the next level in strategic metrics—assessing the role of the workforce in making strategy happen. Their focus is not HR metrics, but workforce metrics in the context of business strategy. Rather than asking, 'How do we measure HR?' they ask, 'What do we need to measure about the workforce to deliver strategy?' At J&J we asked and attempted to answer the same question, one of the reasons we believe *CEO* magazine named J&J a pacesetter in leadership development."

> —*Michael J. Carey, former Vice President, Human Resources,*
> *and Corporate Officer, Johnson & Johnson*

"HR leaders can no longer earn 'strategic partner status' by designing and delivering state-of-the-art programs. Our efforts should result in measurable actions that build the desired culture and develop tomorrow's strategic workforce, while achieving today's customer and ownership objectives. *The Workforce Scorecard* provides practical, results-oriented tools that challenge traditional thinking about human capital management."

> —*Mark Gilstrap, Senior Vice President and Chief People Officer,*
> *American Century Investments*

"I am left unsatisfied by most 'business books,' because while I sometimes violently agree with their arguments, they often ultimately fail to tell me exactly how to implement what they espouse. Two shining exceptions are Ram Charan and Larry Bossidy's masterpiece, *Execution: The Art of Getting Things Done,* and now Huselid, Becker, and Beatty's *The Workforce Scorecard,* which I believe is destined to become a classic, as well.

"'Score-keeping' and 'differentiation' were at the core of Jack Welch's leadership beliefs at GE, from the famous 'A, B, and C player' designations to the revolutionary 'four types' of leaders. Differentiation was rigidly practiced throughout the company, and compensation programs, such as bonuses and stock options, were managed—some might say micromanaged—by Jack, so that they never turned into what he derided as 'another dental plan.'

"Welch scored and differentiated by instinct and by his ability to read workforce performance data as if it were a balance sheet. This book tells you exactly how to do both."

—*Bill Lane was Manager, Executive Communications,
at GE and Jack Welch's speechwriter for twenty years*

"Business strategy and HR strategy are becoming commonplace terms. Workforce strategy is the missing link. This book should be read by line managers and HR managers who together must execute business strategy. It contends that most firms have two strategies (business and HR), but they need a third—a workforce strategy—to successfully execute the firm's strategy."

—*Paul Newton-Syms, Head of HR, Pharma Division,
F. Hoffmann-La Roche Ltd.*

"What gets inspected gets respected. This book addresses the last frontier of competitive advantage: workforce accountability. Organizations don't change, only people do. Holding people accountable for delivering business strategy is imperative for a company's success. This book provides metrics for holding management accountable to close the performance gap . . . a major contribution."

—*Daniel Phelan, Senior Vice President, Human Resources,
GlaxoSmithKline*

"The book makes a powerful statement on how HR can contribute to a firm's competitive advantage—differentiate! It provides a clear rationale why differentiation on the outside must be supported by differentiation from the inside, and provides numerous concrete examples and tools for how this can be done. With this book, the field of HR strategy takes on a new significance."

—*Vladimir Pucik, Professor of International Human Resources
and Strategy at IMD (International Institute for Management
Development), Lausanne*

"If you want to build a high-performance and accountable organization, this book is the place to start. Huselid, Becker, and Beatty present a compelling case for a workforce strategy as *the* key requisite for strategy execution that leads to high performance in any company."

—*Linda Sorrell, Senior Vice President, Talent Strategy, Diageo*

The Workforce Scorecard

The
WORKFORCE
Scorecard

Managing Human Capital
to Execute Strategy

MARK A. HUSELID

BRIAN E. BECKER

RICHARD W. BEATTY

HARVARD BUSINESS SCHOOL PRESS
BOSTON, MASSSACHUSETTS

Library of Congress Cataloging-in-Publication Data
Huselid, Mark A., 1961-
    The workforce scorecard : managing human capital to execute strategy /
  Mark A. Huselid, Brian E. Becker, Richard W. Beatty.
      p. cm.
    ISBN 1-59139-245-4 (hardcover : alk. paper)
  1. Performance standards. 2. Personnel management. I. Becker, Brian E.
  II. Beatty, Richard W. III. Title.
    HF5549.5.P35H87 2005
    658.3'01—dc22

                           2004023599

To Rebecca, Rachel, and Robert

To Henry and Lucy

To Nancy, Sarah, Gracie, and Jake

Contents

Foreword

How do we know? These four words form a simple question. But this question sometimes makes all the difference between desire and delivery, boast and backup, and rhetoric and reality. Too often business initiatives begin with great fanfare and promises, but fizzle and implode without having their intended impact. Often these disappointments come because there is no clear answer to the question, How do we know?

Answering this simple question requires a more complex analysis. Huselid, Becker, and Beatty's thoughtful work *The Workforce Scorecard: Managing Human Capital to Execute Strategy* provides the frameworks and tools to make this analysis possible.

First, the analysis begins by being clear about what we need to know. If we don't know what we need to know, we will never know it. Too often we measure what is easy rather than what is right. In HR, we count the number of days a manager spends in training, the cost of the training, or the satisfaction score from the training because these are relatively easy measures to track, not because they measure what matters most. *The Workforce Scorecard* offers specific and concrete guidance on what matters most with measures of the impact of HR investments.

It is not the activity that counts, but the impact of the activity on organizational outcomes. It is not the number of days of training, but the impact of the training on the individual and the organization. *The Workforce Scorecard* points out that workforce investments should help execute strategy through the culture, mind-set, capabilities, and behaviors created. Executing strategy is not a new concept, but one that has recently been shown to be central to strategic success.[1] It may be easier to craft a strategy than to deliver one; to make promises and claims than to accomplish them. *The Workforce Scorecard* points out that strategy execution is the expected outcome of workforce investments. In addition, successful strategy execution indicates that an HR practice has created workforce success that outlives the HR practice. Workforce success (workforce culture, mind-set, competencies, and behaviors) can become the identity and personality of an organization; they become the link between strategy, HR investments, and the workforce.[2] Investments in training should lead to employees with more strategic clarity—faster in getting things done, more innovative, collaborating more, more talented, able to learn, and with clear accountability for business results. These are the deliverables of HR: workforce success, the firm's capabilities, and the intangibles investors pay for.

The Workforce Scorecard lays out in a cogent and clear manner how to turn strategy into strategy execution by focusing on elements of workforce success that can then be tracked and monitored. Huselid, Becker, and Beatty dissect HR's success into four categories:

- *Workforce success.* These are defined as HR's deliverables, culture, mind-set, competencies, and behaviors that drive operational, customer, and financial strategies, the unique identity of the organization.

- *Workforce mind-set and culture.* Organizations create norms and expectations that the workforce needs to understand. The culture shapes employee behavior, and the behavior shapes the culture. Culture can also be measured and assessed in terms of its impact on the firm's strategic success.

- *Workforce competencies.* Competencies, what each employee is able to do, represent the knowledge, skill, and ability of employees. Competencies for each employee can also be measured and monitored.

- *Workforce behaviors.* Leaders and employees must behave in ways consistent with the strategy for it to be executed. These behaviors can be defined and measured to ensure that leaders and employees do what strategy suggests needs to be done.

With these elements in place, the question of what measures to adopt can be answered. As each of these categories is aligned with business strategy, a perspective is formed about how people can execute the firm's strategy. The scorecard that derives from this perspective becomes a dashboard for gauging a firm's strategic success. Further, with such a dashboard in place, the authors suggest that HR systems, practices, and professional competencies can be defined and tracked. As activities and measures in each of the categories are created, metrics and execution occur. Managers can now be held accountable not only for their words and actions relative to people but also by the workforce success, the mind-set, capabilities, and behaviors they create. A true Balanced Scorecard for guiding and assessing managers will have strategic, financial, operational, and *workforce* measures. No longer will the end justify the means and corporate malfeasance be a by-product of business success. Managers who do not create workforce success can be identified, targeted, and developed, or moved out.

Second, knowing a lot about the wrong thing not only is unhelpful, but can be misleading. *The Workforce Scorecard* points out that not all customers, strategies, or products are equal, which we easily grasp when we seek just the right gift for a loved one, work to define the right strategy for our business, or build intimacy with our target customers. But *The Workforce Scorecard* points out that not all employees or workforces are equal either, which is sometimes harder to face. Investing resources in employees who for whatever reason do not fit, do not add value, or do not deliver is like pouring water into a sieve and wondering why it does not stay. The harsh reality of managing people is that differentiation must occur, with some employees more equal than others. In our work, we have suggested that managers focus on equity, not equality.[3] Equity means that those who give more will get more; equality means that all will be treated equally. Equity only works when managers know what people should give and are confident that they have measures that track their ability to give. *The Workforce Scorecard* lays out frameworks and tools for making equity a reality.

Differentiating both work and employees into "A," "B," and "C" categories requires clear standards and credible measures to build confidence about who belongs in what group. However, making such differentiations will give shape to and link employee behavior and performance, and help employees know what is expected and how they are doing so they can improve. And just as important, line managers can now be accountable for the quantity and quality of the talent they develop. Managers who develop "A" players will be contributing as much or more value to the firm as when they contribute profits. Finding and encouraging managers who supply "A" players will help the firm meet strategic goals over time. These managers should be identified, encouraged, and rewarded. With the measures from *The Workforce Scorecard,* they can be.

For the workforce to have impact, it must have high-quality workforce initiatives multiplied by high levels of acceptance.[4] If the quality of an idea is high and the acceptance of the idea low, it will not have the impact desired. Good measures, even of the right things, not accepted or used will have little total impact. *The Workforce Scorecard* offers specific guidelines for ensuring that good measures are accepted and used. Use of measures means that leaders assume accountability and responsibility for measures of workforce success. Such metrics must be woven into the human resource practices of performance management and consistently communicated.

Integrating workforce success measures into HR practices institutionalizes the measures and ensures that they will endure. HR practices are like the infrastructure of a house: the plumbing, heating, electrical, lighting, and spacing. None of these systems is much noticed unless it is broken. But they often shape the quality of living within a house. Likewise, when workforce success measures are woven into HR practices of work design, staffing, development, performance management, rewards, and communication, the infrastructure is in place to sustain success.

I envision HR leaders paying rapt attention to the metrics advocated in *The Workforce Scorecard.* By so doing, they will see beyond their HR role to the responsibilities of line management. Then, as HR professionals adapt and adjust their HR practices, they will ensure that they deliver real value to the firm. Value is an ultimate outcome of investments in HR.[5] For HR practices, functions, and professionals to deliver value, they must measure and monitor their performance and its impact on the firm's strategic success. *The Workforce Scorecard* provides templates and processes for doing this. HR leaders who want to align their HR investments will savor this book.

So, can we know how we will know? The answer is yes. *The Workforce Scorecard* takes us through the logic of what we should know, how to differentiate what we know into what and who matters most, and how to institutionalize what we know into enduring firm processes. Hopefully, the book will be not only read, but also used by line managers who want to turn practices into strategic results and by HR professionals who want to quantify the value they create.

Dave Ulrich

Preface

This book has been incubating among the three of us for several years. Prior to and since the publication of *The HR Scorecard,* we have had the good fortune be able to work with HR practitioners and other business leaders on the design and implementation of workforce measurement systems across a broad spectrum of firms and industries.[1] While we have seen many of these firms make significant progress in defining and implementing metrics that describe the contribution of the *HR function* to firm success, we have seen much less progress in developing metrics that show the contribution of the *workforce* to firm success.

Why is this the case? Most firms develop explicit strategies to optimize resources such as capital, technology, brands, and so on. But, in our experience, few firms are as articulate in their strategies for their most costly resource: the workforce. We believe that a clear and compelling workforce strategy is a key element of effective business strategy execution, and the nature of workforce strategy should be highly differentiated and customized for each firm. As our research has demonstrated, effective workforce management strategies and practices can have a powerful effect on business outcomes, including productivity, profitability, and shareholder value. Unfortunately, what we most often observe are firms with highly differentiated product strategies but generic or undifferentiated workforce strategies. Drawing on many years of research, consulting, and executive education on this topic, in this book we offer an approach to developing a workforce strategy as well as a *Workforce Scorecard* designed to assess the success of that strategy.

Our aim is to bridge the gap between the development of a business strategy and its implementation through people. Thus, our book is not focused on developing business strategy per se, but on how strategy can be successfully executed. Successful strategy execution, we believe, is predicated on a paradox. In many respects, because of globalization and highly efficient distribution mechanisms for information about how firms compete in the marketplace (e.g., the Internet and the popular press), firms are becoming more similar. Information about Wal-Mart's logistics systems is easy to find, and many firms are using this information to improve their own processes. Yet competitive advantage is created by being different in ways that are meaningful to customers. For that reason, it is important for firms to embrace the difference, to go against the grain, to value differentiation externally and internally. Such a perspective has distinct implications for internal workforce practices, and part of our message is to urge firms to tread cautiously in applying the "best practice" of others to their own circumstances.

In fact, our approach to workforce management and measurement will challenge the status quo in many firms. We have organized our thoughts on this process around the three primary challenges firms face in designing and implementing workforce measurement systems. The first of these, the *perspective challenge,* represents the need for managers to undergo a shift in their thinking about the workforce; from a cost to be minimized to *the* primary source of growth and value creation, especially in the key or "A" jobs throughout the business. The workforce is the single most important renewable source of competitive advantage as firms compete more and more through knowledge capital and "brainware." Those firms that can attract, focus, and motivate the appropriate workforce capabilities and behaviors stand the best chance of not only surviving but thriving in competitive environments. As a consequence, delivering such a workforce is the joint responsibility of the HR function and line management, and this requires a new form of partnership between them.

An important step on the path to effective strategy execution is developing an understanding of the workforce culture and mind-set (i.e., strategic focus) needed to help make the business strategy a reality. Does the workforce understand the firm's business strategy? Do they understand that the business strategy ought to shape their own behavior? Do they understand how their unique capabilities contribute to delivering the *difference* (i.e., the competitive advantage) of the firm? Do HR function and line managers understand that they are (or ought to be) accountable for delivering a workforce that meets the needs of customers and consumers, thereby creating the wealth that sustains the firm? Firms that win in the long run consistently answer all of these questions in the affirmative.

Firms also face a second hurdle—the *metrics challenge*—which requires developing the metrics to assess and help guide the execution of their workforce strategy. For line as well as HR managers, we argue that strategy and metrics should focus on the workforce and not just the HR function. The relevant metrics ought to emphasize the workforce culture, mind-set, competencies, and behaviors that can demonstrate how the workforce executes strategy and impacts the firm's bottom line. Who should be accountable for and measured on the Workforce Scorecard? Those charged with delivering a workforce that can successfully execute the business's strategy: both the HR function and line managers. Since line managers are jointly accountable for the workforce with HR, both ought to be assessed on the same workforce metrics. And in fact, since line managers have a greater day-to-day impact on the workforce than the HR function, we explore this joint accountability by looking at the role of each in influencing the workforce and impacting the Workforce Scorecard.

Finally, firms face an *execution challenge* in designing and implementing a workforce measurement system, and addressing this challenge involves helping managers to use workforce data to improve the quality of decision making in their own businesses. In this process, the CEO, the executive team, line managers, and the HR function each have important roles to play. Our book explores what each of these groups must do and provides examples of metrics for assessing each in discharging its workforce accountabilities.

In summary, we believe that we have articulated both a new way of thinking and a new way of acting to help firms execute their strategies through the workforce. We hope that we have offered important insights for executives, M.B.A.'s, senior HR practitioners, academics, and postgraduate students in HR management and strategy. We have tried to impart practical advice based on our experience with business leaders coping with an increasingly complex, fast-changing business environment, as well as drawing on our research and the research of others.

Much work remains to be done in explicating the concepts of workforce strategy and the Workforce Scorecard. We invite the reader to join us in this process and welcome comments, criticisms, and insights into measuring a firm's "soft" assets and demonstrating their impact on a firm's strategic success.

ACKNOWLEDGMENTS

We are indebted to the inspiration, challenge, and stimulation of our academic colleagues and friends. These include Jim Beatty, John Boudreau, Wayne Brockbank, Paula Caligiuri, Wayne Cascio, Ram Charan, Jac Fitz-enz, Susan Jackson, Steve Kerr, Dave Lepak, Baruch Lev, C. K. Prahalad, Craig Eric Schneier, Randall Schuler, and Charlie Tharp. We are also especially grateful to our friend and colleague Dave Ulrich for contributing the foreword to this book.

We have also gained valuable insights from many firms and appreciate their cooperation in permitting us to publish various materials used throughout this book. Special thanks are due to Garrett Walker and Randy MacDonald at IBM, Tony Rucci and Amy White at Cardinal Health, and Laura Arnold and Elizabeth New at Dell Computer Corporation for their willingness to share their remarkable examples of workforce transformation and measurement. We also wish to thank them as well as Christy Contardi Stone, Katie Outcalt, and Rich Berens at Root Learning for providing the initial draft describing the Cardinal Health and Dell cases that appear in chapter 8.

Many other senior practitioners have been very gracious with their time and expertise in providing feedback, insight, and case examples, including Katy Barclay and John Bridge (General Motors Corporation); Michael Bazigos, Robert Calami, Rich Calo, Larry Hatter, Ted Hoff, Sam Ladah, Tania Le, Donna Riley, and Tom Roden (IBM); Mike Carey (Johnson & Johnson); Joan Crockett and Karleen Zuzich (Allstate Insurance Company); John Donnelly and Renee Hooper (Citigroup); Peter Fasolo and Dominic Fernandes (Bristol-Myers Squibb Company); Ann Gust and Bill Thomkins (Gap, Inc.); Mark Gilstrap (American Century Investments); Steve Grossman (Hoffman-

LaRoche); Bruce Hill (JC Penney); Christian Iversen (LEGO Company); Steve Kerr, Stephen Lindia, and Jake Weiss (The Goldman Sachs Group); Susan Ketterman and Sam Perkins (Aventis); Pam Kimmet and Karen Stanton (Lucent Technologies); Rich Lang (Sun Microsystems, Inc.); Rene Lewin and John Markowski (Wyeth); David Long, Dennis O'Neill, and Chuck Kelly (Perdue Pharma); Hallstein Moerk and Ari Lehtoranta (Nokia); Kathy Oates and Dan Phelan (GlaxoSmithKline); Libby Sartain, (Yahoo, Inc.); Craig Eric Schneier (Biogen Idec); and Sharon Taylor and Bob Crawford (Prudential Financial). Other firms providing important information and access include AstraZeneca, ConAgra, Diageo, Elkay Manufacturing, General Electric Company, Key Bank, and Pfizer, Inc.

Other individuals who have provided insight, examples, and moral support are Tom Banner, Jim Cassady, Lavonne Cate, Diane Coble, Patrick Dailey, Glenn DeBiasi, Jeff Ewing, Lou Forbringer, John Gumpert, Mike Hastings, Paul Johnson, Anand Kumar, Renee Lewandowski, Jeanette Maggio, Kathryn McKee, Linda Merritt, Ralph Meyer, Allan Mitchell, Pete Perez, Jim Porter, John Roddy, Bill Schiemann, and Bernie Wetzel.

Our institutions have also contributed greatly to our work. Mark and Dick would like to thank Dean Barbara Lee at Rutgers-SMLR for providing resources and an enabling culture that continues to encourage our work. Charlie Tharp (who coined the term "disproportionate investments") and Erika Harden provided detailed and very helpful feedback on earlier drafts of the text. Mark would also like to thank his Master's and HR Leadership Executive students in the Workforce Measurement courses at Rutgers-SMLR, who continue to challenge his thinking. We also thank Helaine Randerson, who edited several chapters and deftly juggled multiple revisions of text and graphics. In addition, HRCI and the SHRM Foundation continue to make important contributions to the profession, while supporting the role of workforce measurement in business success.

All three of us would like to thank Melinda Merino and the rest of the editorial team at HBS Press. We particularly appreciate Melinda's wealth of knowledge and gentle persuasion in helping keep us on track. She has been a constant source of encouragement, advice, feedback, and support for our ideas—the best of the best, an editor without peer.

Finally, and most important, we are grateful to our families for their patience and fortitude in the face of the many encroachments on family time that writing a book entails. With appreciation, we dedicate this book to them.

Mark A. Huselid
Brian E. Becker
Richard W. Beatty
January 2005

1

THE THREE CHALLENGES OF
WORKFORCE MEASUREMENT
AND MANAGEMENT

THIS BOOK is based on a very simple premise. Of all the factors affecting firm performance that CEOs and senior managers can directly influence, *workforce success*—or the extent to which a firm can generate a workforce with the culture, mindset, competencies, and strategic behaviors needed to execute its strategy—is the both the most important and most underperforming asset in most businesses. The majority of managers know that despite proclamations that "people are our most important asset," their organizations struggle to make this slogan a reality. In an economic environment marked by hypercompetition and international expansion, where intangible assets are increasingly the basis of competitive advantage and growth opportunities, anything less than optimal workforce success is not just a missed opportunity; in many cases it is a direct threat to the very survival of the firm.

Throughout this book we describe the dimensions of this strategic opportunity and provide clear and unambiguous recommendations for management action. Our approach contains several key elements that some readers might find surprising. First, many managers believe that workforce performance and success is a "people" issue that is largely the responsibility of HR professionals. Instead, our analyses demonstrate, and our recommendations reflect, that workforce success depends on a *shared* responsibility between line managers and HR professionals. As a result, because we define workforce success primarily in terms of successfully achieving business goals rather than HR goals, this book is written for senior line managers as well as HR professionals.

Second, strategic success for the organization requires that both line managers and HR professionals adopt a *different perspective* on managing workforce success. Traditional perspectives on workforce success, which often focus on standardization and cost reduction, have little to do with the demands of successful strategy execution. Indeed, conventional thinking about workforce management may actually work at cross purposes with the firm's larger strategic goals. A central theme in this new perspective is the need for greater *differentiation*—of employees, of jobs, and of the way that firms manage workforce performance—based on the firm's competitive strategy and operational goals. Successful strategies and competitive advantage nearly always rely on some form of differentiation in the marketplace; yet traditional workforce strategies are remarkably undifferentiated both within and across firms. That is, we often see firms with very different organizational strategies adopting highly similar workforce strategies. And as a result, one of the firm's most important strategic assets, the workforce, becomes one of its most underperforming assets. For firms that compete on the basis of their strategic workforce capabilities, this can spell disaster. All too often these same firms end up downsizing the workforce in the hope of improving financial performance.

Finally, we show that this problem is magnified by workforce measurement systems that focus managers on the nonstrategic at the expense of the strategic. This is especially true for commonly used measures of "HR performance" that rely on industry benchmarking studies, which simultaneously focus managers on simple transactions that can be compared across firms and encourage those same managers to reduce strategic investments in the workforce to the lowest common denominator.[1] To provide a solution to these problems, we show how to develop a *Workforce Scorecard* that is focused directly on the strategic measures of workforce success required by senior executives.

THE WORKFORCE SCORECARD

We chose the term *Workforce Scorecard* for a very specific reason. First, while the term *Scorecard* has become increasingly prominent in performance measurement parlance, we use it in the tradition of the Kaplan and Norton Balanced Scorecard framework.[2] Like Kaplan and Norton, we are focusing on a specific kind of business performance: strategy execution. This measurement process is based on a system of leading and lagging indicators of firm success and recognizes the potential importance of both tangible and intangible assets. This is an important distinction because while "scorecards" have become quite common in the management literature, quite often they focus on the operational at the expense of the strategic. Our focus on strategy execution means that the Workforce Scorecard framework is as much about *managing* workforce success as it is about *measuring* workforce success. Indeed, it reflects a different perspective on how to manage workforce success in the same way that it reflects a different approach to measuring that success.

Secondly, we use the term *Workforce* to highlight our focus on the strategic performance of employees rather than the contribution of the HR function to business success. The Workforce Scorecard is intended to provide the CEO and executive team members with timely and strategically relevant measures of workforce performance and the leading indicators of that performance. Figure 1-1 shows how the Workforce Scorecard fits in the larger picture of strategic performance measurement.

We believe that firms need a business strategy, a workforce strategy, and a strategy for the HR function. These strategies are operationalized in the Balanced Scorecard, the Workforce Scorecard, and the HR Scorecard, respectively. As a result, the Workforce Scorecard is a crucial lever in the strategy execution process. The key dimensions of that process include operational and customer success, which in turn help create financial success. Workforce success is often the key performance driver, directly or indirectly, for these other elements of strategic success. Unfortunately, senior executives usually have very limited tools for measuring workforce success or holding line managers accountable for workforce performance. In fact, many of the same firms that have highly detailed information about their inventories and

FIGURE 1-1

Managing Human Capital to Execute Strategy

HR Scorecard ◄──────── Workforce Scorecard ──────► Balanced Scorecard

Financial Success
What specific financial commitments must be met?

Operational Success
What specific internal operational processes must be optimized?

Customer Success
What specific customer desires and expectations must be satisfied?

Workforce Success
Has the workforce accomplished the key strategic objectives for the business?

Workforce Competencies
Does the workforce, especially in the key or "A" positions, have the skills it needs to execute our strategy?

Leadership and Workforce Behaviors
Are the leadership team and workforce consistently behaving in a way that will lead to achieving our strategic objectives?

Workforce Mind-set and Culture
Does the workforce understand our strategy and embrace it, and do we have the culture we need to support strategy execution?

HR Practices
• Work design
• Staffing
• Development
• Performance management
• Rewards
• Communication

HR Systems
• Align
• Integrate
• Differentiate

HR Workforce Competencies
• Strategic partner
• Change agent
• Employee advocate
• Administrative expert

physical plant have almost no information about their own work-forces—presumably one of the key drivers of their strategic success. The Workforce Scorecard is designed to solve that problem.

At the other end of the value creation process is the HR function and the role played by HR professionals. These elements were the focus of our earlier book, *The HR Scorecard,* which highlighted the strategic role HR professionals and the HR management system play in the successful implementation of an organization's strategy.[3] Many of the same themes first introduced in *The HR Scorecard* are carried forward in this book. However, our experiences with HR professionals and line managers in designing and implementing HR Scorecards in a wide variety of firms and industries have made it clear to us that firm success requires an increased emphasis on the roles of the workforce and line managers in the strategy execution process. While HR profes-sionals and the HR management system lay the foundation for build-ing the workforce into a strategic asset, the responsibility for work-force success increasingly falls to line managers, who perform most of the workforce management activities in any firm. Senior executives and line managers need to understand how and why an effective work-force strategy is crucial for the successful execution of their own stra-tegic responsibilities, and there needs to be an appropriate measure-ment system to guide those decisions. *The Workforce Scorecard* fulfills both of these needs.

The arrows at the top of figure 1-1 move from the Balanced Score-card toward the HR Scorecard. This reflects a development process that begins with a clear statement of the firm's strategy and opera-tional goals, as well as a strategy map showing the significant causal linkages in the value creation process. The next step in the process is the development of a workforce strategy and scorecard, and the pro-cess concludes with the development of an HR function strategy and scorecard. However, the value creation process runs in the opposite direction. In other words, the foundation of workforce success begins with the HR function, which is responsible for the design and im-plementation of HR management systems (e.g., recruiting, selection, rewards) that can have a long-term impact on the performance of the firm. As an example of HR's "long shadow," many members of the senior management team in most large corporations have a long tenure in the business, often twenty years or more. Because most HR practices are relatively stable in large companies, this may mean that the current senior management team may have been recruited, selected, and acculturated with an HR management system that was designed forty years ago! Recognizing this responsibility, an organization where HR professionals are solely focused on operational efficiency and administrative compliance can never fully capture the strategic value of its workforce.

The Workforce Scorecard is a key value creating link between the Balanced Scorecard and the HR Scorecard. Does that mean that a firm needs to have all three scorecards in place to benefit from these ideas? We don't believe that it does. Figure 1-1 represents an optimal approach to managing and measuring workforce success. For many firms the most important step is simply a change in direction that begins to move them toward the framework described in figure 1-1, which includes a consideration of HR function, workforce, and business-level outcomes. Adopting a new perspective on workforce success is the foundation of this more formal measurement system, and much progress can be made with the right perspective and a much less formal and comprehensive measurement system. Organizations will often begin by identifying one business outcome (workforce success) and then examining the relationship between that business outcome and a single leading indicator in the Workforce Scorecard (like leadership competencies). This builds a shared enthusiasm for these ideas among line managers and HR professionals and builds the foundation for further elaboration of the framework.

The Workforce Scorecard (figure 1-1) has four dimensions: workforce success, leadership and workforce behaviors, workforce competencies, and workforce mind-set and culture.

Workforce Success

This is the most important dimension on the Workforce Scorecard because it captures "bottom-line" workforce performance. These are the measures that reflect how well the workforce has contributed to the execution of the firm's strategy. They are performance measures with two key characteristics. First, they capture business objectives of greatest concern to line managers. These are the strategic performance drivers that contribute to successful execution of the firm's strategy, and they are the direct responsibility of one or more line managers. Second, these business outcomes are significantly (though not entirely) driven by workforce performance. Take the example of a retail firm that relies on its workforce to create a world-class buying experience for customers, and in turn increase customer satisfaction, sales growth, and financial performance. Workforce success in that firm would be measured by improved buying experience, a key strategic performance driver. Figure 1-2 highlights the perspective that workforce success focuses on the *impact* of your workforce strategy on business success. While business success will ultimately mean financial success, the more immediate impact of interest is on the strategy drivers that execute strategy, which are unique in each firm. Firm-level workforce success would be represented by the cumulative performance of all strategy drivers that are highly workforce intensive.

FIGURE 1-2

Workforce Success: The Impact of Workforce Strategy on Business Strategy Execution

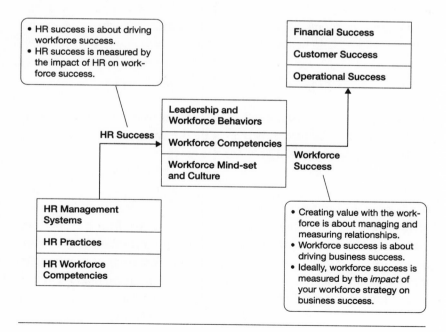

The Workforce Scorecard is designed to reflect a balance of leading and lagging indicators. Workforce success is the principal lagging indicator for measuring workforce performance. But workforce success is not exclusively an attribute of the workforce. In the earlier retail example, it is very likely that customer buying experience is influenced by more than just the workforce. So why do we recommend a business outcome as a measure of workforce success? Because line managers and HR professionals in too many firms treat workforce issues and business issues as separate, and largely independent of one another, when successful strategy execution requires a much more integrative approach. Our measure of workforce success is designed to move the focus of line managers down the value chain and the focus of HR professionals up the value chain so that both accept a shared responsibility for driving strategy through workforce performance.

The other elements of the Workforce Scorecard are leading indicators of workforce success, and elements of workforce management that are strongly influenced by line managers. Compared with workforce success, these measures focus much more on attributes of just the workforce itself. These measures are important because they capture the drivers of workforce success and point to where line managers need to invest in order to maximize workforce success. They also describe those elements of workforce management for which line managers should be held accountable.

Leadership and Workforce Behaviors

As we move back down the value chain from workforce success, the most immediate lagging indicator is the behaviors of the leadership team and the workforce. These are the actual performance behaviors required by the workforce and managers if the firm is going to enjoy workforce success. In the earlier retail example, specific workforce behaviors that influenced the customer buying experience had been identified, e.g., the proportion of frontline staff that were rated as knowledgeable, timely, helpful, and courteous. To capture the key elements of these behaviors, the appropriate points of measurement include both the frontline staff that interact with the customer and the leadership behaviors of line managers responsible for those staff.

Workforce Competencies

Workforce competencies are the knowledge, skills, abilities, and personality characteristics that serve as the foundation for workforce behaviors. We consider competencies a foundational driver of workforce success because they only represent *potential* workforce performance. However, knowing that 90 percent of a workforce segment is "skill ready" or rates as satisfactory or above on a particular competency is just the beginning, not the end, of measuring workforce success. The key aspect of these competencies is not just their level on some generic competency, like teamwork, thought to be important for all workers. It is also important that competency requirements be differentiated by strategic performance drivers. That is, different parts of the business will require different competency profiles, and the entire workforce measurement and management systems need to be sensitive to these distinctions. Line managers responsible for a particular strategy driver (new product cycle time in R&D) need a workforce with the specific competencies required to maximize workforce success for that specific strategy driver (knowledge sharing and cross-functional teaming skills in R&D scientists).

Workforce Mind-set and Culture

Workforce behaviors are in part driven by the larger culture of the organization, particularly around the role of performance. Culture reflects a firm's fundamental assumptions and values about what behaviors are appropriate throughout the organization, and it is critical that a firm have a workforce culture that is both high performance and strategic. This follows from our emphasis on differentiation. Workforce culture needs to reinforce the notion that some jobs (what we will define in chapter 2 as "A" jobs) and positions are more strategic, and more valuable, because of their direct influence on key strategy drivers. Differentiation also means differentiation by workforce performance. A high-performance culture requires that high performers and low performer be identified and both levels of performance be managed effectively. Line managers play the key role in developing and maintaining a high-performance culture.

THE STRATEGIC ROLE OF WORKFORCE MANAGEMENT

We believe that many firms approach workforce management from the wrong perspective, and their financial performance suffers as a result. Instead of focusing on how to execute strategy through the performance of the workforce, in many firms the first priority is cost control, and the focus often begins with the HR *function*. This trend is reflected in common HR metrics such as cost per hire, days to fill an open position, or HR expense per employee.[4] There are several problems with such a focus. First, over the last decade or so, many firms have dramatically increased their HR function "efficiency" through the use of outsourcing, continuous improvement, Six Sigma efforts, and Internet-based or eHR transaction processing. Simply put, in many firms the low-hanging fruit in the domain of HR functional efficiency has largely been collected. Second, since HR operating expenses typically account for just 1 percent of total operating expenses, the potential impact improvement in HR function efficiency on shareholder wealth is limited. Table 1-1 illustrates this point.

Compared with the budget of the HR function, the dollars involved in a firm's total workforce expenditures are considerably greater, typically accounting for 60 to 70 percent of a firm's operating costs. And while a movement from focusing on HR function costs to total workforce costs is certainly an improvement, the emphasis on costs is still too limited. The strategic value of a workforce is a func-

TABLE 1-1

HR Function and Payroll Expense as a Proportion of Total Operating Expenses

HR function expense as a proportion of total operating expenses	0.90 %
Total payroll expense as a proportion of total operating expenses	67.30 %

Source: BNA/SHRM Survey and analyses of 740 publicly held firms.

tion of both benefits and costs. The point of this book is not that work-force costs should be ignored. It's that the benefits, particularly the strategic benefits, of improved workforce performance represent a significant opportunity for improvement in most firms. Simply think of what it would mean to your firm's overall performance if you could improve the extent to which the workforce had the skills, motivation, and focus necessary to execute your strategy by 25 percent or more. In our experience most managers would equate this with winning the lottery, and many consider it about as likely. The problem is not that line managers, or, for that matter, HR professionals, don't have an appreciation that workforce success *could* translate into firm success. The problem is how to get "from here to there" and how to measure that progress. This book is intended to provide a road map for that journey.

In short, we are not arguing for greater HR function budgets or that HR function transactional costs should be ignored. Nor are we arguing that firms should "throw money off the balcony" toward the workforce. What we are saying is that for many years workforce mea-surement has primarily consisted of measuring activities associated with HR transactions and of improving the performance of those ele-ments. As a result, managers quite often focus on the wrong measures, and even if those measures could be driven to zero, it would have little or no influence on the successful execution of the firm's strategy. For example, firms that measure cost per hire and hold HR leaders ac-countable for this outcome will no doubt see lower cost per hire. But the unintended consequence of this action is usually that the quality of hire falls as well, significantly increasing total labor costs over the long run.

In contrast, consider the strategic role of workforce management at IBM. IBM's top management team meets twice per month, and Randy MacDonald, Senior Vice President for Human Resources (SVPHR), gets a significant proportion of that time. More importantly, the focus of his presentation is not a report of HR activities and costs. It focuses instead on key business issues and workforce initiatives designed to respond to those problems. At IBM there is a clear line of sight be-tween workforce initiatives and key strategic challenges, and meas-urement plays a crucial role in managing these linkages.

Human Capital Analysis

Despite the slogans about employees being their most important asset, many managers haven't systematically analyzed how and where human capital drives successful strategy execution in their organizations. Yet this is an important threshold question for both line managers and HR professionals. Can you distinguish employee skills and motivation that play a role in the successful operation of the business, perhaps even have an essential operational role, from those that are genuinely a source of competitive advantage? Does this include all employees and all jobs? Most jobs? Only the highest-paid positions?

The term *human capital* implies an asset with a flow of benefits that are greater than the costs of the asset. From the perspective of the firm, human capital will have the greatest value when those benefits take the form of workforce behaviors that execute strategy. Employee skills (and subsequent performance behaviors) have a market value based on what they are worth to other companies, but *their strategic value is based on the role they play in your firm's strategy execution.* Evaluating that role first requires an understanding of the performance drivers required to execute your strategy, and secondly, the human capital *intensity* of those performance drivers.

We will discuss how to differentiate strategic human capital later in the book, but here is a simple example to illustrate this point. Let's return to our example of a retail organization where the strategic goal is to increase sales growth. This firm's prior analyses have led them to conclude that sales growth is driven in part by increasing customer satisfaction, which is in part driven by an improved buying experience. What is the strategic role of human capital, if any, in this firm? Analyses might reveal that customer service, and in particular the behaviors (courteous, timely, and knowledgeable) of frontline sales staff, has a key influence on that buying experience. The analysis could then go on to identify a series of jobs and specific workforce behaviors required to influence the buying experience (a strategy driver). In this firm, we would conclude that at least one strategy driver in this firm—increased customer satisfaction—is human capital intensive.

In other retail firms, the strategic analysis might result in completely different judgments about the value of human capital. For example, consider the differences in the customer buying experience at Nordstrom's and a discount warehouse such as Costco or the Price Club. At the Price Club, the analysis might reveal that customers simply want a clean store, with ready access to advertised items. In these organizations, the frontline staff have virtually no influence on the buying experience (other than to make sure that the shelves are stocked and that change is made correctly), and their strategic significance is very limited. Or perhaps in this retail segment the buying experience itself is not important to customers, who are much more price driven. The point is that customer satisfaction is a key driver of success in each store, but that the competencies and behaviors of the workforce that drive customer satisfaction differ dramatically in each firm. As a result, the workforce metrics, and the way in which human capital is managed, will need to differ as well.

THE THREE CHALLENGES OF SUCCESSFUL WORKFORCE MEASUREMENT AND MANAGEMENT

The increasing importance of intangible assets, and the associated value of organizational capital, describe a competitive landscape where some portion of a company's workforce has the potential to become a significant strategic asset. Again, we emphasize the word *potential* since among all intangibles, we consider the potential upside opportunity associated with the workforce to be the most significant. Why is this? Because the new role of the workforce and the management systems required to realize its strategic potential represent such a dramatic break with past practice. It requires CEOs and senior managers to think differently about what it means to manage the workforce effectively and, most importantly, how they measure workforce performance at the level of the organization. What questions should the CEO be asking to understand the strategic contribution of the workforce? What measures of performance should he or she be demanding of senior executives and HR professionals? This divide between the traditional approach to workforce management and the unrealized potential of the new approach is represented by three challenges. We call these the *perspective challenge,* the *metrics challenge,* and the *execution challenge* (see Table 1-2). Understanding and overcoming these challenges is the focus of this book.

TABLE 1-2

The Three Challenges of Successful Workforce Measurement and Management

The Perspective Challenge	Do all our managers understand how workforce capabilities and behaviors drive strategy execution?
The Metrics Challenge	Have we identified (and collected) the right measures of workforce success, leadership, and workforce behaviors; workforce competencies; and workforce culture and mind-set?
The Execution Challenge	Do our managers have the access, capability, and motivation to use these data to communicate strategic intent and monitor our progress toward strategy execution?

The Perspective Challenge— An Emphasis on Differentiation

The first challenge of successful workforce measurement and management is to adopt a new perspective on how the workforce can be a source of strategic value to your organization. This new perspective is particularly important for the CEO and senior executives for two reasons. First, line managers, and their direct reports, play a critical role in workforce performance. The senior executive team defines the strategic priorities for the firm and establishes expectations for what's important and what's valued. We aren't calling here for a new round of slogans about the "value of people" or "happy workers are productive workers." Instead, the senior executive management team needs to be asking a different set of questions that focus on workforce performance and its role in the successful execution of the firm's strategy. This requires a much different perspective than one that simply focuses on labor costs. The fundamental distinction is between developing an understanding of the *contribution* of the workforce versus a focus on understanding the *cost* of the workforce. This same perspective must also drive the relationship between line management and HR professionals. It means that HR professionals and line managers will have shared responsibility for workforce success.

This shared responsibility is the second reason that a new perspective for the senior executive team is so important. The HR function has a strategic role to play through its influence on workforce success. The nature of that role and how to measure HR's performance at a strategic level is described in our book *The HR Scorecard*.[5] But the HR function cannot fulfill its strategic role without the cooperation, and indeed the enthusiastic and informed partnership, of senior executives and line management throughout the firm. To the extent that HR has strategic value, such value derives from its role in the strategy execution process. That value can only be realized when the CEO and the senior executive team validate and support that value creation process by the nature of the demands they place on HR professionals. Demands on HR by the top management team to justify its existence based on administrative efficiency will focus HR professionals on those nonstrategic activities. Just because costs are the easiest workforce characteristics to measure does not mean they should be the only measure of workforce performance. Demands that HR demonstrate its contribution to successful strategy execution will instead encourage the kind of focus on workforce performance that creates sustained competitive advantage for the firm. Workforce issues that are legitimately overhead will obviously be managed as efficiently as possible. This new perspective, however, recognizes the wisdom of identifying and separating the strategic, value-creating elements of workforce management from the operational.

This new perspective also requires a new approach to workforce management. The common theme in this new approach is differentiation, which is the focus of chapter 2. The emphasis on workforce differentiation breaks the traditional disconnect between the logic of differentiation at the level of corporate strategy and the tendency toward homogeneity or commonality in workforce management. The foundation of any successful strategy is some basis of differentiation between the value proposition your firm offers customers and the value proposition your competitors offer. Short-term improvements in cost structures based on across-the-board cuts and unfocused layoffs might provide some short-term financial relief, but cannot hope to represent a source of sustained competitive advantage.[6] If for no other reason, it is too easy for competitors to copy. In short, we are advocating a movement away from "plain vanilla" workforce strategies—where all employees are offered the same "deal"—to workforce strategies that are carefully tailored to your business requirements.

Michael Porter makes an important point about strategy, one that is sometimes overlooked. He reminds us that market positioning (e.g., making the decision to become focused on a particular market segment, or deciding to become the low cost producer of goods and services in the industry) is not strategy. Strategy is the result of a unique set of organizational activities that bring the value proposition to the customer. For example, at Wal-Mart an integrated combination of distribution, logistics, just-in-time order fulfillment, considerable focus on stocking stores differentially to meet customer needs in each area, and very close relationships with suppliers helped to create an organizational resource that is difficult for competitors to imitate. The key point is that strategy is as much inward looking as outward looking, and it capitalizes on firm-specific and unique approaches to creating the firm's value proposition. As we discuss in chapter 2, the implication for workforce management is that some positions and some employees are more central to strategy execution than others. This means not only that these positions and employees must be identified, but also that the workforce systems that support, develop, and motivate them are likely to be different from those same systems for nonstrategic workers. In short, not all workforce contribution is created equally, some types of workforce performance are more valuable than others, and this different opportunity for value creation has to be managed differently as well.

To summarize, just as differentiation is at the core of a successful business strategy, it is also at the core of successful workforce management. HR and workforce management systems must be differentiated by jobs and people who make a strategic contribution, and workforce performance must differentiated between "A" performers and "C" performers. If a portion of a firm's workforce genuinely has the potential to become a strategic asset, there is only one measure of that asset value—workforce success. Strategically relevant workforce success needs to be diagnosed and exploited like any other strategic opportunity or any other asset.

The Metrics Challenge—
The Relationship to Strategy Execution

One of the hallmarks of the changing economic environment over the last twenty years has been the increasingly important role of intangible assets as drivers of firm performance. While the general story is no doubt familiar to most readers, it is important to highlight where these developments bear directly on how workforce success contributes to firm success and why a different approach to managing workforce success is required. The acknowledged leader on the subject of valuing intangible assets, Professor Baruch Lev of NYU defines intangible assets as "a claim to future benefits that does not have a physical or financial (a stock or bond) embodiment."[7] Some of the more obvious forms of intangible assets are brands, employee skills (human capital), and patents. More subtle forms of intangible assets, yet arguably the most valuable, are management processes and systems that enable a specific firm to uniquely implement its strategy. Perhaps the best known of the latter would be Wal-Mart's distribution systems, which enable them to execute a distribution and marketing strategy that includes far-flung locations in largely rural areas.

The big picture tells an even more compelling story. Most of us are familiar with the nearly meteoric rise in the market value of firms relative to the book value of their tangible assets. Over the last twenty years the ratio of market price to book value for the S&P 500 has increased nearly sixfold.[8] Even after adjusting this increase for a potential increase in the market value of tangible assets, there is strong evidence that a firm's intangible assets are increasing in both absolute and relative value.

Organizational Capital

Intangible assets take many forms. They can range from the value of a brand (BMW) or customer relationships (the Four Seasons hotels) to the unique skills (R&D scientists in recombinant DNA at Merck) of a firm's workforce. Perhaps the most obvious form of intangible assets is the knowledge capital created through research and development and codified as a patent. Brand-name pharmaceuticals are a typical example (e.g., Lipitor, Prilosec, and Viagra). These intangible assets not only have value because of the value they represent to consumers, but, as importantly, because a firm is able to capture a share of that value since competitors are legally prohibited from copying and selling the same product. The legal protection of a patent is an exception to the norm, however. Most intangible assets are not legally protected from imitation by competitors, yet they can only have sustained value as long as they possess some form of inimitability. As it turns out, for most of these assets it is the very fact that they are intangible that makes them more difficult to imitate.

One such intangible that has gotten increasing attention in recent years is what can be called organizational capital. Organizational capital is reflected in the systems and technologies that transform knowledge and physical capital into a firm's value proposition. What is important about this definition is not that some firms have it and some firms don't, but how much value it represents. Organizations have always combined knowledge and physical capital to satisfy customers. What is important now is that the ways they go about it are increasingly unique and firm-specific, and therefore begin to represent a source of competitive advantage. This is why these systems have an asset value and can legitimately be considered a form of capital. Experienced managers have recognized this trend for years in their own firms. In 1998 the CFO of Coca-Cola described the firm's entire market value as largely a function of the firm's brand and management systems.[9] More recently, Clayton Christensen and Michael Raynor have argued that a firm's organizational capital is one element in the solution to the "innovator's dilemma."[10] Finally, Baruch Lev and his associates conclude that organizational capital accounted for 43 percent of sales growth in the firms in their study from 1989 to 2000.[11] This means that nearly half of the sources of new wealth creation through sales growth were not measured by conventional financial accounting metrics.

Baruch Lev has observed that "optimal use of intangibles . . . requires quality and timely information about these assets."[12] No doubt the same observation could be made for tangible assets as well. The difference is that quality and timeliness is much easier to achieve in measures of tangible assets. Tracking inventory and capital equipment purchases is straightforward. The problem is that we tend to look for the same tangible characteristics even in intangible assets. How many do we have? How much did they cost? How much do we spend to maintain them? But those tangible attributes do not really capture the value creation dimension of intangible assets, particularly the workforce. To the extent that intangibles such as the capability to effectively management workforce performance create value indirectly through more successful strategy execution, measures of the tangible attributes fail to capture the "long shadow" of the workforce systems. And as the saying goes, if you can't measure it, you can't manage it, and you certainly can't improve it.

But does measuring the "long shadow" of intangibles really matter? Research by Christopher Ittner and David Larker demonstrates that it does.[13] They surveyed 157 firms and found that just 23 percent of the firms carefully diagnosed and evaluated the causal linkages between their nonfinancial performance measures and strategic outcomes. Those firms, however, had nearly a 3 percent higher return on assets and more than a 5 percent higher return on equity. The message from the Ittner and Larker study is the same as reflected by Kaplan and Norton's emphasis on strategy maps in the Balanced Scorecard measures, and the same as we highlighted in *The HR Scorecard*. Measurement matters, but not just any measures. It's essential to measure the drivers in the strategic execution process. This doesn't mean that every firm has to establish a quantitative relationship among these strategy drivers, but at a minimum they need to think in terms of those relationships when selecting what to measure. To quote Ittner and Larker: "More successful companies . . . [chose] their performance measures on the basis of causal models, also called value driver maps, which lay out plausible cause-and-effect relationships that may exist between the chosen drivers of strategic success and outcomes."[14]

Developing workforce measures with strategic value is particularly difficult. When managers think of strategic value or contributions to firm performance, their natural inclination is to look for a bottom-line equivalent like the ratio of labor costs to sales, or the training costs as a percentage of all overhead. But these kinds of measures barely scratch the surface of the asset value of the workforce. Even gross productivity measures like revenue per employee tell you nothing about how the workforce is making a contribution. Indeed, the typical workforce measures simply ignore the fact that the workforce is a leading indicator of firm performance. Measures of workforce performance or contribution to firm performance must reflect that indirect line of sight between the workforce and the firm's financial success. This is the focus of the Workforce Scorecard introduced earlier in this chapter.

In chapter 5 we lay out some basic rules to guide the reader in developing these measures. The simplest rule to remember is that *measures are answers to questions*. In some firms, the CEO is asking the right questions, but not always of the right person. Often questions about workforce performance issues are directed first to senior HR professionals. HR is asked to demonstrate its contribution to firm success, but conventional measures of activities and efficiency don't answer the CEO's question. On the other hand, the CEO should also be asking senior executives these same questions because workforce performance, as we argued earlier, should be a shared responsibility of both line managers and HR professionals. In other firms it's a chicken-and-egg problem for HR professionals. Senior executives with a traditional perspective on workforce performance expect to see performance measures that focus on efficiency and cost control, and this gives HR professionals little opportunity to provide more appropriate measures.

The right workforce performance measures follow directly from the strategic role of the workforce in executing your firm's strategy. Unfortunately, the most common source of workforce performance measures takes you in the opposite direction. While many organizations have been devoting increasing attention to people measures, the most common source of those measures is benchmarking surveys. Reliance on benchmarking for these measures is misguided for a number of reasons that will be discussed later in the book. At this point we simply return to the core points developed in this introduction. Workforce performance, and its measurement, should emphasize differentiation and strategic impact. Benchmarking, by its very nature, focuses on commonality, implicitly taking the industry standard as the appropriate measure of success. In addition, it necessarily focuses on operational measures, unless we are to believe that all firms surveyed pursued the same strategy. In short, benchmarking treats workforce performance like a commodity rather than a differentiated source of competitive advantage. Too often, benchmarking simply provides the right answer to the wrong question.

In our view the role of organizational capital, and ultimately its source of value, is very clear. The appropriate forms of organizational capital provide firms with a comparative advantage in the execution of their strategy. As a specific form of intangible asset, the ability to execute strategy (as opposed to the content of that strategy) is an increasingly important source of wealth creation. Larry Bossidy and Ram Charan describe it as "the discipline of getting things done" and the most important challenge facing a CEO.[15] Our own research supports this point. Several years ago we surveyed more than five hundred companies, and one of the questions we asked respondents was to rate the appropriateness of their strategy and how well it had been implemented. We then linked these responses to the firm's current and subsequent levels of financial performance.[16] The results were compelling. It wasn't so much that firms rated their execution all that much higher or lower than the appropriateness of the strategic choice. What was remarkable was how differences on those two answers were related to firm financial performance. The impact of successful strategy execution was six times as large as the effect of choosing the appropriate strategy. We don't conclude from these analyses that choosing the appropriate strategy is irrelevant to the financial success of your organization. Great execution of a poorly crafted strategy will not work, either. Instead, we think this is simply a reflection of differences in firm capabilities. As we've said before, choosing the right strategy is not the real challenge. The challenge is executing that strategy![17]

Implications for Managing Workforce Success

The evidence, both direct and indirect, increasingly points to the prominent role of intangible assets, and in particular organizational capital, as a basis for firm financial success. While these findings point to a major change in the strategic landscape facing a CEO, the senior executive team doesn't manage organizational capital directly.

Workforce management is the most important element of organizational capital because it constitutes the strategic lever with the greatest opportunity for improved performance. What is the potential magnitude of the financial benefits from developing the appropriate systems and processes for workforce management? We've seen that, by one measure, organizational capital explained 43 percent of sales growth in a recent study. Is it unreasonable to assume that having a workforce with the right skills, with the right people in the right jobs, focused on executing the firm's strategy might contribute to half of that impact on sales growth? We don't think so.

For more than a decade, two of the authors, Brian Becker and Mark Huselid, have studied how one aspect of these workforce systems relates to firm performance. Their research focused on what might be considered the most basic element of a firm's system of workforce management, the HR management system. There are many aspects of an HR management system that might have strategic value, and line managers often press HR professionals to demonstrate the efficiency of those systems. How does cost per hire or per trainee compare to industry benchmarks? What is the recruiting cycle time?

Instead of a predominant focus on efficiency, our perspective was different. It was our hypothesis that if the workforce was legitimately a source of competitive advantage, and not just a cost to be minimized, then what was really important about the HR management system was whether it was configured in a way to optimize workforce performance. Since we could not measure workforce performance directly, we surveyed more than three thousand firms over ten years about the characteristics of their HR management systems and subsequently followed their financial performance.

An HR management system typically includes several dimensions, such as recruiting and hiring, development, and rewards and compensation. While some of the questions in our research focused on "how much," such as how many hours of training they provide, many also explored each firm's degree of performance emphasis. For example, respondents were asked about how commonly they used professional validated selection methods or the relationship between employee performance and reward allocations. Our hypothesis was that firms that made greater use of these "high-performance" systems would be more successful. This hypothesis has been supported in each of our surveys and different versions of these questions. Our core finding is that meaningful improvements (about a one-third increase over the average firm) in high-performance HR management systems will produce a 10 to 15 percent increase in shareholder value.[18]

A high-performance HR management system is one of the foundations of strategic organizational capabilities. We have also examined how those capabilities influence firm success. Drawing on the work of our colleague, Dave Ulrich, in a survey of 240 firms in 1999, we asked respondents to rate their firms on various dimensions of their strategic capabilities.[19] These included:

- Speed to market

- Talent acquisition

- Capacity to learn

- Innovation

- Shared mind-set

- Accountability

Figure 1-3 illustrates how firms that rated higher on these strategic capabilities also rated significantly higher on several dimensions of firm performance. First, they systematically invest in more R&D. We take this as at least indirect evidence of greater innovation on the part of these firms. Second, we find that firms rated higher on strategic capabilities are more productive (as measured by cash flow per employee) and more profitable (as measured by return on assets). Finally, we find that the ratio of market to book value is nearly four times larger in firms rated high on these strategic capabilities. Moreover,

FIGURE 1-3

Strategic Capabilities Drive Firm Success

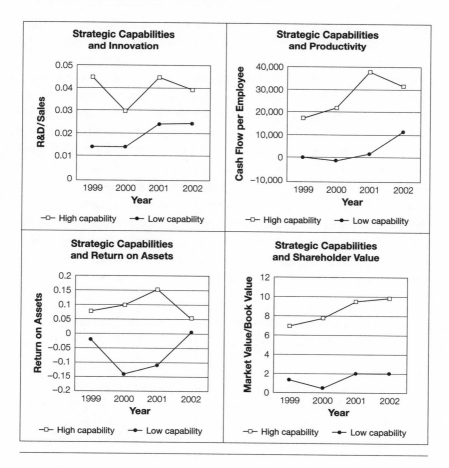

these differences were sustained over the next four years, in a very difficult economic environment.

In short, firms with higher levels of strategic capabilities perform consistently and significantly better than do low-capability firms. Whether measured on innovation, productivity, profitability, or shareholder value, highly capable firms outperform low-capability firms by a significant margin. Based on more than a decade of empirical research, fieldwork, and consulting in these businesses, we believe that high-capability firms leverage their internal assets—most notably strategic capabilities such as speed, talent, learning, innovation, shared mind-set, and accountability—as they create these gains for shareholders.

As appealing as these strategic capabilities appear to be, however, they are not managed directly. Much like Porter's point about market positioning, strategic capabilities are the result of other management systems that combine to produce the financial results we found. Again a new perspective is needed. A key driver for these strategic capabilities, perhaps the most important driver, is effective workforce management. In our empirical work we have also examined how several elements of workforce capability vary by firms rated high and low on their strategic capability. These elements of workforce management practices include differentiating rewards and pay between high and low performers, and differentiating the elements of the workforce management system so they are aligned with the firm's strategy. Once again the differences are dramatic. As we describe in greater detail in chapter 4, firms scoring much lower on these workforce management practices also scored much lower on their strategic capabilities. Our conclusion is that the right HR management systems can enhance strategic capabilities, which in turn drive firm success.

The Execution Challenge—Holding Senior Executives and Line Managers Accountable for Workforce Success

Effective workforce management requires a new perspective on workforce success and a different approach to measuring that success. Jeffrey Pfeffer and Bob Sutton identified a "knowing-doing" gap in general management practice, arguing that it isn't that managers don't know what to do—the problem for many managers is *implementing* and *executing* effective management practices, that is, doing it.[20] There is a similar challenge in implementing world-class measurement systems. A new perspective requires a different cognitive understanding of how and why the workforce can be a strategic asset. A new measurement system translates those same ideas into an organizational-level system for measuring workforce performance. The third challenge, the execution challenge, requires line managers to manage by measurement in a way that is unfamiliar and sometimes uncomfortable. However, it isn't much help to spend the energy to develop an effective workforce measurement system if no one understands its implications or how it can be used to help make better decisions about the workforce.

Effective execution means new ways of embedding workforce success measures into routine managerial decision making and thereby making strategic workforce performance a key component of managerial decision making. It also requires that the senior executive team, line managers, and the HR leadership team develop a clear business strategy, an associated workforce strategy, and an HR strategy and operational plan for the HR function to help execute that strategy. They also need scorecards to monitor their progress.

To develop this type of accountability as a strategic capability, the CEO and the senior executive team must be very clear about their expectations for the workforce in delivering business success. Different strategies require different workforce competencies and behaviors for successful execution; different competencies and behaviors require unique and different HR management systems; and different HR management systems require specific cultures and mind-sets among the workforce to be optimally effective. Thus, a key role of the senior management team is not only to make clear its expectations about the firm's culture, but also to help enact it. Effective strategy execution requires culture and mind-set by design, not by accident.

Part of this process will require a different relationship with HR professionals, and the nature of the conversation with those professionals will need to differ as well. HR professionals will be held accountable for their contribution to workforce success, not just the efficient administration of the HR management system. Similarly, senior executives and line managers will be held accountable for the effective management of workforce success. This also means that Workforce

Scorecard measures will be included in both the performance reviews and compensation decisions of line managers because they have a direct influence on the successful execution of the firm's strategy.

Finally, ensuring that communication and learning programs are in place for the Workforce Scorecard is also a key element for successful strategy execution. Making sure that the workforce knows and understands the firm's strategy, embraces this strategy, and has the skills and capabilities to execute the strategy is a necessary, but not sufficient, condition for strategic success; the workforce must also have access to the appropriate workforce data and be prepared and motivated to use it. Thus, addressing the execution challenge requires a communication and learning strategy for workforce metrics.

THE ORGANIZATION OF THIS BOOK

The book is organized around the three challenges described earlier in this chapter. Chapter 2 focuses on the perspective challenge. It describes in considerable detail what we mean by the focus on workforce, job, and HR management system differentiation, and what new approaches to workforce management are required of line managers to help create a differentiated workforce. The key elements of this approach are the need to move from viewing people and people management systems as a cost to be minimized to viewing them as a primary source of competitive advantage. Here we introduce the concept of *disproportionate investments* and show how disproportionate investments in "A" players in "A" positions is essential for the effective execution of workforce strategy.

The next three chapters focus on a solution to the metrics challenge. Chapter 3 lays out in detail our concept of the Workforce Scorecard and provides a clear rationale for the measures in each of the four categories (workforce culture and mind-set, workforce competencies, leadership and workforce behaviors, and workforce success). Each of these elements helps determine the needed HR management systems and metrics that can ensure strategic success. We believe that it is only after you are clear about the strategic objectives and workforce capabilities that you can effectively develop a Workforce Scorecard. Thus, the process begins with a clear statement of firm strategy and the identification of the key or "A" roles that disproportionately contribute to firm success—as well as "A"-level performance within those roles.

Figure 1-1 highlighted the central role of the Workforce Scorecard, but also recognized a key role for the HR function and HR professional within the HR Scorecard. Chapter 4 describes the HR Scorecard in depth and is designed to refocus the strategic relationship between line managers and HR professionals by redefining HR's strategic performance in terms of its contribution to workforce success. Chapter 5 completes the discussion of the metrics challenge by focusing on a set of principles that managers should keep in mind as they consider what measures to develop and how to incorporate them into their decision making.

For workforce information to provide a source of competitive advantage and to help leverage firm success, it is also very important to effectively address the "information failure" around human capital. That is, the right people need to have the right workforce metrics at the right time—and they also need to know how to use them. Chapters 6, 7, and 8 conclude our approach to the three challenges by focusing on the execution challenge. Chapter 6 focuses on the role of the CEO senior executive leadership team in the strategic success of the workforce. We describe how executives can use workforce measures to help negotiate performance agreements and to hold managers accountable for the quality of the workforce. We also describe the process of aligning compensation and incentive systems with workforce metrics for strategic advantage. Chapter 7 covers those same topics for line managers and the HR function.

Chapter 8 focuses on data analysis, decision making, and communication of workforce metrics. Here we make the point that developing a world-class workforce measurement system isn't enough to ensure strategic success; these metrics must also be *understood* by the intended audience and *used* to make better decisions about the workforce. Using a variety of tools, we show how to help managers use workforce metrics as a practical tool to enhance strategic decision making.

We conclude in chapter 9 by summarizing the key lessons for creating, managing, and measuring human capital, and provide a road map for managers wishing to develop more effective workforce measurement systems in their own firms. Chapter 9 is also intended to be used as a diagnostic tool that will allow readers to quickly evaluate how their organization's approach to the management and measurement of workforce success compares with the ideas discussed in this book. Some readers may want to begin with chapter 9 to get a sense of what the organizational landscape ought to look like when these ideas are successfully implemented.

PART ONE

The Perspective Challenge

2

DIFFERENTIATING YOUR
WORKFORCE STRATEGY

I N CHAPTER 1 we outlined three challenges companies face
as they attempt to manage the workforce as a strategic asset.
The first of these, the perspective challenge, is the focus of
this chapter. At the foundation of the perspective challenge is an
increased emphasis on *differentiation*—of employees, jobs, and performance. Such a shift in focus may represent a new approach to
workforce management for most firms. Indeed, we find it interesting
that while most managers appreciate the value of differentiation as an
attribute of products and services, we don't observe the same emphasis on the role of differentiation in the execution of workforce strategies. For example, managers routinely evaluate the key elements of
their customer value proposition or marketing strategies and readjust
when necessary. Yet they rarely apply the same discipline to managing
and measuring the foundational driver of strategy execution: workforce performance and the HR management processes and systems
that drive it.

The goal of a workforce strategy is to *drive effective strategy execution*. In terms of both the content of the workforce strategy and the
execution of that strategy, there needs to be a much greater emphasis
on differentiation if a firm's workforce strategy is to meet that goal.

Just as the effectiveness of a corporate strategy can be analyzed in terms of quality of its content and the comprehensiveness of its execution, the same approach can be used for evaluating a firm's workforce strategy. The foundation of a workforce strategy is the HR management system that selects, develops, and rewards the workforce. These systems are often very complex and can range from recruiting strategies and channels to compensation and executive development systems. The second dimension of the workforce strategy, the quality of its execution, is largely a function of how line managers use that system to implement the firm's strategy. To the extent that their execution of the workforce strategy is ineffective and doesn't reflect the potential strategic role of the workforce, the workforce strategy itself becomes less successful, and ultimately the larger corporate strategy is jeopardized.

In our experience, far too many firms emphasize homogeneity and commonality in the development of organizational systems that drive workforce performance. In particular, when an initiative is designated as "strategic," it tends to focus on corporatewide strategic themes or goals and attempts to influence the behavior of all employees in a similar way. Indeed, in some firms the strategic character of such initiatives is measured by how many employees it touches and how closely its rationale is linked to a high-level corporate goal. Whether this focus is designed to gain support for the initiative or genuinely reflects a belief in the direct relationship between these change efforts and strategic success, these initiatives are often of limited value because they do not focus directly on the *drivers* of strategy execution. It's like a surgeon operating with a dull knife instead of a scalpel. Unfocused initiatives typically fail because they attempt to influence the strategic goal *directly* rather than tailoring separate initiatives to each of the performance drivers that drive the strategy execution process throughout the firm.

Take, for example, an organization that includes some variation of "customer focused" as a strategic theme. The problem with translating such a global business strategy into a workforce strategy is that the implications for workforce success are much different in R&D than they are in sales. Or in retail they are much different for distribution and logistics than they are among frontline staff. While it may be considered strategically important to have a customer orientation across diverse segments of the workforce, it is equally important to have a workforce strategy that reflects the diverse ways in which each of these workforce segments actually implements that strategic theme.

This book is intended to improve how line managers manage workforce performance in general, but in particular how they manage strategic workforce performance, or that part of workforce performance that executes strategy. Part of the answer is in designing organizational systems that optimize workforce performance, but an equally important ingredient is changing the way line managers actually manage those systems. Once again, differentiation is paramount. Consider these two perspectives on the familiar "employer-of-choice" strategy:

> ***Firm A:*** *As a key component of our employer-of-choice strategy, we want to communicate to potential employees that this is a great place to work. In support of this goal, we provide extensive benefits, job security, and great pay for everyone. We are proud that we have won a number of awards for innovative benefit packages and for becoming an employer of choice. As a result, our applications are up considerably and turnover is down across the firm. Once employees join our firm, they rarely want to leave. We are very proud of our achievements with our workforce.*

> ***Firm B:*** *The last thing we want to be is an "employer of choice." All that does is dramatically increase the number of unqualified or marginal applicants, which increases the probability of selection and placement errors and increases the transaction processing costs of our selection systems as we deal with many applicants who don't fit our organization. This is very expensive and unnecessary if we are effective in communicating the appropriate message to our potential workforce. Our strategy is to build a distinct employment brand by seeking the "employee of choice" and differentiating among the best candidates in the marketplace by having them self-select even before they apply. We want all applicants to understand that this is a demanding, high-performance organization, and to make a determination of whether this is a place where they will fit, where their skills and motivation will fit our culture. To achieve this, we try to communicate in every*

possible interaction that this is a place that values excep-
tional talent and exceptional effort. For those employees, we
provide exceptional pay and exceptional developmental op-
portunities. We cannot be everything to everyone, and we do
not want to be.

Differentiation is not just how you execute workforce strategy, but also a part of the cultural DNA of the organization. Employer-of-choice strategies *might* reinforce that differentiated strategy *if* the right applicants are attracted to the firm and the wrong ones choose to look elsewhere. Such efforts represent one approach to winning the war for talent, but they must lead to hiring a disproportionate number of high performers and keeping them. Otherwise, they are just another good idea with unintended consequences.

The more common examples of undifferentiated workforce strategies are in the areas of rewards and performance management. In most firms there is simply too little differentiation between high performers and low performers, or "A" players and "C" players, to use our terms. The result is that the high-performance talent is undermotivated and more likely to leave, while the less productive talent is overcompensated and less likely to leave. Over time this leads to a decline in overall workforce performance and a decline in the effectiveness of strategy execution. Eventually the underperformance increases the need for layoffs of underperforming groups that could be avoided if these performance differentials were handled appropriately in the first place. It's really a form of "pay me now or pay me later." In a world where product market competition allows no tolerance for organizational slack, performance-based differentiation cannot be avoided.

Our emphasis on differentiation in the execution of workforce strategy is not new. It has been the practice at AlliedSignal, GE, Microsoft, and PepsiCo for many years and also incorporates the concepts of Topgrading described by Bradford Smart.[1] Similarly, Larry Bossidy and Ram Charan describe differentiation as "the mother's milk of building a performance culture."[2] Indeed, while the importance of executing strategy has been widely acknowledged, as has the importance of differentiating among employees, there are two key elements that have not been sufficiently emphasized. First, managers need to focus significantly greater attention and resources on the "A," or strategically critical, jobs and in making sure that the firm has "A" players in the "A" positions. Second, managers need a new set of workforce measures, not only to signal what's important and what's not, but also to provide a method to hold managers accountable for how they manage the workforce. These ideas come together into what we describe as *disproportionate investments in "A" players in "A" positions*. In sum, it simply isn't enough to focus on "A" players. Managers need to disproportionately focus their efforts on the best employees in the firm's most important jobs. And managers must have the appropriate performance measures to facilitate such a shift. Developing and implementing just such a measurement system is one focus of our book.

DIFFERENTIATING THE CONTENT OF WORKFORCE STRATEGY

We've described workforce strategy as consisting of two dimensions: the content of the workforce strategy and system and the quality of its execution. In this section we explain what differentiating your workforce *system* really means, and why doing so creates a form of organizational capital that can represent a source of competitive advantage. Figure 2-1 describes the evolution of this differentiation strategy.

FIGURE 2-1

Workforce Differentiation Drives Strategy Execution

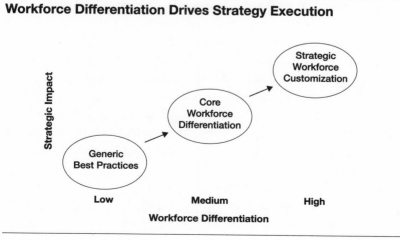

Generic Best Practices—the Foundation

The foundation for transforming your workforce into a strategic asset that can drive strategy execution is the HR management system, or the bundle of HR policies and practices that constitute your approach to managing the workforce. For those firms where workforce performance represents a significant driver of successful strategy execution, the HR management system is where it all begins. The HR management system determines who is hired and in many cases who stays with the firm. Perhaps more importantly, once employees have joined the firm, the HR management system is constantly sending signals about what's valued and what's appropriate, particularly in terms of performance. It is the key to building a high-performance culture because if the workforce gets conflicting signals, and the HR management system develops and motivates in conflict with the message from senior leadership, there is a problem. The typical example of such misalignment is rewarding A and hoping for B.[3] More systemically, the problem is hiring for A, rewarding for B, training for C, and hoping for D.

HR professionals have traditionally faced competing objectives when developing an HR management system. Administrative efficiency, legal compliance, employee advocacy, and workforce performance all have an influence in varying degrees. But the focus required for the HR management system to drive strategy execution is unambiguous; the focus must be on workforce performance. While we refer to this as a best practice in figure 2-1, it is more of a philosophy than a practice. Every firm has many choices about how to select, develop, reward, and motivate the workforce. In other words, there are many practices available that will provide the foundation for strategic workforce performance, but HR professionals have to understand that it is workforce performance that is the bedrock of strategic success. This perspective and philosophy must be their number one priority when architecting the system of HR practices that will constantly reinforce, or undermine, that perspective.[4]

An example of a best practice perspective with respect to pay is that a strong link exists between levels of performance and pay. The form of the pay could include profit sharing, gain sharing, options, or merit increases, or a mix. The point is that whatever practice is chosen the "best practice" element of that decision, there is a clear business logic for how pay will drive workforce performance. In fact, as we move up the differentiation curve in figure 2-1, that performance logic will become increasingly clear and easier to define.

An HR management system incorporating "best practices" is the most elemental level of differentiation, and its value should not to be discounted. Too many firms don't even get this far. But even firms that have adopted best practice HR management systems often fail to focus those systems in a way that meaningfully improves the quality of overall strategy execution. This can happen when managers, often with the very best intentions, adopt "best in class" HR policies and practices across the broad spectrum of job design, recruiting, selection, and so on. The fundamental problem with doing this is that while a particular practice may well be "best in class" in its "native" firm, there is no reason to expect that the "best practices" taken from a wide variety of firms and industries will work together in a synergistic manner, let alone do a good job in helping to execute the firm's strategy. From the perspective of the workforce, this type of misalignment can be painfully obvious.

In order for a firm to transform its system of managing workforce performance into a strategic asset, that system must contribute more directly to strategy execution. Instead of relying on best practices, this requires the development of workforce strategies that are increasingly differentiated *between* firms and *within* firms. It is this increasing differentiation that is the hallmark of the workforce systems we describe next.

Core Workforce Differentiation—High-Level HR Management Systems in Support of High-Level Business Strategies

Figure 2-1 describes this first step toward differentiation as *core workforce differentiation*. We use that term because differentiating by a firm's core strategy is the most common approach to differentiating the workforce strategy. By core strategy we mean that most strategic frameworks identify a small handful of strategic choices that a firm has available. Michael Porter, for example, identifies three market positioning strategies: cost leadership, differentiation, and focus. Miles and Snow's popular framework uses categories like Prospector (innovation) and Defender strategies.[5] Whether the firm uses these categories or some variation, the main point is that there is an over-arching market strategy that shapes the future of the firm. Firms that exhibit core workforce differentiation attempt to match each of the elements of the workforce strategy to this overarching business strategy. As a result, the defining characteristic of a core workforce strategy is its homogeneity or consistency within a particular firm. Focusing the workforce system at that level implies a core set of skills, competencies, and behaviors that when taken together will achieve this goal.

One example of core workforce differentiation is the framework developed by Dave Ulrich and Dick Beatty.[6] Following Treacy and Wiersema, they differentiate the workforce strategy based on the value proposition the firm chooses to offer the customer.[7] This is the same framework used by Kaplan and Norton to articulate the customer segment of the Balanced Scorecard.[8] In this framework there are three core strategic options: price, innovation, or customization. Product leaders competing primarily through product and/or service innovations offer some form of product or service innovation that customers "must have." These firms enable customers to obtain products that may be referred to as the "new way" (e.g., fashion designers such as Ralph Lauren, automobiles such as the PT Cruiser, or other designer goods), whereas competing through cost and price requires extreme standardization. Low-price marketers continuously attempt to drive variance out of their systems to minimize cost and thus offer customers *the* lowest price. Those firms offer little variation or customization to customers. What they are offering is what the market perceives as "their way" (e.g., McDonald's, Wal-Mart, Southwest Airlines, Best Buy, IKEA, Home Depot). Finally, customization is "you can have it your way," although firms have been able to differentiate by creating the perception that "you could have it your way," when, in fact, it may not necessarily be that differentiated in *how* it is produced (e.g., Burger King). But consumers perceive the product as uniquely tailored to meet their needs.

Workforce differentiation in this framework is similar to the notion of core competencies in that it delivers a comprehensive workforce capability for this overarching value proposition. The focus is on one company-wide description of the workforce capabilities required for the particular core strategy. For example, in a firm competing on the basis of cost, the primary focus of the work system would be on lowering costs. Figure 2-2 illustrates an example of how one dimension of workforce success, core mind-set, would be differentiated across three alternative core strategies.

The core workforce differentiation approach has several advantages. First, it is relatively easy to implement for an organization making its first efforts to align its workforce strategy with a larger corporate strategy. In effect there is only one point of alignment, the core

FIGURE 2-2

Strategic Choice and People "Fit"

Operational Excellence Cost	Product Leadership Innovation	Customer Intimacy Solutions
Core Workforce Mind-set		
• Identifies with process • Trainable/can learn • Follow the Battle Plan • Dedicated to organization • Shorter-term focus • Avoid waste and cost • Driven by incremental improvement • High concern for output quantity • High concern for process • High comfort with stability • Lower level of risk taking • *Not:* **Free spirits/ostentatious**	• Identifies with, values, and is humbled by the discovery process • Challenges the possibilities/ the status quo • Antibureaucratic • Longer-term focus • Versatile • Driven by learning • Higher concern for outcomes • Higher tolerance for ambiguity • Greater degree of risk taking • *Not:* **Structured/streamlined**	• Identifies with customers • Shares "secrets" readily, easily • Seeks customer intelligence • Adaptable/flexible • Makes customer results happen • Quick study • Driven by customer success • Anticipates customer needs • *Not:* **Clones**
Typical Behaviors		
• Teamwork • Working to fit in/find a role • Relatively repetitive and predictable behaviors • Primarily individual activity as part of process	• Problem solving • Challenging one another • Cross-functional collaboration • High degree of creative behavior	• Share ideas and solutions • Thinks/works across boundaries • Develops broad-based skills • Networks effectively • Customer management
Examples		
Federal Express, Dell, Nucor, Wal-Mart, UPS, Home Depot, Lowe's, Best Buy, IKEA, McDonald's, Carrefour	Sony, Glaxo, Merck, 3M, Intel, Nike, Microsoft, Burberry	Four Seasons, Airborne, Cott, Roadway, Cable & Wireless, Circuit City

Source: Adapted from Dave Ulrich and Dick Beatty, "From Partners to Players: Extending the HR Playing Field," *Human Resource Management* 40, no. 4 (2001): 293–307.

value proposition. This approach doesn't require that the firm fully articulate all of the performance drivers that characterize successful strategy execution, yet provides general strategic guidance to HR professionals and line managers attempting to leverage workforce success. Alternatively, it is just a first step. Descriptions of workforce capabilities remain at a very high level given the immediate challenges facing an individual line manager charged with executing his or her part of the overall strategy. It suggests that just as there are only three core strategies, there are only three workforce strategies that a firm might adopt. The relatively small number of options for the workforce strategy and their relative transparency probably limits the potential of these workforce strategies to develop into a significant source of competitive advantage. In fact, the academic research that has attempted to measure the value of this type of core strategic alignment has found little evidence of any incremental value creation beyond the contribution of a high-performance HR management system.[9]

Strategic Workforce Customization—Differentiated HR Management Systems in Support of Strategic Value Drivers

The concept of strategic workforce customization takes differentiation one step further and differs from core workforce differentiation in several important ways.[10] First, in core workforce differentiation, the focus on strategy execution is more implicit than explicit. Workforce strategies are mapped, as a whole, onto broad corporate strategies rather than the elements of those corporate strategies that drive their execution. Strategic workforce customization involves a more explicit linkage between the workforce strategy and the strategy performance drivers. It means that there is not just one homogeneous workforce strategy for a particular corporate strategy, but rather the workforce strategy will be differentiated across the firm's strategic performance drivers. In some cases, depending on the particular human capital demands of those performance drivers, this may mean considerable variation in workforce strategies within the same organization. For example, even a firm that is predominantly focused on cost reduction may well have areas of the workforce that receive very high levels of investment, as required by their strategy.

What is the business case for this level of differentiation? The premise of this book is that workforce performance is an unrealized strategic asset in most organizations. In order to achieve that unrealized value, firms, and in particular line managers, need to be much more effective at improving that part of workforce performance that genuinely drives strategy execution. But line managers don't manage the entire strategy—they manage parts of the strategy, what we call strategy or performance drivers. Therefore, to the extent that workforce performance is going to more effectively drive strategy execution, it has to be designed and managed at the level of the performance driver.

The rationale for strategic workforce customization follows directly from Michael Porter's concept of the strategy-activity system.[11] Porter argues that the underlying strategic activities that drive success in the marketplace are in fact the essence of strategy. Once again Wal-Mart provides a useful illustration. The company's integrated combination of distribution, logistics, just-in-time order fulfillment, considerable focus on stocking stores differentially to meet customer needs in each store, and very close relationships with suppliers has helped to create an organizational resource and first-mover advantage that is very difficult for competitors to imitate. The important point is not simply that a system of internal organizational activities might have *operational* value in any organization, but rather that this activity system has *strategic* value in large part because it will *differ across competitors*. In other words, simply choosing a core strategy like customer intimacy does not imply a particular strategic activity system, or in our case a particular workforce strategy. As Porter observes, "strategic positioning means performing *different* activities from rivals or performing similar activities in *different ways*."[12] The implication is that there are multiple ways, or activity systems, to implement a particular competitive strategy.

This distinction is important because the strategic value of workforce performance turns on its implication for value creation in the firm. The purpose of a strategy, however, is not only to create value for the customer, but also to allow the firm and its stakeholders to share in that value creation. A wildly successful value proposition that is easily imitated by competitors is of little or no strategic value. The question then becomes how does the firm develop a set of strategic "activities" that creates value for the customer and is not easily imitated by the competition? From the perspective of the appropriate workforce strategy, it's a two-stage process. First, the organization must articulate the system of those strategic activities that will describe and define the elements of successful strategy execution. This articulation process is similar to the development of a strategy map described by Kaplan and Norton.[13] The process essentially defines the key performance drivers in the strategy execution process and their relationship to one another. The second stage in this process is to differentiate the core workforce strategy sufficiently to meet the unique human capital demands of each performance driver. Unlike core workforce differentiation, which differentiates the workforce strategy on just two or three core strategies, performance drivers within those core strategies are also potential points of differentiation. The point is that not only will workforce strategies differ *across* firms that have different core strategies, but they will differ *within* firms as well.[14]

Strategic workforce customization is similar to the manufacturing concept of mass customization. You deliver exactly what the customer needs; and the customer is the line manager responsible for one or more strategic performance drivers. What is different about the customer analogy and a traditional internal customer focus for the HR professional is the value proposition. The traditional value proposition for the internal customer focuses on timeliness, efficiency, and cost of HR services. The *strategic* value proposition for the line managers has to focus on the execution of strategy so HR's deliverable, and shared responsibility, is the strategic performance driver(s) for which the line manager is held accountable. This is a new perspective for both line managers and HR professionals.

An Illustration of Strategic Workforce Customization

Further differentiation of your organization's workforce strategy beyond the adoption of generic best practices introduces some degree of strategic workforce customization. When should this become a consideration? The answer is that strategic workforce customization should be considered when the *different* elements in the strategy execution system increasingly require *different* workforce behaviors, mind-sets, and competencies. Instead of merely searching for the lowest common denominator that links the human capital dimensions of these strategic elements (drivers) together, organizations should give equal or more attention to the *differences* in those human capital dimensions. This is particularly true where employees and positions are primarily associated with one or two elements of the strategy execution process rather than organizations where all positions have equal importance across the entire execution process. For example, at the Four Seasons hotel the primary business strategy is one of customer intimacy and providing a world-class experience for guests, whatever it takes. However, the billing and procurement functions at this luxury hotel add value based on an efficiency and cost-reduction strategy. Differentiated workforce strategies will recognize and support each of these strategic imperatives.

What might an example of strategic workforce customization look like? Earlier we mentioned the elements of Michael Porter's strategic activity system as the basis for workforce customization. Another example is Robert Kaplan's notion of strategic themes.[15] Figure 2-3 illustrates the notion of strategic themes for the Wells Fargo Online Financial Services unit and demonstrates how a strategy can be differentiated by the major themes or capabilities required to implement that strategy. In this case the key organizing themes focus on adding and retaining high-value customers, increasing revenue per customer, and reducing cost per customer. In the actual case the workforce strategy depicted in the learning and growth segment of the strategy map is broadly focused, and the workforce measures do not have the same strategic significance as traditional financials.

This relatively unfocused workforce strategy makes it difficult to manage the workforce as a strategic asset and develop the type of performance measures that will capture that impact. An alternative would have been to examine the opportunities for several, more customized workforce strategies based on strategic themes. For example, to the extent that the job structure in this unit reflects those strategic themes, the organization will benefit from increasing customization across those three themes. In other words, the appropriate workforce mindset, leadership behaviors, workforce capabilities, and certainly the notion of workforce success should be much different in positions primarily responsible for adding and retaining high-value customers versus those positions focused on reducing cost per customer. Likewise, the HR management systems that support those workforce strategies

FIGURE 2-3

Strategic Themes as Basis for Customized Workforce Strategy

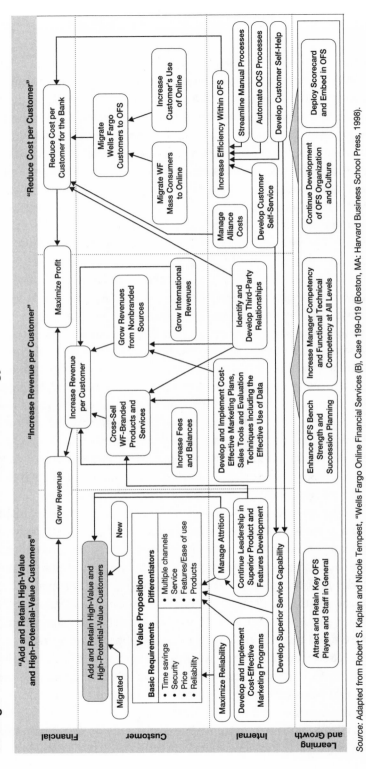

Source: Adapted from Robert S. Kaplan and Nicole Tempest, "Wells Fargo Online Financial Services (B), Case 199-019 (Boston, MA: Harvard Business School Press, 1998).

would also be customized to the point where we should expect to see different selection, development, and reward systems across those workforce strategies.

IBM provides an example where HR took the lead in developing and validating a strategy map that would provide the business logic for various workforce initiatives. The development process was very collaborative with business unit managers and included unique maps for each business unit, as well as a corporate map. This in turn allowed IBM to customize its workforce strategy as necessary by the unique requirements of each unit. Several of IBM's business units such as Global Services and BCS have such a unique approach they consider their strategy maps—and the resulting HR management systems—to be proprietary. This approach represents a significant advance over generic or firmwide strategy maps.

Returning to figure 2-1, the differentiation of your organization's workforce strategy represents a choice along a continuum. Most organizations will always have a strong core element to their workforce strategy, one that serves to reinforce the common brand throughout the firm. An example would be the "Credo Culture" at Johnson & Johnson—an ethical framework that guides managerial decision making across J&J's many different businesses. Nevertheless, introducing an element of customization to that workforce strategy has the potential to significantly improve the execution of the larger business strategy.

Strategic workforce customization requires a different perspective not only about the value creation potential of the firm's workforce strategy, but also on the investment required to realize that value. We find it curious that for the last several years there has been a lot of discussion about the strategic value of human capital and the workforce being the most important asset in many businesses. But in many cases that discussion seems to proceed as if this particular intangible asset is immune to the same influences that create value in other assets. Creating a sustained source of competitive advantage through a workforce strategy is not as simple as following five simple rules or copying best practices in the industry. The concept of inimitability, the equivalent of barriers to entry for intangible assets, should remain a prominent consideration in the design of an HR management system. We are always surprised at how freely companies are willing to share information about their workforce systems and at the same time claim that they have such strategic value. Strategic workforce customization is *not* easy to implement, which ironically is part of the source of its value. It requires an entirely new perspective on workforce strategies for both line managers and HR professionals. It is not a strategy that you copy from the industry leader. It requires a unique investment by your firm and in return promises to maximize the strategic value of workforce performance and contribute to a sustainable source of competitive advantage. More importantly, because it is largely firm-specific, even if another firm did copy your strategy, it wouldn't have the same value unless that firm had the same strategic activity system as the foundation of its strategy execution. This in turn elevates the workforce strategy to the level of organizational capital described in chapter 1.

To summarize, we argue that firms should increase the differentiation of their workforce strategies. We described three points along the differentiation continuum. They should be considered a hierarchy and not as substitutes for one another. At the foundation is a high-performance HR management system that focuses on workforce performance as the guiding development principle (generic best practices). The next level is what we call core workforce differentiation, where the workforce strategy is fitted to the overarching core strategy of the firm. It is a strategy that focuses on those elements of workforce success (mind-set, competencies, and behavior) that are required of the entire workforce if the core strategy is to succeed. Finally, we introduce the notion of strategic workforce customization. This level of differentiation emphasizes the need to customize the workforce strategy to the unique demands of the performance drivers that execute the core strategy.

DIFFERENTIATING THE EXECUTION
OF WORKFORCE STRATEGY

Execution is the second dimension of workforce strategy. Just as the content of workforce strategy requires more differentiation, so too does the execution of that strategy. They are related in part because increasing differentiation in the content of the workforce strategy implies increased differentiation in the execution of the strategy. Not all positions have the same strategic importance, and being able to identify and act on differential performance within those "A" positions takes on even greater importance when the firm has developed a detailed and specific business strategy. Therefore, while execution of the workforce strategy is in part a shared responsibility of line managers and HR professionals, it is foremost the responsibility of line managers. It falls to line managers to adopt the principles of differential execution if the workforce strategy, and ultimately the core strategy, is to be successful.

The Problem

Firms that don't emphasize differentiation in the execution of their workforce strategy will underperform, but the source of the problem won't be obvious. Without the right perspective, the line of sight between the execution of the workforce strategy and firm performance is in most cases simply too indirect. In our experience the simplest indication that there is a problem is in how HR generalists allocate their time. In "low-differentiation" firms, HR professionals spend too much time on employee performance problems; specifically they spend too much time on employees who should no longer be with the firm and should never have been hired in the first place. This marks a failure to differentiate by HR at the point of hire, but perhaps more importantly a failure to differentiate by line managers once the performance problem is obvious.

The misallocation of HR resources follows directly from the workforce decisions of line managers. HR managers respond to requests of supervisors and managers to solve specific workforce performance problems—especially of underperforming employees. These are problems that should be solved between the individual employee and the line manager, but many of these problem employees become HR's problem. The key is to deal with the root cause—never to hire low performers in the first place—and secondly to have measurement and information systems that enable and encourage line managers to quickly fix or exit problems in the workforce.

The responsibility for a new perspective on workforce strategy falls squarely on the shoulders of the line manager. But just as we call for a new shared responsibility for workforce performance, the reliance on an undifferentiated strategy in large part reflects the perspective of most HR professionals and the HR management system. HR professionals' understandable attention to legal compliance issues and administrative efficiency encourages an emphasis on *homogeneity* (i.e., treating all employees the same regardless of role or performance level), which tends to drive variance out of the system. Even where line managers might prefer a more differentiated system, every tool, every form, and very often the firm's culture make it nearly impossible to treat the execution of the workforce strategy as anything more than an administrative chore.

Moreover, the costs and benefits of this new perspective are not equally apparent. The problem is that the immediate costs are obvious and often tangible in terms of both financial investments and increased effort. Differentiation takes effort. At a minimum it requires a clear explanation of what the firm is looking for in the way of employee performance. By contrast, because workforce success is a leading indicator of firm performance, the benefits necessarily "lag" the more obvious costs. Make no mistake, however—the benefits are substantial. The overarching benefit is increased strategic success. At its core, our argument is that in firms where workforce performance is crucial for strategic success, the status quo results in strategic underperformance. By treating all jobs more or less equally, the organization underinvests in high-return ("A") positions and overinvests in low-return ("C") positions. These losses are compounded by underinvestments in high-return employees ("A" players) and overinvestments in low-return employees ("C" players). As a result, high performers leave and low performers stay, which over time creates a drag on firm performance and the need for significant, and often unfocused, layoffs.

Differentiation by Roles—Identifying the "A" Positions

Managers are paid to differentiate. In the case of workforce strategy, this takes the form of disproportionate investments in high-return positions and high-return individuals. The challenge is to think of these investments as strategic decisions and bring the same discipline and effort to investing in intangibles as to making tangible investments decisions.

The first step toward differentiating the execution of a workforce strategy is to recognize and accept that some positions and roles in the organization have a more important influence on the execution of strategy than others. We use the term "A" positions to describe those positions that have a significant influence on the execution of the firm's strategy. There is no rule of thumb regarding the percentage of the workforce that might be included in this designation. The lesson of the first half of this chapter is that firms will vary by how they execute their strategy, and this differentiation will translate into a differentiated workforce strategy. What we can say is that a choice will have to be made regarding the importance of a position, and that the choice should be driven by how the firm has chosen to execute its strategy.

What should be clear is that the decision about which positions will be designated "A" positions will follow directly from the nature of the differentiation in the workforce strategy. For example, if the firm has adopted a core workforce differentiation strategy (figure 2-1), the positions will map directly onto the overall approach to delivering value to the customer. If your firm has extended the differentiation of the workforce strategy to strategic workforce customization, the choice of "A" positions will be linked directly to the system of performance drivers that populate the firm's strategy map. In either case, identifying the "A" positions should be considered an integral part of the organization's workforce strategy. This is one of the key points of intersection between the corporate strategy and the workforce strategy and should be a *key strategic responsibility* of line managers. As we discuss in chapter 3, it is also an essential element in the development of your Workforce Scorecard.

An "A" position (e.g., R&D scientist) is a job that has a *critical impact* on the formation of one or more of the strategic capabilities (e.g., new product development) the firm needs to execute its strategy. As a result, "A" positions are critical to the firm's competitive advantage. Note that these positions have nothing to do with a firm's hierarchy, which experience has taught us is often an "A" position criterion proposed by executive teams. Resist this temptation! "A" positions can be found in a wide variety of places throughout the organization. In R&D it could be a biochemist; in joint ventures, a manager of new business development; in marketing, a field sales representative; in government relations, the chief lobbyist; in retail, a cashier, and so on.

An example of a firm that has developed a clear workforce strategy and identified "A" positions is IBM. IBM's overarching strategy is to go to market as "One IBM," which means leveraging its resources in hardware, software, and consulting to provide a systemic solution that is uniquely tailored to the business needs of each client. A key element of this strategy is ensuring that IBM can develop into an "on-demand" business. IBM Chairman and CEO Sam Palmisano defines an on-demand business as an enterprise whose business processes—integrated end-to-end across the company and with key partners, suppliers, and customers—can respond with speed to any customer demand, market opportunity, or external threat.[16]

IBM believes that an on-demand business requires an "on-demand workforce"—one that is responsive to market requirements—adaptively brings the right skills and expertise to meet client demand, is resilient to market forces, and provides strong leadership. Key elements that help to create an on-demand workforce include deploying programs that recognize accomplishments, regarding people development as an investment, differentiating performance and rewards, nurturing leadership capacity, driving accountability, and balancing its human asset utilization. In other words, IBM intends to use its HR management system to help deliver value to its customer, the business.

IBM's new business strategy relies on considerably more cross-IBM collaboration than ever before. This in turn requires more and better workforce management systems. IBM needs to be able to assemble workforce capabilities to meet client needs wherever they may be in the world, and they need to be able to do it quickly. The challenge in doing this is that 49 percent of the workforce has less than five years' experience with the firm, and more than one-third of the workforce do not work out of a traditional IBM building, but are considered mobile workers. As a key element of their execution strategy, IBM has developed what it describes as an Adaptive Workforce (ADWF) in its services business. In essence, ADWF is the application of supply chain management principles to the workforce. In IBM's case, the key question is "How do we optimally match resources to client demands, across units within IBM and throughout the world?" Including contract workers, IBM has more than 475,000 employees throughout the world. The problem is that historically, the resources have been in a variety of supply pools and difficult to aggregate leading to suboptimized response to client needs. To deal with this issue, IBM has included approximately 65 percent of the workforce (primarily technical, client-facing employees) in their ADWF program, which is a multimillion-dollar transformation project integrating strategy/ policy, process, organization, and technology to ensure that the resource supply and demand information is available throughout the business to match critical skills to client needs, on demand.

As a result of this type of analysis, IBM has identified membership on the Strategic Leadership Team as a key "A" position. The SLT consists of about three hundred people, or about 1 percent of total (full-time) employment. Selection to the SLT reflects both the significance of the positions held by these employees and their leadership skills. Members of the SLT are expected to be role models and drive the strategy down through the organization.

Another example of an "A" position at IBM involves "major dealmaking." IBM's strategy of going to market as "One IBM" requires developing and selling *business-transformational systems solutions* that leverage the firm's capabilities in hardware, software, services, and consulting. This is an important part of the firm's comparative advantage over firms such as Accenture (whose primary focus is on consulting and software) or HP (hardware and software). The economic impact of a successful "systems sell" can be significant. For example, a "clothed" server (i.e., one with software applications installed) will generate on average several million dollars more in revenue over its service life than will a "naked" server (one without software). Developing sales leaders with the breadth of experience to master major deals and leveraging the IBM's full brand to help generate business transformational solutions for clients is a key objective for the firm. This is an important part of the firm's focus on developing cross-unit initiatives that can drive growth and innovation.

It is important that line managers and the senior executive team understand that identifying the strategic "value" of a job should not be left to an outside method of job evaluation. Effective processes for identifying "A" positions do not include scientific methods of job evaluation that rationalize the value of jobs in one organization in comparison with the value of jobs in another organization. There is no market equivalent for the strategic value of a job, because of the unique way in which "A" jobs contribute to your firm's strategic success. Designing and implementing a workforce strategy requires investing in a mix of intangible assets (strategic human capital) that contribute *uniquely* to the success of your firm's strategy. This is in stark contrast to job evaluation systems intended to develop an internally consistent set of job values that ultimately are independent of the firm's strategy. Said differently, if seniority and job level explain 90 percent of the variation in pay in your organization, you probably need to take another look at how jobs are valued in your firm.

Differentiating by Employee Performance— Rewarding the "A" Players

Differentiating by position is only the first step in executing a workforce strategy. Equally important is differentiating by actual and potential employee performance. At a minimum this means distinguishing and increasing investment in in the high-performing "A" players, and at the same time limiting your losses and typically exiting the "C" players. "A" players make a disproportionate contribution to the success of your strategy, so it is entirely appropriate that the organization make a disproportionate investment in identifying them, developing them, and motivating them. Ultimately, the goal is to have an organization where all of the "A" positions are populated by "A" players. Equally important is that "C" players be removed from "A" positions. Ideally, the HR management system will avoid hiring them in the first place, and subsequent development opportunities will identify any hiring mistakes earlier rather than later. Again, this is not to say that there may not be a role for "C" players in the organization, but you do not want them in positions where their underperformance can do significant damage to the execution of the strategy.

A simple example of such disproportionate investment would be to establish salary structures normed to the seventy-fifth or eightieth percentile for "A" positions, but to the fortieth percentile for "C" positions. For example, a major manufacturer identified its engineering group as an "A" position and invested in a competency growth model for these positions. The increased emphasis on competency development allowed R&D to increase productivity and reduce engineering head-count. This contrasts with a large chemical company that didn't differentiate and ultimately faced a situation where thousands of scientists lacked the talents to contribute to the strategic projects that were being planned.

Great talent in critical positions is a source of a firm's competitive advantage and, if not present, an obstacle to strategy execution. The importance of identifying "A" players and how they may be described is shown in "Jack Welch on What Characterizes 'A' Players." Here examples of "A" players are described by Welch for finance, engineering, manufacturing, and sales positions. However, an executive team may wish to develop more specific criteria for describing "A," "B," and "C" players, as shown in figure 2-4.[17] This is a generic example, designed and used by an executive team to assess managerial and executive talent in its first efforts to make significant workforce differentiation decisions. Subsequently, the firm evolved to using even more specific "A," "B," and "C" criteria, beginning with separate managerial and technical grids and evolving to "A," "B," and "C" grids for technical positions. Obviously, the ideal is to have specific grids for each "A" position, but the patience of an executive team (and HR) is often taxed before this can be accomplished.

JACK WELCH ON WHAT CHARACTERIZES "A" PLAYERS

In finance, for example, "A's" will be people whose talents include, but transcend, traditional controllership. The bigger role is one of full-fledged participant in driving the business to win in the marketplace—a role far bigger than the counting that once defined and limited the job.

In engineering, "A's" are those who embrace the methodology of Design for Six Sigma. "A" engineers can't stand the thought of "riding it out" in the lab, but rather relish the rapid pace of technological change and continually re-educate themselves to stay on top of it.

In manufacturing, "A" players will be people who are immersed in Six Sigma technology, who consider inventory an embarrassment, especially with a whiff of deflation in the air—people who understand how to drive asset turns and reduce inventory while at the same time increasing our readiness to serve the customer.

In sales, "A" players will use the enormous customer value that Six Sigma generates to differentiate GE from the competition, to find new accounts, and to refresh and expand the old ones—as contrasted with "C" players whose days are spent visiting "friends" on the "milk-run" circuit of customer calls.

This is now the business of your Company: "A" products and "A" services delivered by "A" players around the globe.

—1995 General Electric Annual Report

FIGURE 2-4

Using "A," "B," and "C" Players in Selection Decisions

SAMPLE "A," "B," AND "C" CRITERIA
POSITION: BUSINESS UNIT LEADER

	"A" Player	"B" Player	"C" Player
Overall Talent Level	Top 10% of those at this salary level	65th–89th percentile at this salary level	Below the 65th percentile at this salary level
Vision	Facilitates the creation and communication of a competing and strategically sound vision	Vision lacks credibility; is somewhat unrealistic or strategically flawed	Embraces tradition over forward thinking
Intelligence	130 or higher IQ; a "quick study"; able to rapidly perform complex analyses	120–129 IQ; smart, but not as insightful an an "A" player	110–119 IQ; has difficulty coping with new, complex situations
Leadership	Initiates needed change; highly adaptive and able to "sell" the organization on change	Favors modest, incremental change, so there is lukewarm "followership"	Prefers the status quo; lacks credibility, so people are hesitant to follow
Drive	Passionate; extremely high energy level; fast paced; 55(+)-hour workweeks	Motivated; energetic at times; 50- to 54-hour workweeks	Dedicated; inconsistent pace; 40- to 49-hour workweeks
Resourcefulness	Impressive ability to find ways over, under, around, and through barriers; invents new paradigms	Open-minded and will occasionally find a new solution	Requires specific direction
Customer Focus	Extremely sensitive and adaptive to both stated and unstated customer needs	Knows that "customer is king" but does not act on it as often as "A" players	Too inwardly focused; misjudges the inelasticity of demand for the firm's products and services

Topgrading	Hires "A" players and employees with "A" potential; has the "edge" to make the tough calls and remove chronic "C" players	Hires mostly "Bs" and an occasionally costly "C" player; accepts less than top performance	Hires mostly "C" players; crises occur due to low talent level; tolerates mediocrity
Coaching	Successfully counsels, mentors, and teaches each team member to "turbo-boost" performance and personal/career growth	Performs annual performance reviews and some additional feedback; is "spotty," inconsistent in coaching	Inaccessible, hypercritical, stingy with praise, and late/shallow with feedback; avoids career discussions
Team Building	Creates focused, collaborative, results-driven teams; energizes others	May want teamwork but does not make it happen	Drains energy from others; actions prevent synergy
Track Record	Exceeds expectations of employees, customers, and shareholders	Meets key constituency expectations	Sporadically meets expectations
Integrity	"Ironclad"	Generally honest	"Bends the rules"
Communication	Excellent oral/written skills	Average oral/written skills	Mediocre skills

Source: Adapted from Bradford D. Smart and Geoffrey H. Smart. "Topgrading the Organization," *Directors and Boards* 21, no. 3 (1997): 28.

This also means that talent development is taken seriously, and the organization may even take some risks to develop that talent. For example, at a company where workforce performance is not managed like a strategic asset, leadership development might be limited to annual off-site programs, little attention by the senior executive team, and "A" players spending too much time in "B" positions. By comparison, at companies like Johnson & Johnson that excel at leadership development, "A" players are rotated regularly though a wide range of positions, often creating opportunities for P&L responsibilities largely for developmental reasons. Every rotation is a test, and even though the test "location" may not benefit immediately, the organization benefits in the long run from the bench strength developed for the "A" positions in the firm.

IBM is another example of a company that has recently become much more aggressive in the way it differentiates on performance. Traditionally, even employees with low performance ratings were receiving salary increases and bonuses. This has changed. Salary increases are now going to just 50 to 60 percent of the workforce, and a disproportionate share has been allocated to the top performers, the "A" players (three times the amount) compared with the "B" players. Similarly, the "A" players get up to twice the bonus received by the average performer. The bottom 5 to 15 percent of employees (the "C" performers) gets no bonus at all. This is combined with a new emphasis on performance management for the "C" players. The HR function has taken the lead in encouraging managers to exit serial low performers as soon as possible, and at the same time find some relief from hiring limitations for replacements.

INCREASING LINE MANAGER ACCOUNTABILITY FOR WORKFORCE PERFORMANCE

The Workforce Scorecard, described in the next chapter, is premised on two significant changes in the role of line managers in managing workforce performance. We have alluded to both, but they need to be articulated in some detail. First, the view that a firm's workforce strategy is a key driver of business strategy execution means that line managers will be held accountable for workforce success. The Workforce Scorecard provides a basis by which the senior executive team and the

CEO can evaluate each line manager's performance on this dimension of strategy execution, and at the same time is a management tool that line managers can use to manage their piece of the workforce strategy. Second, this greater accountability means that many of the workforce decisions that line managers had made in the past will be made differently. In some cases those were decisions that had been left to HR professionals. Figure 2-5 compares the execution of a differentiated and an undifferentiated workforce strategy.

Performance Management and Compensation

The most important element of implementing a differentiated compensation policy is that performance feedback and pay actually vary by *strategic performance* rather than being driven by level and tenure. For example, in most firms there is simply too little variance in many managers' performance ratings based on real differences in employee performance and, as a result, little subsequent variance in the compensation allocation.

For example, if a firm has a 4 percent salary increase (or merit) budget, the suggested range may be zero to 12 percent. But in practice it is often much narrower, typically between 2.5 percent and 6.5 percent, or even less. Thus, "A" performers, especially in "A" positions, are not rewarded commensurate with their contributions. This situation is often most severe in the case of high-performing junior employees. They tend to have relatively low base salaries and as a result will receive the same merit pay (or less) as "B" or "C" players, depending upon how long the "B's" or "C's" have been with the organization. Firms that execute a more differentiated strategy will have more variance in performance ratings as well as in reward consequences. For example, we are increasingly observing the situation that when long-term, often highly compensated individuals underperform, the organization may actually reduce their salary in an attempt to send the appropriate pay-for-performance message and reinstate performance reward equity within the firm. This would be unheard of where an undifferentiated strategy is the norm. Familiar examples of this approach can be seen at GE, Microsoft, and Siebel Systems, Inc.[12] Siebel Systems developed a policy called the Workforce Improvement Initiative, modeled after the GE approach. Not only does this initiative

FIGURE 2-5

Workforce Differentiation

Line Manager's Responsibility	Common Practice	Differentiated Workforce Practices
Performance Management and Compensation	• Little range in incentive pay • Pay takeaway unheard of • Low performers get about the same as average performers • Bonus pool fixed % across firm • Base pay strategy same/consistent across positions (e.g., market midpoint) • Under-rewards best performers • Little variance in performance ratings • Highly lenient ratings/few low ratings • Performance expectations remain the same from year to year • Little honest feedback, if any • Rating based on effort/competencies • Managers not held accountable for workforce performance • Considering forced distributions	• Great range in incentive pay • Takeaway not unusual • Low performers get nothing • Size of bonus pool varies by strategic role of position • Base pay strategy varies between strategic and non-strategic positions (e.g., Q3 versus Q1) • "A" players in "A" positions highly rewarded • Much variance in performance ratings • Lower average ratings • Performance expectations increase annually • More accurate and honest feedback • Ratings based on strategic contributions/results • Managers held accountable for workforce performance
Selection	• Little detail on performance expectations used in selection decisions • Little attention paid to "A" players • Little attention paid to "C" players • Little effort to retain employees because turnover only seen as administrative cost, yet few leave, usually best performers • Managers' performance evaluations not related to strategic turnover—it's HR problem • Overall firm turnover metrics used	• Much detail on performance expectations in selection decisions • Considerable attention paid to "A" players • Systematic focus on exiting "C" players • Considerable effort to retain "A" players; few leave; strategic talent maximized • Managers rewarded for retaining "A" players and exiting "C" players • Turnover measured by strategic positions
Training and Development	• Peanut butter approach—a little for everyone regardless of performance or potential • Random or ad hoc developmental assignments • Career management owned by employees • Competency growth models not likely • Mangers not assessed/rewarded on workforce development	• Investment dollars targeted to "A" players and "B" players with "A" potential • Focused developmental assignments, especially for "A" positions • Career management owned by top management for "A" positions • Competency growth models often used, especially for "A" positions • Managers are rewarded for developing strategic talent

tie performance management, coaching, feedback, and rewards tightly together, but every six months the lowest-performing 5 percent of the firm's employees are discharged.

Selection

In a differentiated strategy, workforce selection doesn't end at the point of hire. Instead, selection is an ongoing process where the manager is continually making "selection" decisions regarding who should be provided with additional development opportunities and who should be "selected" for reassignment to less important roles and perhaps exited from the organization. Selection is first about making predictions about an individual's future performance and, second, about acting on those predictions. Firms with undifferentiated workforce strategies typically have ambiguous, and very rarely exceptional, performance expectations as selection criteria. Managers in these organizations devote little time and attention to deselecting "C" players or to differentiating "A" players for promotion possibilities. Tenure is the primary promotion criterion. In these firms, turnover is simply considered an administrative cost, and managers are not held accountable for the loss of "A" players. In firms with a differentiated strategy, managers are held accountable for setting performance expectations, exiting of "C" players, and reducing turnover of strategic talent. There are consequences when managers lose "A" players or do not exit "C" players. In these firms, measures of turnover are not overall (i.e., firmwide) metrics, but are differentiated by strategic positions, strategy driver, and performance. Managers are held accountable, based in part on the common observation that "employees join organizations, but leave supervisors." These firms expect that turnover of "A" players in "A" positions is close to zero, while the turnover of "C" players in any position (but especially in "A" positions) is close to 100 percent. In short, a differentiated strategy requires both a change in performance expectations for line managers and different measures to capture that performance.

Training and Development

Designing and implementing effective training and development systems is a particular challenge because all the costs are borne in the present, while all the benefits accrue in the future. Firms that follow undifferentiated strategies are unwilling to absorb those costs or fail to recognize the benefits. They tend to let employees manage their own careers, give everyone equal access to the development budget, and largely provide ad hoc development assignments. Most importantly, the tone is set at the top. Managers are not held accountable, supported, or rewarded for the development of their workforce. These are companies where internal success stories say things like "I was lucky early in my career. . . ." There should be no luck involved. In firms with a differentiated strategy, development investments are targeted at "A" players and "B" players with "A" potential. The focus is on the use of competency growth models and development opportunities that focus these current and future "A" players on "A" positions. "C" players receive few, if any, development resources.

Sometimes this calls for some difficult choices. As much as we might like to develop all "B" and "C" players into "A's", it simply isn't a wise use of limited resources. In the reality of most organizations, it is difficult for line managers (or the human resource function) to influence such dramatic turnarounds, no matter how much they may wish to do so. In viewing employees from an investment perspective, it is more appropriate to consider where the firm might best invest its scarce resources to obtain the greatest return in terms of strategic success. Remember, failing to invest in "B" or "C" players does not necessarily mean they have no future with the organization. It does mean, however, that they should play no key role in the execution of the firm's strategy.

MEASURING AND MANAGING "B" POSITIONS AND "B" PLAYERS

Readers should keep an important qualifier in mind as they consider the main ideas presented in this book. This book is not intended to cover all aspects of workforce or HR management; it is about managing the human capital dimensions of the strategy execution process. There are a wide range of HR problems and challenges that any organization would normally consider important, and indeed are important, but that are not part of the focus of this book. For example, the reader will note that we focus most of our attention on "A" positions and players (roughly the top 10 to 15 percent in each category), and "C" positions and players (roughly the bottom 10 to 15 percent). The Workforce Scorecard described in the next chapter is in part based on metrics that highlight the "A" and "C" jobs, and "A" and "C" players. What about the rest of the organization? Are these other jobs and employees unimportant? The answer is no. These "B" positions and "B" players are not unimportant, they are just not strategic. This is an important distinction.

Most organizations have a number of important "B" positions and "B" players. They typically play an important supporting role in determining firm success. Not all jobs are strategic, however, because not all jobs are directly linked to the execution of strategy. Since the focus of our book (and The Workforce Scorecard) is on managing the strategic aspects of jobs and of workforce performance, we highlight those key roles. As we have described earlier, most firms have highly differentiated product market strategies, yet undifferentiated workforce strategies. For us, the key issue is to begin the process of internal differentiation, and the process should begin by ensuring that the firm has "A" players in "A" positions. The second differentiating priority is to begin to deal effectively with the "C" players, especially if they are in "A" positions. In essence, it is important to design and measure for exceptional, not average performance. This means that for the workforce as a whole we tend to focus on the two ends of the distribution, and hence our focus on "A" and "C" positions and players.

ADDRESSING RESISTANCE TO WORKFORCE DIFFERENTIATION

It would be nice to live in a world where we didn't have to make tough choices concerning the workforce, but we don't. We recognize that highly differentiated work systems may not be for everyone. However, markets are so competitive that the firms with the better work systems and talent will always win—and drive out firms that don't differentiate. Once-dominant firms like AT&T and Lucent Technologies are a salient reminder that market dominance is not a given, and in the case of these firms, the failure to differentiate was a significant factor that led to their underperformance. Indeed, the bankruptcy courts are filled with businesses dominated by low-performing workforces.

Because none of us lives in Lake Wobegon, where all the children and (presumably) employees are above average, it should come as no surprise to find that resistance to an increased emphasis on differentiation will not be normally distributed throughout the workforce. High performers generally embrace it, while low performers are generally opposed. Bradford Smart said it very well: "C players don't hire A players. . . . If I'm a C player, why in the world would I hire someone who could get my job?"[19]

Indeed, we have worked with many HR professionals who have said to us that "it is counterculture to tell some employees that their jobs are strategically more important than others. We want all employees to feel strategic." While we are sympathetic to this concern, we also feel that this view is symptomatic of the wider problems associated with an undifferentiated workforce strategy. Strategy is as much about deciding what you *won't* do as it is deciding what you *will* do. The same culture that won't allow the tough decisions about the workforce isn't likely to make the tough decisions about the execution of strategy, either. The resulting underperformance is likely to threaten the livelihood of and developmental opportunities for all employees, not just the low performers. Without customer security, there can be no job security. And customer security is most effectively created with a high-performing workforce.

For us, the essence of the issue is the distinction between equity and equality norms. One of the legacies of the historical development of the HR profession is that there is often significant energy devoted to ensuring that all employees are treated the same, with similar or equal access to rewards, developmental opportunities, promotions, and so on. As we've described, the current economic environment is shifting the norm from one of *equality*—everyone gets the same "deal"—to *equity*—the "deal" depends on a particular individual's role in the business as well as her performance within that role. As a result, we believe the message ought to be that "we invest in all employees, but we disproportionately invest in the very best employees in our mission-critical positions."

A NEW STRATEGIC ROLE FOR HR PROFESSIONALS

A differentiated workforce strategy has three significant implications for the traditional role of HR professionals. First and foremost, it means a new definition of the term *strategic partner*. HR professionals have long been encouraged to add the role of strategic partner to their traditional responsibilities, yet have often found this to be a difficult challenge. Much of the frustration has been the result of a focus on strategic planning and strategy content. In other words, find a role for senior HR professionals in the strategy development process. The message of this book is that while being "at the table" during the formulation of a strategy has some value, it is even more important that HR professionals (and line managers) view themselves as strategy managers. HR's strategic partnership should focus first on a shared responsibility for the execution of the firm's strategy, since that is where HR's real strategic contribution is to be found. This means HR professionals need to accept and embrace a responsibility for a range of deliverables that are outside the normal range of the HR function. Second, a differentiated workforce strategy has implications for what HR professionals do and how they approach the HR management system. There will be much more focus on how the HR management system drives workforce performance *at the level of the line manager*. Strategic no longer means just firmwide and general strategic goals. It means delivering workforce performance to those strategy drivers that have a clear line of sight to those strategic goals. Finally, senior HR professionals and the senior executive team need to think differently about how HR's performance is measured. In addition to traditional efficiency metrics, new performance measures like the HR Scorecard need to capture how well HR is delivering strategic workforce performance.[20]

Figure 2-6 highlights some of these new roles for HR professionals. Foremost will be different conversations between the senior HR leader and the CEO. Firms with undifferentiated workforce strategies are typically characterized by CEOs who are frustrated with HR's role, don't understand it, and can't satisfactorily measure HR's performance. There is much attention to performance against benchmarking data and best practices, but little insight into how HR is contributing to successful execution of the firm's strategy. In firms with a differentiated workforce strategy, HR is held accountable for tracking and developing "A" players in "A" positions. HR provides data to each manager on the extent of "A" players in "A" positions and the developmental plans for each. HR provides data to each manager's boss on the extent of "A" player incentive pay equity and the range of allocation, what was given to the "C" players, and so on.

FIGURE 2-6

The Impact of Differentiated Work Practices

	Common Practice	Differentiated Workforce Practices
CEO Conversation with HR Leaders	• CEO increasingly frustrated with failure to understand and measure HR's contribution	• HR held accountable for tracking and development of "A" players and "A" positions building strategic capabilities
HR Professional Competencies	• Measures of workforce competencies are nonexistent or undifferentiated	• HR provides data to each manager on the extent of "A" players in "A" positions and the developmental plans for each
	• HR ensures salary budget compliance and permits "salary savings" distribution in base salary increases to other workers	• HR provides data to each manager's boss on the extent of "A" players' performance incentive pay retention, development plans, incentive pay
	• Little attention to strategic HR metrics	• Considerable attention to strategic HR metrics in the HR practice design
	• Considerable use of external best HR practice, not necessarily strategic practices	• Strategic differentiation is basis of HR practices, not best practices
Substantial HR Time Devoted to . . .	• Salvaging of "C" players	• Rewarding, growing, and retaining "A" players
HR Selection Strategy	• Employer of choice	• Employee of choice
Workforce Culture	• Workforce drafts culture or value statement—culture by accident	• Culture aligned with strategy and brand—culture by intent

This same strategic perspective has to be applied to the HR management system as well. This means much more attention to the systemic effect of the HR management system on workforce performance and by implication to the overall alignment of that system with strategy drivers. In part this will require a different perspective by HR functional specialists and perhaps new competencies on their part as well. If HR is going to play a strategic role, functional specialists need to focus much more on understanding how to *differentiate* their practices within the organization. Designing a Workforce Scorecard that is intended to help facilitate such strategic differentiation is the subject of the next chapter.

PART TWO

The Metrics Challenge

3

BUILDING THE WORKFORCE
SCORECARD

T HE NUMBER of different elements of the workforce that could potentially be measured in any organization is overwhelming. There are literally hundreds of different metrics that can be collected—some useful, some irrelevant, and some actually counterproductive to effective strategy execution. To further complicate the situation, in many firms the lack of an overall workforce strategy—coupled with the very real need executives often feel to measure "something"—can lead managers to create different and often inconsistent metrics in various parts of the firm. Besides the obvious duplication of efforts, very often these metrics aren't aligned in any meaningful way. This can result in different parts of the organization working very hard to meet goals and objectives that are internally inconsistent, causing them to work at cross-purposes.

In these firms the senior management team has missed an important opportunity to communicate its strategic intent to the workforce by developing a comprehensive and integrated series of measures that show how strategy needs to be executed. To identify the "critical few" measures that really matter, managers need two frameworks—the first to help them understand the categories of workforce measures that really make a difference in the execution of strategy, and a second framework to help them understand the process through which these measures are developed and implemented throughout the business. Such frameworks are important, because without really understanding what it is we are measuring—without developing models that show "what causes what" throughout the business—we'll end up with a series of unrelated metrics, not a holistic system of metrics designed to help execute strategy.

In chapter 2 we outlined the key elements of the perspective challenge by describing the importance of differentiation in the design of a workforce management system. This is the first of three chapters focused on the solution to the metrics challenge, or the design and collection of workforce metrics that are intended to help execute strategy. In this chapter we describe the elements of the Workforce Scorecard and demonstrate its development in a company we call "Big Pharma." The thrust of our basic model is that business strategy determines the needed culture and mind-set, which help to generate the requisite workforce competencies and behaviors, which in turn help create workforce success. Each of these elements helps determine the needed metrics that can ensure strategic success. As we've described in chapters 1 and 2, the process begins with a clear statement of firm strategy and the identification of the key or "A" jobs that disproportionately contribute to firm success—as well as "A"-level performance within those jobs. To develop these ideas more fully, we begin this chapter by describing the key elements of the Workforce Scorecard in greater detail.

KEY ELEMENTS OF THE WORKFORCE SCORECARD

An important decision that must be made concerns categories of metrics that appear on the Workforce Scorecard. To be effective, a framework for workforce metrics must be *practical* (i.e., the data can actually be collected), *easily understood* throughout the firm (i.e., all employees can grasp the concepts), and *actionable* (i.e., managers can use them to improve key business processes). It should be grounded in the relevant research. The metrics should also be cascaded throughout the value chain in such a way that success at lower levels leads to success at higher levels.

The academic and practitioner literature on the factors that determine firm success is voluminous. Much of this work focuses on broad firm-level elements such as competitive strategy. For example, Michael Porter's work focused on the "five factors" that he believes determine the level of industry competition and subsequently firm profitability.[1] Prahalad and Hamel have focused on firm-specific "core competencies," arguing that to be successful, a firm must identify and leverage its own firm-specific capabilities in the marketplace.[2] We have no doubt that some industries are more profitable than others, and that within a given industry, some strategies will be more effective than others. Our focus here is on the internal infrastructure over which managers have some direct and immediate control—that is, the workforce and the quality of strategy execution. We assume that for the vast majority of firms, improved execution of strategy will improve firm performance. Thus, we are interested in gaining a better understanding of—and developing metrics for—the elements of the workforce that drive strategy execution.

As we described in chapter 1, Kaplan and Norton's Balanced Scorecard framework consists of financial, customer, internal operational, and learning and growth categories.[3] These categories work well when applied to an entire firm. They don't perform well, however, when applied to elements of the workforce. We have seen many HR professionals who have tried to apply these four "boxes" to HR functions and/or the workforce, and they have been consistently frustrated by the outcomes. The problem is that the categories, which were intended to be used to describe how *all* of the elements of firm success contribute to the bottom line, don't work well when we are interested in highlighting the contribution of a single element—for example, the workforce. It's not that there is anything inherently wrong with these categories; it is just that these elements simply aren't consistent with the processes through which the workforce creates value.

The elements of the workforce aren't a microcosm of the entire firm, so it is reasonable to expect that different categories will be needed to describe the contribution of the workforce to firm success. Clearly, specific elements need to be developed (or identified) for the Workforce Scorecard, as we described in chapter 1. While the primary objective of a publicly held firm is to maximize profit and shareholder value, it is important to recognize that profits are generated through the productive behaviors of employees, consistent with the firm's strategies and operational goals. One way to think about this is that financial results require very specific operational results—which we call *workforce success*. Workforce success is the product of very specific leadership and workforce behaviors. Leadership and workforce behaviors are in turn a function of workforce competencies. Finally, competencies, behaviors, and results are a function of the firm's culture and mind-set. Said differently, mind-set and culture enable competencies; competencies enable the right behaviors; the right behaviors enable workforce success. These elements prompt for us the questions shown in figure 3-1, which provides a graphical representation of these relationships. We describe these elements in greater detail next.

Workforce Success

To paraphrase Steven Covey, we need to begin with the end in mind by identifying in very specific terms what the workforce needs to deliver to flawlessly execute the firm's strategy. Here the key question that must be answered is, Has the workforce accomplished the key strate-

FIGURE 3-1

Elements of the Workforce Scorecard

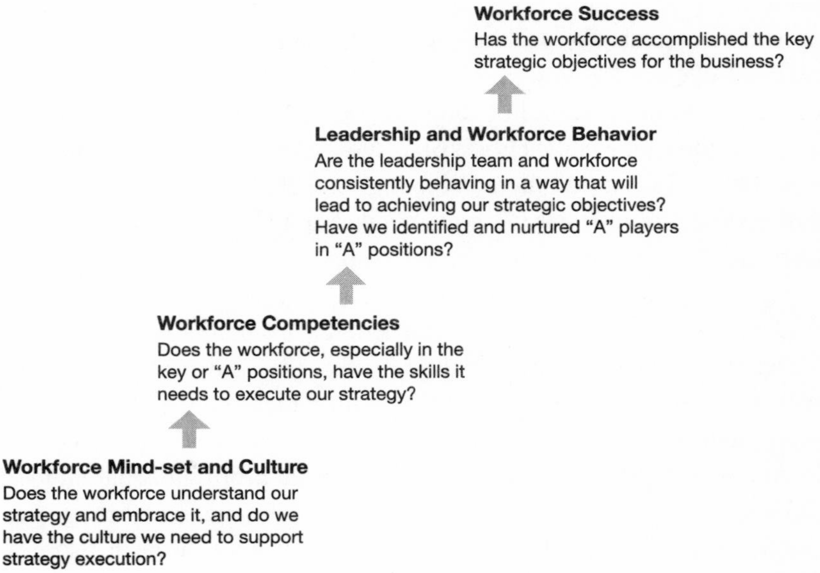

Workforce Success
Has the workforce accomplished the key strategic objectives for the business?

Leadership and Workforce Behavior
Are the leadership team and workforce consistently behaving in a way that will lead to achieving our strategic objectives? Have we identified and nurtured "A" players in "A" positions?

Workforce Competencies
Does the workforce, especially in the key or "A" positions, have the skills it needs to execute our strategy?

Workforce Mind-set and Culture
Does the workforce understand our strategy and embrace it, and do we have the culture we need to support strategy execution?

gic objectives for the business? Often, the focus of workforce measurement has been on either attributes of the HR function or perhaps attributes of employees. While these elements are no doubt of importance, at the end of the day we need to focus on whether or not we are making specific progress toward achieving our strategic objectives. Or as one of our colleagues likes to say, "I don't just want you to push the rock, I want you to *move* the rock."

We call this category *workforce success* because the measures are: (1) directly related to executing the firm's strategy and (2) driven directly by employees' competencies and discretionary efforts. As we will see later, workforce success is defined by your most profitable, or "A," customers. For example, in a semiconductor business, this might be cycle time for the introduction of major new products (for the R&D function), and yield rates for these new chips (in manufacturing). For a bank wishing to expand share of customer wallet, revenues procured from cross-selling would be a key measure of workforce success. In a retail sales environment that is focused on customer loyalty, share of customer wallet, intent to repurchase, profit per customer, and willingness to recommend the store to others become the key metrics. More generally, in manufacturing, uptime of the line, scrap rates, and product quality are typically key indicators. In an R&D environment, number of patents and cycle time to the introduction of significant new products are typically measured. Example measures of workforce success can be found in table 3-1.[4] The reader will quickly note that there are a great many metrics presented in this and in the following tables—many more than should be presented in any firm's Workforce Scorecard. This is by design. The point that we are trying to make is that there is no shortage of *possible* metrics. They key challenge is to select *useful* metrics, which should be guided by your firm's strategy.

Leadership and Workforce Behaviors

Workforce mind-set and competencies are a necessary but not sufficient condition to produce results—people have to be actually motivated to perform to execute strategy. In this category the key question that needs to be addressed is, Is the workforce consistently behaving in a way that will lead to achieving our key strategic objectives? We all know highly competent people who didn't deliver—either because

TABLE 3-1

Measures for Workforce Success

KEY QUESTION: HAS THE WORKFORCE HELPED TO ACCOMPLISH
THE KEY STRATEGIC OBJECTIVES FOR THE BUSINESS?

Average price premium versus competition

Customer complaints as a proportion of sales

Customer repurchase intent

Customer repurchase volume

Customer service representative ratings by secret shoppers

Number and quality of customer complaints

Number and quality of customer praise

Number of customer complaints resolved satisfactorily

Number of customer suggestions received and/or acted upon

Number of new distributors

Number of new product offerings unlike anything sold by the competition

Order-to-delivery time

Percent customer retention

Percent customer satisfaction

Percent gift returns (in retail)

Percent of "A" customers retained

Percent of "C" customers transitioned to the competition

Percent of clients extremely satisfied with service

Percent of current shareholders liquidating assets per year

Percent of customer orders achieving "perfect order" status

Percent of customers for whom we are suppliers of choice

Percent of customers who believe employees can resolve product/ service problems

Percent of customers who believe their issues/concerns are listened to and addressed

Percent of customers who report that their product/service expectations have been met

Percent of new shareholders per year

Percent of orders shipped in twenty-four hours

Percent of product sales resulting in return

Percent of products delivered defect-free

Percent of profit or cash flow generated from organic growth (versus acquisitions)

Percent of proposals that result in product orders

Percent of recurring customer complaints

Percent of revenue from lost sales accounts

Percent of revenue generated from organic growth (versus acquisitions)

Percent of revenues from new customers

Percent of revenues from new products

Percent of sales from new distributors

Percent reduction in COGS in a given year

Percent reduction in SGA per year

Percent returns due to product defects

Product value perception of "A" customers

Product value perception of "C" customers

Public perception of the company as a market leader

Quality of brand awareness

Quality of customer brand awareness

Quality of new product introductions

Rate of new product introductions

Reduction in cycle time for product design to first shipping order

Response time for customer inquiries

Sales revenue of new versus existing customer accounts

Sales volume due to customer referrals

Share of all customers' wallets (market share)

Share of wallet (market share) of "A" customers

Share of wallet (market share) of "C" customers

Shareholder evaluation of quality of firm governance

they were unmotivated or (more frequently) because there was some sort of constraint in the environment or culture that kept them from performing in their roles. Perhaps even more dangerous are highly motivated but incompetent employees—they can cause a lot of trouble in a hurry. Since workforce behaviors are what managers, manage, being very clear about what we would like the workforce to actually do is very important for the measurement process. And as we'll see, doing so effectively can have a very significant impact on the performance of the firm.

For example, Peter Fasolo, VP of Leadership Development and Organizational Effectiveness at Bristol-Myers Squibb (BMS) notes that at BMS the urgency to clearly define these elements came directly from the senior executive team.[5] CEO Peter Dolan recently challenged the organization to come up with a series of leadership and workforce behaviors that would support the execution of BMS's strategy and enable a high-performance culture with the highest integrity. HR leaders, in partnership with line managers designed, validated, and implemented the resulting measures that were based upon these behaviors, which then became the core elements of the BMS leadership model.

What are now called *Core BMS Behaviors* include not only clear statements about what is expected form the workforce, but also explicit behavioral anchors at different levels of the workforce. These behaviors will become part of the performance management process later this year with a portion of variable tied to actual performance of the leadership behaviors. The key point is that BMS managers are rewarded not only on *what* they accomplish but also on *how* they accomplish it. Moreover, because these behaviors are seen as so important for BMS's strategic success, managers view them as proprietary and do not want them released to the general public. BMS's approach contrasts starkly the common practice in many firms of relying on generic competencies and benchmarking to define their own performance expectations. Long-term competitive advantage cannot be generated by following the approaches that might have been used by other firms in the past—strategic success requires a uniquely differentiated strategy and a uniquely differentiate workforce to execute that strategy. Example measures of leadership and workforce behaviors can be found in table 3-2.

TABLE 3-2

Measures for Leadership and Workforce Behaviors

KEY QUESTION: ARE THE LEADERSHIP TEAM AND THE WORKFORCE CONSISTENTLY BEHAVING IN A WAY THAT WILL LEAD TO ACHIEVING OUR KEY STRATEGIC OBJECTIVES?

Average change in performance-appraisal rating over time

Consistency and clarity of messages from top management and from HR

Effectiveness of information sharing among departments

Effectiveness in dealing with poor performers

Employee turnover by performance level and by controllability

Extent of adherence to core values, such as cost consciousness, by the leadership team and workforce

Extent of cross-functional teamwork

Extent of organizational learning

Extent to which employees will put forth the extra or discretionary effort when a job really needs to be completed

Knowledge sharing of best practices

Number of subordinate managers receiving ≥ 4.3 on 180° feedback on leadership

Number of programs available to customers to recognize employee behavior/accomplishments

Percent acceptance of Key Talent offers

Percent female and minority promotions

Percent intern conversion to hires

Percent of eligible employees taking certification exams (e.g., Series 9)

Percent of employees involved in self-appraisal

Percent of employees making suggestions

Percent of employees who are recognized by customers for outstanding performance

Percent of employees who are satisfied with the level of coaching feedback received on the job

Percent of employees who feel they are empowered to act on the customer's behalf

Percent of employees who met goals for customer satisfaction

Percent of employees who report leaving the company for compensation reasons

Percent of employees who report satisfaction with current information-sharing practices

Percent of employees who report satisfaction with how pay decisions are determined

Percent of employees who report they believe messages delivered through formal channels

Percent of employees who report training has improved their effectiveness on the job

Percent of employees with experience outside their current job responsibility or function

Percent of executives indicating the culture helps the company adapt to competitive challenges

Percent of identified new skills acquired within a specific time period

Percent of managers achieving black-belt status by due date

Percent of original ideas that are implemented

Percent of positions filled on or before agreed-upon date

Percent of service technicians who check out on service expansion sales training

Percent of those attempting Series 7 and 9 exams who pass on the first attempt

Percent of those experiencing customer service training who pass the skills checkout on first attempt

Percent of workforce that is promotable

Percent repatriate retention after one year

Percent retention of core competency workforces

Percent retention of high-performing key employees

Percentage improvement in key indicators of customer satisfaction

Perception of consistent and equitable treatment of all employees

Performance of newly hired applicants

Planned development opportunities accomplished

Requests for transfer per supervisor

Retention rates of critical human capital

Success rate of external hires

Workforce Competencies

Producing the needed workforce behaviors and workforce requires that the workforce possess the needed *competencies*. In this category the key question that needs to be addressed is, Does the workforce, especially in the key or "A" positions, have the knowledge, skills, abilities, and personality characteristics it needs to execute the strategy? All managers know that there are significant differences in the competencies of the people who work for them. But competencies without motivation won't get you anywhere. It doesn't matter how hard your people try—if they don't have the requisite competencies, the work won't get done. Simply put, managers need to ask, What specific skills and competencies does the workforce possess? Are these the *right* skills to help us execute our strategy? You need both to win—the right competencies and the right motivation. Example measures of workforce competencies can be found in table 3-3.

Workforce Mind-set and Culture

All organizations have a culture, and all organizations have a mindset. Organizational culture is one of the most studied aspects in the management sciences; there are literally hundreds of different research articles and books on this topic. While many different definitions are in use, Denise Rousseau describes organizational culture as being comprised of five layers: fundamental assumptions, values, behavioral norms, patterns of behavior, and artifacts.[6] Culture and mindset are important because they help produce the behaviors and competencies needed for strategy execution.[7] For example, Lou Gerstner stresses the importance of a firm's culture on the ability of the firm to be successful in executing the firm's strategy:

> *I came to see, in my time at IBM, that culture isn't just one aspect of the game—it is the game. . . . I have a theory about how culture emerges and evolves in large institutions: Successful institutions almost always develop strong cultures that reinforce those elements that make the institution great. Reflect the environment from which they emerged. When that environment shifts, it is very hard for the culture to change. In fact, it becomes an enormous impediment to the institution's ability to adapt.[8]*

TABLE 3-3

Measures for Workforce Competencies

KEY QUESTION: DOES THE WORKFORCE, ESPECIALLY IN THE KEY OR
"A" POSITIONS, HAVE THE SKILLS IT NEEDS TO EXECUTE OUR STRATEGY?

Bench strength (at least 3:1) of highly qualified "eligibles" for all executive openings

Compra-ratio status of critical human capital (e.g., Percent > Q3)

Degree of financial literacy among employees

Depth of "excess capacity" of executives and HR to export to recent acquisitions

Depth of bench strength of change agents to deploy to needed business situations

Depth of workforce understanding of linkage of incentive measures to business measures

Diversity of race and gender by job category

Effectiveness of information sharing among departments

Employee commitment survey scores

Employee competency growth

Employee development/advancement opportunities

Employee job involvement survey scores

Employee satisfaction with advancement opportunities

Employee turnover by performance level and by controllability

Exit rate of "C" players in "A" positions

Exit rate of "C" players in "B" or "C" positions

Exposure of cross-functional job experiences

Extent of automation of common HR processes

Extent of cross-functional teamwork

Extent of organizational learning

Extent of understanding of the firm's competitive strategy and operational goals

Extent to which employees have ready access to the information and knowledge that they need

Extent to which hiring, evaluation, and compensation practices seek out and reward knowledge creation and sharing

Extent to which HR does a thorough job of preacquisition soft-asset due diligence

Extent to which HR is helping to develop necessary leadership competencies

Extent to which HR leadership is involved early in selection of potential acquisition candidates

Extent to which required employee competencies are reflected in recruiting, staffing, and performance management

Extent to which the firm has turned its strategy into specific goals and objectives that employees can act upon in the short, medium, and long run

Extent to which the firm is known for having *accountability*—that is, you are able to define and hold people accountable for results

Extent to which the firm is known for having *innovation*—able to create and produce new products and/or services

Extent to which the firm is known for having *outstanding talent*—able to attract and retain the best talent

Extent to which the firm is known for having *shared mind-set*—able to demonstrate a common or shared culture among employees and customers

Extent to which the firm is known for having *speed*—able to move faster to market with ideas or products, quickly able to make change happen

Extent to which the firm is known for *capacity to learn*—able to generate and implement ideas with impact

Extent to which the firm shares large amounts of relevant business information widely and freely with employees

Extent to which the *senior executive team* is seen by the workforce as effective in communicating a mission and vision

TABLE 3-3

Measures for Workforce Competencies *(continued)*

Extent to which the *senior executive team* is seen by the workforce as effective sources of motivation and energy for the rest of the organization

Extent to which top management shows commitment and leadership around knowledge-sharing issues throughout the firm

Gap between current and needed capabilities in "A" positions

Growth rate of human capital in "A," "B," and "C" positions

Internal talent bench strength; availability ratio per vacancy

Managerial competence in subordinate development

Number of subordinate managers receiving ≥ 4.3 on 180° feedback on leadership

Percent agreeing that rapid change is essential for our business's success

Percent exit of "C"-level technicians

Percent of "C" players in "A" positions

Percent of "A" players versus "B" and "C" players

Percent of employees assessed to be "highly capable"

Percent of employees assessed to be "highly motivated"

Percent of employees recognizing that our costs are 2 percent greater than our competition's

Percent of employees understanding that all customer guarantees must be met or exceeded

Percent of employees understanding that competency growth is essential for job security

Percent of employees understanding that new product offerings are the foundation of our survival

Percent of internal customers that rate staffing function highly

Percent of new hires performing satisfactorily within six months

Percent of newly promoted employees performing satisfactorily after six months

Percent of service technicians who check out on service expansion sales training

Percent of skill availability for "A" positions

Percent of skills gaps for "A" positions closed per year

Percent of those attempting Series 7 and 9 exams who pass on the first attempt

Percent recognizing that our costs are 2 percent greater than our competition's

Percent retention of core competency workforces

Proportion of employees not meeting basic skill requirements

Proportion of employees receiving a decrease in evaluation during latest performance review

Proportion of employees receiving an increase in evaluation during latest performance review

Proportion of local versus expatriate employees

Proportion of non-entry-level job openings filled with internal candidates

Proportion relevant candidates ready for international assignments

Quality of employee development and advancement opportunities

Retention rate of "A" players in key positions

Retention rate of "A" players in noncore positions

Retention rate of critical human capital during organizational transition/transformation

Retention rates of critical human capital (y-o-y) during strategic transition

Success rate of external hires brought in to "seed" the change effort

Without an understanding of where the firm is to go, how it can measure its progress, and what is in it for members of the firm, little strategy execution will result. To execute its strategy, every member of the firm should understand the firm's business model, the role of the workforce, and that leaders at all levels will be held accountable for financial success, customer success, business process, *and* workforce success. Larry Bossidy referred to firm culture in his book *Execution,* stressing that an important component of a high-performance culture is accountability:

> *[W]ork for cultural change that creates and reinforces a discipline of execution. This approach is practical and completely linked to measurable business results.*
>
> *The basic premise is simple: Cultural change gets real when your aim is execution. You don't need a lot of complex theory or employee surveys to use this framework. You need to change people's behavior so that they produce results. First you tell people clearly what results you're looking for. Then you discuss how to get those results, as a key element of the coaching process. Then you reward people for producing the results. If they come up short, you provide additional coaching, withdraw rewards, give them other jobs, or let them go. When you do these things, you create a culture of getting things done.*[9]

To execute strategy, the workforce must understand, be capable, and *do* what is necessary to deliver the firm's strategy. With respect to the measurement of mind-set and culture, the primary question of interest is, Does the workforce understand the strategy and embrace it, and do we have the culture and mind-set that we need to support strategy execution? This means that the measurement issue isn't just to measure culture—it is to measure whether or not that culture supports the firm's strategy. Example measures of mind-set and culture can be found in table 3-4.

While organizational culture is a broad and overarching construct that describes "what's important and what it is like to work around here," mind-set is a narrower construct that describes employees' own performance orientation and their understanding of their own role in

TABLE 3-4

Measures for Workforce Mind-set and Culture

KEY QUESTION: DOES THE WORKFORCE UNDERSTAND THE STRATEGY AND EMBRACE IT, AND DO WE HAVE THE CULTURE WE NEED TO SUPPORT STRATEGY EXECUTION?

Consistency and clarity of messages from top management and from HR

Degree to which a "shared mind-set" exists

Depth of workforce understanding of business strategy

Depth of workforce understanding of linkage of incentive measures to business measures

Diversity of ideas

Employee commitment survey scores

Employee engagement survey scores

Employee job involvement survey scores

Employee knowledge of status of change efforts by measures (e.g., mind-set, operational, financial)

Employee mind-set readiness for strategic transition

Employee mind-set/mind-set change to fit strategic direction (or strategic change)

Employee satisfaction with advancement opportunities, compensation, and so on

Extend to which values are clear and widely understood

Extent of access to business information to facilitate decision making

Extent of understanding of the firm's competitive strategy and operational goals

Extent to which all employees understand how the firm's performance management and appraisal process operates

Extent to which culture allows the firm to attract, develop, and retain a diverse array of "A" players

Extent to which employees are clear about the firm's goals and objectives

Extent to which employees are clear about their own goals

Extent to which employees are seen primarily by senior management as a cost to be minimized versus a source of value creation

Extent to which employees can make decisions and take action, without

approval, when they have the information and experience to do so

Extent to which employees feel that managers are helpful in problem solving on the job

Extent to which employees feel that their contributions are recognized

Extent to which employees feel they have some say in their workload and timing of projects

Extent to which employees perceive managers as inflexible or whether they are open to new ways of doing things

Extent to which employees take pride in working for the company

Extent to which employees will willingly take on extra work to meet some organizational goal

Extent to which strategy is clear and widely understood

Extent to which the average employee can describe the firm's HR strategy

Extent to which the average employee can describe the firm's strategic intent

Extent to which the average employee in your firm understands how his or her job contributes to the firm's success

Extent to which the culture promotes good communication among the workforce

Extent to which the culture supports differential outcomes for "A" versus "C" performers and "A" versus "C" positions

Extent to which the firm has executed strategy effectively

Extent to which the firm has turned its strategy into specific goals and objectives that employees can act upon in the short, medium, and long run

Extent to which the firm shares large amounts of relevant business information widely and freely with employees

Extent to which the firm's competitive strategy is broadly understood throughout the firm

(continued)

TABLE 3-4

Measures for Workforce Mind-set and Culture (continued)

Extent to which the organization's culture supports an appropriate level of risk taking (i.e., doesn't punish good decisions that had bad outcomes)	Extent to which the workforce is receptive to receiving feedback from multiple sources
Extent to which the senior management team has clearly articulated competitive strategy	Extent to which the workforce judges the competitive strategy to be appropriate
Extent to which the workforce believes that high performers are more likely to get promotions and raises than low performers	Extent to which there a broad-based commitment to executing this strategy throughout the firm
Extent to which the workforce believes that it has challenging and important work	Extent to which there is a process for broad-based discussions and decentralized decision making around obstacles to executing strategy
Extent to which the workforce believes that managers will willingly provide relevant performance information	Extent to which top management shows commitment and leadership around knowledge-sharing issues throughout the firm
Extent to which the workforce believes that the firm deals effectively with low performers	Extent to which vision is clear and widely understood
Extent to which the workforce believes that the senior management team is planning effectively for the future	Level and change in employee mind-set
Extent to which the workforce believes there is a strong positive culture or "team spirit" among the group	Percent of managers who report that the company culture creates a positive environment for decision making
	Strength of employment "brand"

firm success. Culture is an organizational-level attribute while mind-set is an individual-level attribute. Mind-set is a very specific deliverable of management, and it addresses the fundamental question What do employees need to know and understand about the business? At Sears, the realization of the wrong mind-set—around the business main strategy as well as its operational details—led the management team to develop specific measures of culture and mind-set that it tracked carefully. Sears's executives have found that higher scores on these dimensions have an economically and statistically significant impact on Sears's financial performance.[10] It should also be noted that more than 150 additional items that Sears regularly collected from employees were *not* found to be related to firm performance. The importance of this point is that the Sears team had the discipline to test its assumptions about the workforce and to empirically validate the measures that it would use in its scorecard. We describe the data collection and validation processes necessary to perform these analyses in greater detail in chapter 5.

Similarly, in our empirical work we have shown that firms with a strategic workforce mind-set—defined as the extent to which employees understand the firm's strategy, embrace it, and have the competencies and desire to execute it—do a better job at strategy execution. We found that an increase in strategic workforce mind-set had a significant impact on the quality of strategy execution. As mind-set improves, so does the quality of strategy execution.[11]

In summary, firms that systematically win in the marketplace achieve excellence in not just one or two areas, but across *all* of the areas that are central to their strategic success. These firms have the right culture and mind-set, develop and retain the right workforce competencies, elicit the correct behaviors from the workforce in the "A" jobs, and achieve the right business outcomes that are directly linked to the firm's strategy. These firms also recognize that there is a causal order inherent in this process, and that you can't manage results directly; you need to identify and nurture the drivers of firm success. We provide an example of how this process can operate below.

DEVELOPING A WORKFORCE SCORECARD
AT BIG PHARMA

Up to this point, we've emphasized that workforce culture and mind-set, workforce competencies, workforce leadership and behaviors, and workforce success are key drivers of strategy execution. We now turn to showing how the elements of the Workforce Scorecard work together, by describing the case of "Big Pharma." Big Pharma is a multinational pharmaceutical firm whose overall strategy is to discover, produce, and market drugs that enhance the quality and longevity of human life (because of privacy concerns, Big Pharma is a pseudonym that represents a compilation of our experiences in numerous firms over the last decade). Like many other firms in the industry, Big Pharma operates on a global scale, in 140 countries. Historically, the company has been very profitable. However, while sales have been increasing on a global basis, the industry (and Big Pharma) faces significant challenges from governmental regulations, numerous drugs going off-patent, global competition, and a diminished pipeline for new products.

Industry consolidation and the globalization of both the R&D and manufacturing processes have also changed the competitive landscape in pharmaceuticals. Huge mergers in this industry have produced potent competitors. Pfizer's hostile takeover of Warner-Lambert, the mergers of Glaxo Wellcome and SmithKline Beecham into GSK, and the recent formation of AstraZeneca have all helped to make this industry more global as well as more competitive. As a result, many jobs were lost in the 1990s, with more consolidation likely in the coming years. More specifically, disintermediation of the sales channel—because of increasingly Web-savvy physicians who expect to receive more of their medical information online—has led Big Pharma to think very carefully about how to (and who will) market their products. Big Pharma's senior management believes that there are still very significant opportunities ahead for Big Pharma, but that the environment will continue to be highly challenging and competitive. Customers are more knowledgeable than ever before, and the governmental agencies and the investment community worldwide have placed the entire industry under increased scrutiny.

Big Pharma's challenge is to move from a strategy of considerable wealth and success—where all employees, regardless of position or performance level, have the opportunity to access Big Pharma's considerable compensation and developmental resources—to a more targeted and strategic workforce strategy, especially in selection and workforce development. Historically, they have spent money like, in the words of one senior manager, "drunken sailors." This had led the workforce, over time, to develop a significant "entitlement mentality" with regard to pay, benefits, and even performance expectations. In addition to more targeted spending for workforce development, Big Pharma needs to do a better job on soft-asset due diligence prior to any acquisition, do a world-class job on cultural and strategic integration after the merger, and retain some of the small-firm biotech culture from some of its many acquisitions, where appropriate.

Big Pharma is organized into three divisions within each of four geographic areas that reflect its primary value-creating processes: R&D,

manufacturing, and sales and marketing. Because of their size and geographic dispersion, they often duplicate efforts in R&D, while perhaps missing significant opportunities in other areas. Similarly, in sales this may mean that some physicians might receive several Big Pharma sales calls for different drugs, while others don't see any. In manufacturing this means that they just don't have the workforce competencies that they need in a certain area, while redundancies are common in other parts of the firm. There is also a tight labor market for some of the high-end skills, greater opportunities to use those skills (e.g., Big Pharma is now facing more aggressive competition for talent from universities, which see faculty as a potential source of revenue), and greater mobility of talent (poaching by competitors). Fifty-eight percent of Big Pharma's operating budget goes to wages, training, or other HR support—but there is little accountability or measurement for the managers who are entrusted with these resources.

To begin to address these challenges, Big Pharma developed a Workforce Scorecard for its businesses. It began with developing a clear statement of its business strategies and the strategic capabilities needed to execute those strategies.

Clearly Defining Business Strategy and Organizational Capabilities at Big Pharma

Big Pharma, like most other publicly held firms, is focused on growing earnings, revenue, return on assets, and ultimately shareholder value. Despite Big Pharma's large size, its strategy must be one of focus. Because it takes approximately seven to ten years to move a drug from compound identification to Phase I of clinical trials to approval by the FDA, the firm cannot afford to get it wrong at any step in the process. As a result, it needs to focus its R&D efforts in a few key areas. Promising molecules and compounds must be identified early, while less promising projects must be encouraged to "fail fast."

New drugs are not enough, of course. Big Pharma needs to be able to perfectly manufacture these medicines and effectively distribute them to doctors, pharmacies, and hospitals throughout the world. To deliver on this strategy, Big Pharma's senior management team identified the following key objectives for the business:

- Increase the product pipeline by shortening R&D cycle time and effectively licensing external compound acquisitions.

- Enhance sales force marketing competence and cross-selling.

- Enhance the speed with which drugs go through the approval process, and leverage licensing opportunities wherever economically viable.

- Enhance manufacturing efficiencies—zero tolerance for defects.

Identifying "A" Jobs at Big Pharma

The identification of key or "A" positions at Big Pharma was relatively straightforward and followed directly from Big Pharma's needed strategic capabilities (e.g., R&D, licensing/acquisitions, sales/marketing, government relations, quality, and leadership). Big Pharma's senior leadership team asked the key managers from each area of the business to look closely at their businesses and to determine the key roles that were "make or break" for business success. These managers were also asked to provide specific data, wherever possible, about the range of employee performance in each of these key positions. In essence, managers were asked to define, in very specific terms, "A" performance for their "A" positions. Big Pharma's senior leadership team made it very clear that this task was a strategic priority for the business, and it provided internal consultants to help the managers accomplish this work. Once the managers had accomplished this task, the Big Pharma senior management team assembled the group and asked each manager to report his or her findings.

Initially, several of the managers did not provide the necessary degree of clarity or specificity and were asked to go back to their business units and collect more information. Some of these managers wanted to assert that all employees above a certain level in the business held "A" jobs, while other managers did not want to differentiate among jobs, because they felt that all jobs were important. The senior leadership team at Big Pharma made the point that while all jobs were important (otherwise the firm wouldn't continue to fund them), some roles were simply "mission critical" to Big Pharma's success. Moreover, these mission-critical positions cannot simply be identified by looking at organizational level. There could well be midlevel positions in the business that were critical and senior-level positions that were much less so.

Based on these discussions and analyses, the Big Pharma management team concluded that to effectively deliver on its business model, it needed to ensure that it would have world-class performance from the following categories of employees:

- R&D scientists

- Manufacturing managers and supervisors

- Sales representatives

Big Pharma's management team also noted that an important organizational capability was in the domain of regulatory affairs. Because Big Pharma is heavily regulated by the FDA, which imposes very strict guidelines that must be followed if a drug is to receive approval, ensuring that the correct infrastructure is in place is crucial to Big Pharma's success. However, while all acknowledged the importance of the regulatory affairs function, several managers noted that the firm had been able to select or develop very high-quality managers in this division on a consistent basis, and currently the bench strength for this role was deep. Thus, although the regulatory affairs role was important, Big Pharma's management team did not believe that it was as crucial to the firm's success as R&D, sales, or manufacturing.

"A" Performance in an "A" Position— Measuring Workforce Success in R&D

Big Pharma's vision in R&D is to develop leading-edge pharmaceuticals to help improve and prolong patient life. At the end of the day, workforce success at Big Pharma means delivering new "blockbuster" drugs through R&D and to a lesser extent licensing, manufacturing, and distributing medicines that were developed by competitors. While everyone at Big Pharma understands the importance of developing such new drugs, what is less well understood are the *processes* through which this happens. It is not enough to simply identify which roles disproportionately contribute to firm success—Big Pharma also needs to understand the factors that distinguish between low and high employee performance *within* each of those roles. Effective strategy execution requires that managers help to consistently enable "A" performance in "A" positions—and for the "A," or most important, customers.

To better understand these processes, Big Pharma initiated a study of successful and unsuccessful drug-development processes at its firm. As a result of these analyses, it introduced the following measures into its Workforce Scorecard:

New products. The number of new products that progress to Phase I of clinical trials is a key indicator of Big Pharma's success in new product introductions.

Therapeutic area knowledge. The breadth and depth of therapeutic area knowledge among R&D scientists is also a key driver of successful new product development.

New technologies. Introduction of new discovery and development technologies helps to leverage employee knowledge and competencies. It also helps support the business indirectly, by increasing retention of high-performing scientists. Big Pharma has learned that the best scientists highly value access to the very best and latest laboratory equipment.

Speed to market. Cycle time from discovery to Phase I is also a key driver of Big Pharma's success.

"A" Performance in an "A" Position—
Measuring Workforce Success in Manufacturing

Big Pharma's vision in manufacturing is to develop operational excellence in a Six Sigma environment, where there is zero tolerance for product defects. At Big Pharma, manufacturing excellence isn't just "nice to have," it is absolutely critical to the business. Not only is there a clear moral obligation not to produce ineffective or, worse, harmful drugs, but the negative economic consequences for a breach in quality are extremely high in the pharmaceutical industry. Such a lapse in quality, which may be caused by manufacturing impurities or even mislabeling, will almost always result in a product recall. Such recalls can result in hundreds of millions of dollars of direct losses and reputational damage.

Big Pharma's analyses also showed that the competencies and behaviors needed for manufacturing excellence are quite different from those needed for R&D innovation. As a result, they began to track the following measures:

Index of overall quality. Quality is crucial. Quality is also a multidimensional and multifaceted construct. Big Pharma developed an index of overall manufacturing quality that included compound purity, yield rates, and wastage. While we discuss the construction and interpretation of indexes in more detail in chapter 5, the basic point of using an index in this context is to provide a single number that reflects Big Pharma's performance in a specific domain—in this case, product quality. All variables were standardized and equally weighted.

Order fulfillment rate. This is the extent to which orders are shipped complete within twenty-four hours of the time promised to customers.

Standard cost performance. Big Pharma measures its total manufacturing costs against internal benchmarks.

Working capital ratios. Big Pharma's management team is held accountable for managing working capital and cash flow in each of the manufacturing sites.

Lost-time injuries. The number and duration of worker injuries are closely monitored by Big Pharma, which places particular emphasis on worker safety in all areas of the business.

Work stoppages. The number and duration of plant shutdowns (for any reason) are reported on a monthly basis.

Overall productivity. Finally, each of Big Pharma's manufacturing plants reports an index of overall productivity.

"A" Performance in an "A" Position— Measuring Workforce Success in Sales

Big Pharma's goals in sales are to build trust, enhance sales force education and product knowledge, and generate market share for each of the key constituencies—patents, physicians, and institutions. Of all of these, the amount of time that a salesperson is able to spend in direct contact with a prescribing physician is the key driver of success. High-performing salespeople ("A" players) are able to "triage" their sales prospects effectively, spending a disproportionate amount of time with the high-potential leads. "C" players, in contrast, tend to be more egalitarian in their distribution of time across sales prospects. The net result is that salespeople performing at the ninetieth percentile sell nearly ten times more than do average salespeople—a very substantial difference.

As a result, there is a real need for the sales force to move well beyond the role of order taker to partnering with the physicians and institutions (hospitals, HMOs, insurers) to provide information as well. This requires world-class communication and selling skills, in addition to a well-developed understanding of how and why physicians make decisions about prescriptions. The sales force needs to be adept at providing the information necessary to help doctors make decisions. Big Pharma identified the following metrics as key drivers of sales force success:

Market share of therapeutic area or drug class. Much as with any other business, a key driver of profitability for Big Pharma is the ability to capture market share.

New prescriptions versus total prescriptions versus quota. Big Pharma's sales force doesn't sell medications directly to physicians. They provide information and samples to doctors and hospitals, and encourage them to write prescriptions for their patients. Big Pharma tracks the number of new prescriptions and the total number of prescriptions sold per doctor, and compares these numbers with each salesperson's quota. Increasing market share means that currently served physicians write more prescriptions, but that new physicians are encouraged to do so as well.

Product and competitor knowledge. Big Pharma's analyses showed that its most successful salespeople have a deep understanding not only of Big Pharma's product line, but the products of their competitors as well. This allows the sales force to portray Big Pharma's products favorably, when appropriate.

Sales calls greater than five minutes with the physician. A key driver of sales force success is gaining access to physicians, which is a significant challenge in this industry. Big Pharma's analyses showed that sales increased significantly when salespeople spent more than five minutes with a physician.

Sample productivity. Finally, Big Pharma also tracks the extent to which sample medications distributed by the sales force are related to subsequent prescriptions. Because samples can be quite expensive, this helps the firm to make the most effective use of its marketing budget.

Measuring Leadership and Workforce Behaviors

Big Pharma's analyses showed that workforce success was generally associated with four broad outcomes: the quality of leadership, the extent to which knowledge was shared willingly and effectively, the extent to which teams worked together in a cohesive and effective manner, and the extent to which high-performing employees were retained—and low-performing employees exited the business. While they found some differences in how these processes operated across each of the "A" positions, the general high level of consistency in the findings led them to use the same measures for each key position but to report the results separately. Big Pharma uses an index of items to reflect performance in each domain.

Leadership profile index. This reflects the weighted average score on a validated 360-degree leadership survey.

Knowledge-sharing index. This reflects the weighted average score on a validated scale of knowledge sharing. There are two versions of this scale—one that is used for intact teams and a more general form that is used for all employees.

Team performance index. This reflects the weighted average score on a validated 360-degree performance-appraisal tool. It is only used for intact teams.

Proportion of "A" players retained and proportion of "C" players exited. Big Pharma knew that the overall turnover could be a highly misleading number. It hoped to manage turnover such that the exit rates of low performers were high and the exit rates of high performers were low.

Measuring Workforce Competencies

Big Pharma's analyses also showed that employee competencies had a significant impact on the new-product development process, sales, and manufacturing. The firm used the following measures for each of the key positions, each of which is specifically designed to tap a different dimension of workforce differentiation:

Total percentage of "A" players. Big Pharma tracked the proportion of employees in each strategic job category who were rated as "A" players. Big Pharma's goal was to first ensure that it had "A" players in "A" positions.

Percentage of "B" players with "A" potential. Big Pharma also tracked the proportion of "B"-rated employees whose managers felt could be developed into "A" players. These employees were targeted for special developmental programs.

Percentage of training and development budget spent on "A" players. In the past, Big Pharma had tended to overinvest in "C" or low-performing employees, many of whom should never have been hired. Big Pharma's workforce strategy is now focused on ensuring that a higher proportion of its developmental monies is spent on the most promising employees.

Percentage of pay at risk for "A" players, percentage of options and restricted shares granted to "A" players, and *percentage of bonus for "A" players.* Big Pharma's strategy was to significantly increase the pay at risk (earnings potential) for its very best employees, and these three measures tracked its progress toward that goal.

Skills checkout rating, score on sales-call role-play exercise (in sales), and new product test scores (in sales). Big Pharma developed skills and proficiency tests for many of its key positions, and these metrics track the proportion of the workforce with "Pass" or "High Pass" scores on these tests.

Bench strength rating on 360-degree potential assessment tool. Big Pharma was also very concerned about its bench strength in many of its key roles. This measure reflects the extent to which each key position has one or more ready replacements—that is, employees who are currently qualified to be promoted.

Measuring Workforce Mind-set and Culture

Finally, workforce mind-set and a supportive culture are also needed prerequisites to ensure successful strategy execution. Big Pharma developed the following measures to help track progress in this area:

Percentage of the workforce with a clear understanding of Big Pharma's overall strategy—as well as Big Pharma's strategy as it pertains to their jobs

Percentage of the workforce that is clearly committed to Big Pharma's strategy

Percentage of the workforce that has the requisite skills to execute Big Pharma's strategy

Percentage of the workforce that believes that Big Pharma's culture supports strategy execution

Each measure is collected via electronic survey. One-twelfth of the workforce is randomly surveyed every month, so the leadership team is constantly aware of the current state of workforce mind-set.

INTEGRATING THE WORKFORCE SCORECARD
AT BIG PHARMA

Big Pharma's integrated Workforce Scorecard is shown in figure 3-2. In addition to the key strategy drivers associated with mind-set, competencies, behaviors, and results, Big Pharma tracks a series of financial outcomes associated with the workforce, such as total employment, total compensation, total budget for training and development (T&D), total bonus payouts, and total options granted. These measures are reported separately for each of the key or "A" positions, to help the leadership team track its level of investment in each of the key roles.

FIGURE 3-2

Workforce Scorecard for Big Pharma

"A" Position	R&D R&D Scientist	Manufacturing Manufacturing Supervisor	Marketing and Sales Sales Representative	All Others
Workforce Success	# of new compounds generated that progress to Phase I Breadth and depth of therapeutic area knowledge Introduction of new discovery and development technologies Cycle time from discovery to Phase I	Quality index Order fulfillment rate Standard cost performance Working-capital ratios Lost-time injuries Work stoppages Productivity	Market share of therapeutic area or drug class New Rx versus total Rx versus quota Product and competitor knowledge Sales calls > 5 minutes with doctor Sample productivity	
Workforce Behaviors	Knowledge-sharing index Team performance index Leadership profile Index Retention % of "A" players Exit % of "C" players	Knowledge-sharing index Team performance index Leadership profile Index Retention % of "A" players Exit % of "C" players	Knowledge-sharing index Team performance index Leadership profile Index Retention % of "A" players Exit % of "C" players	Knowledge-sharing index Team performance index Leadership profile Index Retention % of "A" players Exit % of "C" players

Workforce Competencies	Total % "A" players % "B" players with "A" potential % T&D for "A" players % pay at risk for "A" players % options to "A" players % bonus for "A" players Skills checkout Bench strength rating on 360	Quality indexTotal % "A" players % "B" players with "A" potential % T&D for "A" players % pay at risk for "A" players % options to "A" players % bonus for "A" players Skills checkout Bench strength rating on 360	Market share of therapeutic area Total % "A" players % "B" players with "A" potential % T&D for "A" players % pay at risk for A" players % options to "A" players % bonus for "A" players Score on sales role-play New product test scores	Total % "A" players % "B" players with "A" potential % T&D for "A" players % pay at risk for "A" players % options to "A" players % bonus for "A" players Skills checkout Bench strength rating on 360° feedback
Workforce Mind-set/Culture	% understand strategy % committing to strategy % have skills to execute strategy % feeling culture supports strategy execution	% understand strategy % committing to strategy % have skills to execute strategy % feeling culture supports strategy execution	% understand strategy % committing to strategy % have skills to execute strategy % feeling culture supports strategy execution	% understand strategy % committing to strategy % have skills to execute strategy % feeling culture supports strategy execution
Workforce Financials	Total employment Total compensation Total T&D budget Total bonus payouts Total options granted	Total employment Total compensation Total T&D budget Total bonus payouts Total options granted	Total employment Total compensation Total T&D budget Total bonus payouts Total options granted	Total employment Total compensation Total T&D budget Total bonus payouts Total options granted

Common and Unique Elements of the Workforce Scorecard

An important issue to address in developing a Workforce Scorecard is the extent to which all of the elements are the same across the "A" positions, or whether the metrics will differ dramatically for each different "A" position. The answer is that the closer you get to the specific measures of workforce success, the more differentiated the measures must become. As can be seen in Big Pharma's Workforce Scorecard, the measures for mind-set, competencies, and behaviors are largely the same, while the measures for workforce success differ considerably among the R&D, manufacturing, and marketing and sales positions. The behaviors and accomplishments can be very different across the key roles. In addition, culture and mind-set in R&D and in manufacturing can differ dramatically—both in content and how they are managed. However, it is likely that we will use the same *types* of measures to interpret these attributes in each case—even though their *interpretation* might differ. This finding highlights for us the importance of reporting these elements separately for each key element of the workforce, but ensuring that managers are held accountable for the quality of workforce mind-set, competencies, and leadership within each of their respective areas of the business.

What Can Be Learned from the Workforce Scorecard?

As we described previously, there are an almost unlimited number of elements of the workforce that can be measured in any organization. At Big Pharma, the key challenge was to focus on the critical few measures that really drive strategy execution—for those critical few "A" jobs. Big Pharma's management team learned (to its surprise) that it actually measured many things about the workforce. However, many of those elements were redundant, focused on transactions (e.g., cost per hire or time to fill an open position), and/or were "legacy metrics"— elements that the management team had been tracking, but not using, for many years. Unfortunately, very few of those metrics really told the team anything about its progress toward strategy execution. As a result, until the development of the Workforce Scorecard, workforce measurement had a very poor reputation at Big Pharma. For other attributes of an effective Workforce Scorecard, besides a focus on the critical few elements, see "Attributes of an Effective Workforce Scorecard."

ATTRIBUTES OF AN EFFECTIVE
WORKFORCE SCORECARD

A Workforce Scorecard should *describe the process of strategy execution.* Effective workforce metrics are based on a model of workforce success that is comprehensive, mutually exclusive, and only minimally redundant. Organizations have the unfortunate tendency to measure the easy things many times and the more difficult things rarely, if at all. For example, many firms measure return on sales (ROS), return on assets (ROA), return on net assets (RONA), and return on invested capital (ROIC), and give them all equal weight when evaluating the performance of the firm. The problem with these measures is that they are so highly correlated that they all provide essentially the same information. For example, ROS, ROA, and RONA all have the same numerator (net income), so interpreting any differences in these ratios is essentially measuring the differences between sales (which can vary significantly from year to year) and assets (which usually don't vary much from year to year). Similarly, ROIC (which also uses net income in the numerator) has as a denominator invested capital, which is very highly correlated with total assets (much like ROA). The implication of these results is that while there will be differences in the *levels* of these variables (e.g., 4.2 percent versus 6.8 percent versus 7.0 percent versus 7.6 percent) in the same firm in any given year, these measures are so highly *correlated* that they all contain roughly the same information. Managers could just choose one of them and come to the same conclusions about performance. Where is the harm in using all four? This is certainly an option, as long as the presence of redundant items doesn't confuse the audience and crowd out other measures.

A Workforce Scorecard should *help managers execute strategy more quickly by improving the quality of decisions about the workforce.* The primary objective of workforce measurement should be to provide the data and insight needed to improve workforce management. Such metrics should be based on a *strategy map* that describes "what causes what," or the *causal logic* underlying the process of strategy execution through the workforce. The metrics should also be matched with a clear and compelling process to help managers understand how to use them. Most large organizations actually have many more measures than they should have. The problem is that without an overall integrated framework, managers lose focus and create ad hoc metrics and reporting frameworks. Because these frameworks are rarely widely accepted, they tend to not be actionable, even as they proliferate. Thus, developing an overall set of metrics can actually save a lot of expense, if it can help to crowd out such legacy metrics.

A Workforce Scorecard should *have a solid base in empirical research*. Managers should recognize that there is a negative correlation between the accessibility of a metric and its utility—if it were easy, metrics (and HR) wouldn't likely be such a source of competitive advantage. To help guide the selection of the metrics that really matter, managers should recognize that there is a substantial body of empirical research that has explored the determinants of firm success. Not surprisingly, this literature finds that some metrics matter more than others. Without a clear link to a research base, the easy becomes the enemy of the good.

A Workforce Scorecard should *contain a mix of leading and lagging indicators of firm success*. To effectively drive behavior, measures need to help generate a clear "line of sight" such that: (1) employees know what their role is in the organization and how it contributes to firm success, and (2) success at each lower level in the firm helps to create success at the next higher level.

A Workforce Scorecard should *focus on the critical few elements that really drive success*. Managers should identify the minimum number of key measures that communicate and help to evaluate the firm's strategic intent—and focus on those measures—no more, but certainly no less.

A Workforce Scorecard should *differentiate—customers, jobs, and employees*. As we described in chapter 2, one of the key attributes of successful workforce management is *differentiation*. As a result, effective workforce measures should highlight the key or "A" positions in an organization, and provide a very clear description of "A" performance in those roles as well. Average levels of culture, competence, or turnover aren't particularly helpful to managers—the measures of strategic relevance focus on those attributes in our most important positions, and for the high performers, not the lowest performers.

A Workforce Scorecard should *serve as a teaching tool*. You can't assume that employees understand their role in the firm's success—or even the firm's key mission and vision. For example, at Sears executives were dismayed to learn that employees held a much-distorted view of how the firm operated as well as what was expected of them.[a] Senior executives asked hundreds of employees, "What do you think is the primary thing that you get paid to do here every day?" Instead of an answer that highlighted the importance of "delighting the customer," more than half the workforce said, "I get paid to protect the assets of the

[a]See Rucci, Kirn, and Quinn, "The Employee-Customer-Profit Chain at Sears," *Harvard Business Review* (January–February) 1997: 83–97.

company"—that is, keep customers from stealing the merchandise! When they asked these same employees, "How much profit do you suppose Sears keeps on every dollar of revenue?" the median response was forty-five cents! The actual answer was two cents. Measures and metrics can help employees come to understand the firm's goals and objectives and their own role in contributing to firm success. As a tool to teach the workforce about strategy, workforce metrics should help focus the workforce and drive alignment between strategy end behaviors.

A Workforce Scorecard should *show actionable and clear objectives for improvement.* World-class Workforce Scorecards highlight strategy-linked as well as actionable elements of the workforce, and provide managers with a clear sense of what to do next if the scores on the measures don't meet the objectives. One of the most robust findings in all of the social sciences literature is that employees and groups that set specific, challenging goals outperform those who set no goals or set unrealistic goals.[b] An important part of the workforce measurement process is to facilitate goal setting, cascading of goals throughout the workforce, providing feedback on results (goal attainment), and, finally, facilitating links to compensation.

A Workforce Scorecard should *identify specific initiatives that will drive improvement.* The elements of the Workforce Scorecard need to be actionable, not just informative. Measures not only need to include specific and challenging goals for improvement, but also should be matched with specific initiatives to drive workforce improvement. We demonstrate how to match goals and objectives with initiatives for improvement in the next chapters.

A Workforce Scorecard should *encourage continuous learning and experimentation.* Measures reflect management's best hypothesis about how the workforce creates value in an organization. As with all hypotheses, the goal is to validate these predictions with actual data. Some managers can be quite uncomfortable with uncertainty. We are reminded of the old story of the middle-aged person who resisted going back to college to get a degree, saying that in four years, she would be fifty. Of course, the key question in response has to be, How old would you be in four years if you *didn't* go back to school? Measurement of the workforce is a bit like this predicament—the key elements that drive your strategy will be in operation whether you choose to measure them our not. In the spirit of continuous improvement, we believe that the best time to start is now.

[b]Mark E. Tubbs, "Goal setting: A Meta-analytic Examination of the Empirical Evidence," *Journal of Applied Psychology* 71, no. 3 (1986): 474–483.

The Workforce Scorecard helped Big Pharma's leadership team address a number of key challenges associated with strategy execution. The first key outcome of the process was that Big Pharma's management was now able to effectively facilitate a discussion with the workforce about the role of key or "A" jobs in the business. By highlighting the importance of R&D, manufacturing, and sales, the leadership team was able to more completely describe the value creation process to everyone in the business. By positioning all of the other roles at Big Pharma as supportive of those key positions, it was able to describe the importance of these roles in the value creation process, while at the same time making it clear that the firm would never win unless it was successful in R&D, manufacturing, and sales. Simply put, the Workforce Scorecard provided the management team with a tool to describe the process of strategy execution.

As a corollary, Big Pharma's leadership team discovered that there is no such thing as "overall" workforce performance. A "high-performing" sales manager is doing very different things than a top R&D scientist or even a manufacturing supervisor, and it is very important that the workforce metrics used by a firm highlight these differences.

A second key outcome of the process was an improvement in managers' decision quality about the workforce. Over the long run, firms that win differentiate—customers, jobs, and employees—and they focus on the critical few elements that really drive business performance. This was in many ways counterculture at Big Pharma, where historically all employees and jobs received more or less the same levels of investment. As a result, they had too much talent in some nonproductive roles and not enough talent in some critical roles. As a direct result of developing the Workforce Scorecard, Big Pharma was able to reallocate some of its scarce workforce development resources to its most productive uses.

A third key outcome of the process was that Big Pharma set clear objectives for improvement. Effective workforce management requires specific goals and targets for improvement as well as specific initiatives to help drive the needed behaviors. Now that Big Pharma has made clear the specific behaviors and outcomes that are needed from the workforce, the next step in the process is to design an HR management system to ensure that the firm's key strategic objectives are met. In the next chapter, we show how to link the specific elements of the Workforce Scorecard to an HR Scorecard that can help to deliver the desired results.

4

LINKING THE WORKFORCE
AND HR SCORECARDS

Strategy Execution Through
HR Management Systems

I N THE LAST CHAPTER we described the key elements of the Workforce Scorecard and provided a detailed example of its design and implementation at "Big Pharma." We also made the point that measurement alone won't lead to improved business performance. Significant and lasting change in organizations isn't likely without a plan. For workforce metrics to effectively help leverage strategy execution and drive shareholder value, they need to be systematically linked to both specific targets for improvement (stretch goals) and specific initiatives designed to enhance performance.

In this chapter we focus on cascading the key elements of the Workforce Scorecard into specific actions and accountabilities that managers can understand, own, and act on. In doing so, our goal is to help ensure that the firm's HR management system elicits the needed competencies and behaviors from the workforce, which ultimately drives firm success. The tool that we use to do this is the *HR Scorecard*.[1]

DELIVERING WORKFORCE SUCCESS WITH HR MANAGEMENT SYSTEMS

Delivering results with the Workforce Scorecard means we need to cascade the firm's strategic goals and objectives—such as shortening R&D cycle time or improving quality and productivity in manufacturing—into specific HR management systems and an HR Scorecard that will help ensure the achievement of these goals. But just as we need to know and understand the firm's strategy before we can develop an effective Workforce Scorecard, we must also understand the firm's workforce strategy before we can build an effective HR Scorecard. The Workforce Scorecard highlights the key workforce outcomes that each senior manager needs to focus on providing to the business. The HR Scorecard, in contrast, is intended to "drill down" below the elements contained in the Workforce Scorecard to address the question: What type of HR management system is required to deliver a workforce capable of successful strategy execution?

THE KEY ELEMENTS OF THE HR SCORECARD

Based on our research over the last decade, we have identified a series of measurement categories, shown in table 4-1, that we believe senior HR leaders need to focus on to help them drive workforce success and strategy execution.

TABLE 4-1

Five Key Elements of the HR Scorecard

Workforce Success	Have we delivered on each of the key elements contained in the workforce scorecard—that is, workforce success, leadership and workforce behaviors, workforce capabilities, and workforce mind-set and culture?
Right HR Function and Workforce Costs	Is our total investment in the workforce (not just the HR function) appropriate (not just minimized)?
Right Types of Alignment	Are our HR practices aligned with the business strategy and differentiated across positions where appropriate?
Right HR Practices	Have we designed and implemented world-class HR management policies and practices throughout the business?
Right HR Professionals	Do our HR professionals have the skills they need to design and implement a world-class HR management system?

FIGURE 4-1

The Five "Rights" of HR Measurement

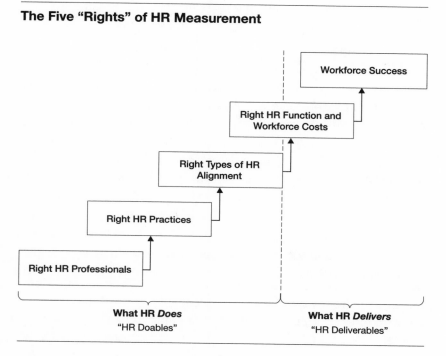

Figure 4-1 shows the interrelationships among the five elements of the HR Scorecard. Having the right HR professionals and designing a system of HR management practices that is aligned with the firm's strategy is largely the responsibility of the HR function. Making sure that these practices are effectively implemented, at appropriate cost levels, is a responsibility that is shared by HR and line managers. The key element to remember is the importance of having a causal logic that describes the processes needed to develop and implement an effective system for workforce management.

The HR Scorecard is designed to link directly with the Workforce Scorecard, as we described in chapter 1. In essence, line and HR leaders share responsibility for the elements contained in the Workforce Scorecard, while HR managers have primary responsibility for the elements in the HR Scorecard. Next we describe the elements of the HR Scorecard in greater detail. Returning to the example we began in the last chapter, we then show how an HR Scorecard can be developed at Big Pharma.

Workforce Success

As we described in detail in the last chapter, we believe that these are the fundamental questions that need to be asked about the workforce: Has the workforce accomplished the key strategic objectives for the business? Have we produced the right types of workforce success, leadership and workforce behaviors, workforce competencies, and workforce mind-set and culture? Measures of workforce success are taken directly from the Workforce Scorecard, which is intended to demonstrate that line and HR managers need to be held accountable for the same outcomes. Placing the same workforce success factors on each scorecard consistently reminds both HR and line managers that they are being held accountable for the same results.

Right HR Function and Workforce Costs

In developing metrics to help track the right HR function and workforce costs, the key question to be asked is, Is our total investment in the workforce (not just the HR function) appropriate (not just minimized)? We believe that this question is fundamental, because we frequently observe HR functions making some well-intentioned but ultimately counterproductive decisions with the intent of lowering costs. This can be seen most clearly in the use of HR function metrics such as cost per hire or days to fill an open position. With respect to the workforce, the relevant costs are the *total costs* or ROI of the firm's workforce for the expected level of productivity—not just the costs associated with the HR function. As we described in chapter 1, total workforce costs average nearly 70 percent of operating expenses in the S&P 500, while HR function costs generally average about 1 percent of operating expenses. Over the last few decades, most HR functions have become much leaner and more efficient, and have placed much greater emphasis on outsourcing, centers of excellence, and so on. As a result, it is becoming increasingly difficult to take costs out of the HR function, and some firms are finding that reducing HR function budgets can actually be quite counterproductive (and expensive). At Verizon, for example, HR leaders found that a shift to lower-cost recruiting sources for call center employees had the desired impact of lowering cost per hire. But it also had an expensive unintended consequence, because the employees hired from "lower cost" pools had lower performance and shorter tenures, thus increasing total workforce costs.[2]

Similarly, in search of cost reductions, many firms lay off employees, only to hire them back later at perhaps 140 percent of their previous salaries, with significant and negative economic consequences for the firm.[3] This happens for at least two reasons. First, firms frequently use a one-size-fits-all approach to layoffs and cut employees before they meaningfully restructure work. So, what ends up happening is that the employees leave but their workload doesn't, leaving the remaining employees stressed and lobbying for more help. Since the recently departed employees know the firm and the work the best, they are often brought back into the firm to address a specific business problem. Second, because such "temps" aren't counted in the firm's overall head-count, layoffs can help managers meet their numerical goal for head-count reduction. However, hiring temps can increase the firm's overall wage bill while decreasing productive efficiency. The solution to this situation (in addition to managing the workforce in such a way that layoffs are seldom likely) is to hold line and HR managers accountable for the *total* costs of the workforce for the appropriate level of productivity, not the *HR function* costs. Example measures of right workforce costs can be found in table 4-2.[4] As with the metrics presented in the last chapter, the reader will quickly note that there are a great many metrics presented in this and in the following tables— many more than should be presented in any firm's HR Scorecard. This is by design. The point that we are trying to make is that there is no shortage of *possible* metrics. They key challenge is to select *useful* metrics, which should be guided by your firm's strategy.

Right Types of HR Alignment

Measuring HR alignment requires that we ask, Are our HR practices aligned with the business strategy and differentiated across business groups, where appropriate? Alignment can take two forms. *Internal alignment* reflects the extent to which our workforce management practices fit together in a cohesive whole and are mutually reinforcing. *External alignment* reflects the extent to which the firm's entire bundle of workforce management practices effectively helps to execute

TABLE 4-2

Measures for Right HR Function and Workforce Costs

KEY QUESTION: IS OUR TOTAL INVESTMENT IN THE WORKFORCE (NOT JUST THE HR FUNCTION) APPROPRIATE (NOT JUST MINIMIZED)?

Absenteeism rate by job category and job performance

Accident costs

Accident safety ratings

Accuracy of HRIS data

Attendance

Average employee tenure (by performance level)

Benefits cost per employee (e.g., $, trend)

Benefits costs as a percent of payroll or revenue

Benefits as a percentage of total compensation

Competency development expense per employee

Compliance with federal and state fair-employment practices

Compliance with technical requirements of affirmative action

Compra-ratio status of critical human capital (e.g., percent > Q3)

Comprehensiveness of safety monitoring

Competency development expense per employee

Cost of HR-related litigation

Cost of injuries

Cost per grievance

Cost per hire (by job classification and employee performance)

Cost per trainee hour

Firm salary/competitor salary ratio

FTE head-count by diversity representation in HR

FTE head-count by gender in HR

HR expense per "A" employee

HR expense per "C" employee

HR expense/total expense

Incidence of injuries

Litigation filings/litigation costs per employee

Lost time due to accidents

Lost work days

Measures of cycle time for key HR processes by level of customer satisfaction

Number of applicants per recruiting source (by quality and by key position)

Incentive compensation differential (low versus high performers)

Number of days lost to safety incidents

Number of hires per recruiting source (by quality)

Number of recruiting advertising programs in place

Number of safety training and awareness activities

strategy. Example measures of both types of alignment can be found in table 4-3.

The implications of both internal and external alignment are that while it is important that each of the HR management practices that a firm adopts be carefully linked to its strategy, it is also crucial that the bundle of HR practices a firm adopts be internally consistent and linked together in a meaningful way. Because HR practices are often developed and managed independently by various subfunctions within the HR department, we wouldn't expect (and in fact don't often find) those elements to work together in a way that makes sense to the workforce. For example, one HR leader recently told us that he has a

TABLE 4-2

Measures for Right HR Function and Workforce Costs *(continued)*

Number of stress-related illnesses	Retention rates of critical human capital
Number of training days and programs per year	Sick days per full-time equivalent per year
Offer-to-acceptance ratio	Speed of salary action processing
OSHA audits	Time for new program design
Payroll expense per employee	Time needed to orient new employees
People expense/earnings	Time to fill an open "A" position with an "A" player
People expense/earnings before people expense	Total compensation as a percentage of earnings or cash flow
People expense/revenues	Total compensation as a percentage of revenue
Percent and number of employees involved in training	Total compensation expense per employee
Percent correct data in HR information system	Total HR investment/revenues
Percent payroll spent on training	Turnover by recruiting source
Processing cost per benefit transaction	Turnover costs
Productivity gains through use of HRIS ($ and response time)	Turnover rate by job category and job performance
Rate of EEO complaints	Variable labor cost as percent of variable revenue
Rate of employee grievances	Worker's compensation costs
Ratio of offers to acceptances in critical human capital positions	Worker's compensation experience rating
Recruitment to fill time in days for "A" players	Workforce cost as percent compared to industry index
Requests for transfer per supervisor	Workforce cost per unit of production
Response time per benefit information request	Workforce investment per employee (all relevant costs)
Response time per information request	

hard time getting his benefits director to work with his compensation director! In this business, it is hard to imagine that the compensation and benefits programs will work together in a way that creates real value for both employees and shareholders.

Misfit, or misalignment, among HR management practices isn't usually the result of willful incompetence by managers. We're convinced that misalignment is a naturally occurring phenomenon in organizations. Like entropy in social systems, over time management systems tend to fall into disarray—even if they started as perfectly aligned. Thus, developing effective alignment requires consistent monitoring by managers.

TABLE 4-3

Measures for Right Types of Alignment

KEY QUESTION: ARE OUR HR PRACTICES ALIGNED WITH THE BUSINESS STRATEGY, INTEGRATED WITH EACH OTHER, AND DIFFERENTIATED ACROSS EMPLOYEE GROUPS, WHERE APPROPRIATE?

Extent to which customer expectations are addressed by learning programs

Extent to which employees are held accountable for their own performance

Extent to which employees are rewarded for desired behaviors

Extent to which employees believe that the performance management system largely determines promotions and raises/bonuses

Extent to which employees can influence the content and degree of challenge associated with their own development plan

Extent to which employees feel the performance appraisal standards are specific, challenging, and fair

Extent to which employees have ready access to the information and knowledge that they need

Extent to which employees see a clear link between the performance appraisal process and their compensation

Extent to which employees see the performance management system as clearly linked to firm strategy

Extent to which employees understand what is expected of them throughout the performance management process

Extent to which hiring, evaluation, and compensation practices seek out and reward knowledge creation and sharing

Extent to which HR does a thorough job of preacquisition soft-asset due diligence

Extent to which HR is helping to develop necessary leadership competencies

Extent to which HR leadership is involved early in selection of potential acquisition candidates

Extent to which HR measurement systems are seen as credible

Extent to which information is communicated effectively to employees

Extent to which level of reward is appropriately matched with level of accomplishment

Extent to which most employees feel that the performance appraisal process is fair

Extent to which required employee competencies are reflected in recruiting, staffing, and performance management

Extent to which the average employee understands how his or her job contributes to the firm's success

Extent to which the average employee understands how his or her job contributes to *customer satisfaction with your products and services*

Extent to which the average employee understands how his or her job contributes to *financial results* (e g., profitability and shareholder value)

Extent to which the average employee understands how his or her job contributes to *key business processes* (e.g., cycle time and quality)

Take, for example, the situation illustrated in figure 4-2. A firm has recently adopted a competitive strategy focused on customer intimacy. The firm believes that this strategy will require shorter cycle times and customer responsiveness throughout its business, but especially in its R&D, procurement, billing, and sales and service operations. Based on an systems analysis of its work processes inspired by the work of Peter Senge, the firm believes that a broad-based movement toward teams is crucial to the success of its new strategy.[5]

TABLE 4-3

Measures for Right Types of Alignment (continued)

Extent to which the firm's organizational design (i.e., the way in which jobs and work are structured) effectively supports your firm's strategy

Extent to which the firm's training and development programs effectively support strategy execution

Extent to which the performance management and appraisal process effectively supports employee behaviors required to execute strategy

Extent to which your firm has developed a set of behavioral competencies for hiring, developing, managing, and rewarding people

External (with business strategy) alignment index

Focus group findings on line executives' (and line managers') perceptions of HR alignment

HR workforce's perception of HR's "tool kit" integration (practice by practice)

Internal (among HR practices) alignment index

Internal (consistency of HR policies and practices) alignment index

Internal talent strength; availability ratio per vacancy

Line manager satisfaction with compensation outcomes

Line manager satisfaction with culture change initiatives

Line manager satisfaction with executive development outcomes

Line manager satisfaction with performance management outcomes

Line manager satisfaction with recruiting and hiring outcomes

Line manager satisfaction with training outcomes

Line manager feedback on HR strategy alignment with business strategy (survey scores)

Line manager satisfaction with new hires

Magnitude of correlation between customer satisfaction ratings and reward issuance

Management satisfaction with HR contributions to organizational transformation efforts

Percent of HR leadership time spent on HR alignment issues

Quality of training content delivered

Satisfaction of "A" players with compensation package

Satisfaction of "C" players with compensation package

Success in implementing alignment initiatives

Extent to which the firm develops leadership talent consistent with the business needs

Extent to which the firm's compensation and rewards policy supports the implementation of strategy

---

Based on what worked for this business in the past, its job descriptions were fairly narrowly drawn. For example, an Accountant 1 only did accounting work. Consequently, employees were hired and promoted based on individual skills—that is, individual contributors. Consistent with this situation, performance management and compensation systems were linked to performance on individual, as opposed to group or team, goals. Finally, training and management development systems were based almost entirely on the development of individual skills.

FIGURE 4-2

Archetypes of Failure: Adoption of Teams

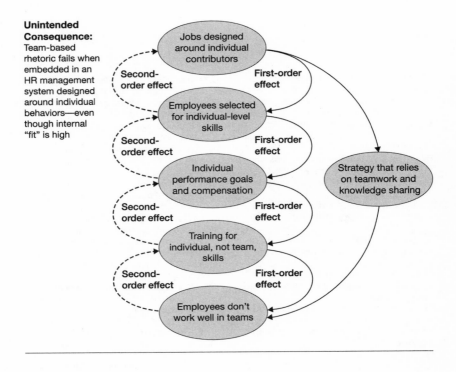

Not surprisingly, many of the firm's employees had a very difficult time making the adjustment to working effectively in a team-based environment. In fact, some of the employees who had previously been rated very highly found that they subsequently received very poor performance appraisal ratings in the new milieu.

The same logic can also be extended to evaluating the types of HR metrics that are likely to be used in this business. In the preceding example, the managers in charge of the firm's recruiting efforts are held accountable to a budget figure—for example, cost per hire. As a result, recruiting managers strive for efficiency and cost-effectiveness in the new-hire process, and hire the skills currently required by the organization at the going market rate. As a direct result of this strategy, new hires are not likely to have the competencies required to become promotable more than a level or two above their current positions. Consequently, the firm's training energies (and budget) will be directed toward ensuring that the firm has a promotable cadre of employees, as opposed to increasing the skill sets of the highest-level employees. As a result, these high-potential employees will become more likely to leave the firm, because they are not being developed as quickly as they might be elsewhere. Thus, the firm must either promote below-par candidates or hire additional employees from outside the firm. As a result, the tertiary effect is that that firm must increase its recruiting efforts and budgets to deal with the increased recruiting needs at all levels of the business not only because of the absence of promotable employees, but also because of the increased turnover of high-potential employees (often due to the lack of perceived promotion opportunities, to the extent they are competing with external candidates). In addition, the firm may simultaneously have to increase training efforts at all levels throughout the firm.

What is going on here? Certainly the firm has achieved a very high level of internal "fit," in that all of the current policies and practices work together in a balanced outcome—to produce undesirable results. In fact, this system contains so many different balancing and feedback loops (first- and second-order effects) that effecting a significant change in it will prove very difficult indeed. We describe this as an "archetype of failure" to reflect the fact that they are commonly occurring systems; we encounter them on a regular basis.

The converse of these negative synergies or misalignment could occur when all of the elements of a firm's work system "pull together" to create a form of alignment or synergy. For example, in many businesses, we are witnessing a shift to "upstream" strategies that require leveraging the firm's knowledge and intellectual capital as a key element of success. Imagine a firm, as shown in figure 4-3, that has developed explicit strategies for the development of knowledge and intellectual capital. This firm has embraced the "learning organization" rhetoric, which requires both the creation of strategically relevant new knowledge throughout the business, and efficient and effective sharing of this knowledge throughout the business. As a central part of this process, the firm provides training for the mechanics of knowledge sharing within and across teams, and subsequently provides meaningful opportunities for employees and teams to demonstrate these newly

FIGURE 4-3

Archetypes of Success: Knowledge Management Strategy

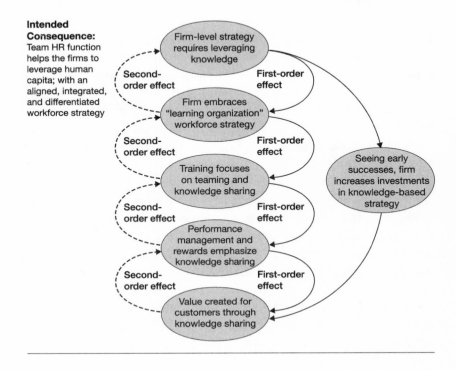

Intended Consequence: Team HR function helps the firms to leverage human capita; with an aligned, integrated, and differentiated workforce strategy

acquired behaviors back on the job. In addition, the firm has transformed its performance management and incentive compensation systems to recognize and reward knowledge sharing. As a result of these processes, synergy and real value are created through the sharing and leveraging of knowledge.

For example, at Quantum, a manufacturer in the computer industry, the management team uses the concept of *value behaviors* as a set of organizing principles for the HR function.[6] In the hard drive industry, product life cycles are very short. As a result, one of Quantum's key strategic objectives is to minimize what it calls *time to volume,* which is the total amount of time needed from product concept to when products are shipping in the volume necessary to meet customer needs. The more typical measure in this industry, *time to launch,* was found to have some unintended negative consequences, because engineers cut corners to meet launch deadlines, only to find manufacturing or design flaws once the product was shipping. What is important about Quantum's approach is that the firm carefully developed a system of HR management practices in support of the key value behaviors, which in turn supported the reduction of time to volume. These systems encourage managers to develop employees and take the long view of the firm's success while simultaneously meeting the needs of Quantum's clients. As one of Quantum's senior managers stated, "You can't simply 'get results' too often while leaving a trail of dead bodies behind you."

The common elements for all of these examples are the existence of balancing loops that reinforce and in many cases magnify the effects of the initial actions. The implications are that such systems are very difficult to change, and also that marginal changes in one or two elements of the system are not likely to affect the desired results. In contrast, such "system dynamics" can also work in the firm's favor, creating a sort of first-mover advantage that is very difficult to replicate—and harder still to compete with. Indeed, in both our empirical research and our consulting experiences, we have consistently found that the most effective firms leverage internal as well as external "fit" in the creation of distinctive capabilities—capabilities that are very difficult for competitors to overcome.

Right HR Practices

The key question that managers need to ask concerning HR practices is, Have we designed and implemented strategically aligned world-class HR management policies and practices throughout the business? While this question might seem quite basic, firms actually differ dramatically in the quality with which they manage the workforce. For example, over the last decade, we have conducted a series of empirical studies that focused on assessing the quality of a firm's HR management system, the importance of aligning that system with a firm's strategy, and the effects of such a system on corporate financial performance.[7] These results, which have now been replicated in a number of countries throughout the world, are clear: Designing and effectively implementing a high-performance work system (HPWS) can have an economically as well as statistically significant effect on firm performance. In our research, we have consistently found that the following attributes affect employee turnover, productivity, profitability, and shareholder value:

- Selection and hiring practices designed to identify and acquire workforce capabilities needed to execute the firm's competitive strategy and achieve operational goals

- Reward systems that reinforce strategy execution in all aspects of the performance management and appraisal processes

- Development strategies that emphasize the nurturing of employee competencies needed for strategy execution

While these elements represent the core facets of an HPWS, the ways in which they are implemented will differ across firms, consistent with each firm's strategy and operational goals. Said differently, adopting the right HR practices is a necessary but not sufficient condition for firm success—making sure that the elements of an HPWS are implemented effectively, are operationally appropriate, and are carefully tailored to strategy is crucial as well. Example measures of HR practices can be found in table 4-4.

Up to this point, we've argued that investments in appropriately aligned HR management systems can help create the type of strategic capabilities that drive firm success. Strategic capability, a concept we introduced in chapter 1, consists of speed, talent, learning, innovation, shared mind-set, and accountability. Our analyses have shown that firms with higher levels of strategic capabilities do a better job designing work systems, have more effective training and leadership development processes, do a better job with performance management and rewards systems, and are much more likely to clearly articulate the types of competencies that they are seeking in the workforce. We have also examined the impact that specific HR management practices have on a firm's resultant strategic capabilities. As we show in table 4-5, compared with low-capability firms, high-capability firms systematically invest at a much higher level in HR management practices that are directly linked to the execution of their strategy.

Right HR Professionals

The implications of the preceding analyses are that a properly designed and implemented system for managing the workforce, specifically

TABLE 4-4

Measures for Right HR Practices

KEY QUESTION: HAVE WE DESIGNED AND IMPLEMENTED STRATEGICALLY ALIGNED WORLD-CLASS HR MANAGEMENT POLICIES AND PRACTICES THROUGHOUT THE BUSINESS?

Average *differential* in merit pay awards between high-performing and low-performing employees

Average economic value (NPV) of employee suggestions

Average merit increase granted by job classification and job performance

Average time for managers to respond to suggestions

Current percentile ranking on total compensation for "A" players

Current percentile ranking on total compensation for "C" players

Extent to which the workforce has access to business information to facilitate decision making

Extent to which a validated competency model is used as the basis for hiring, developing, managing, and rewarding employees

Interviews-per-offer ratio in "A" positions (selection ratio)

Customer satisfaction with hiring process

Exit rate of "C" players in "A" positions

Exit rate of "C" players in "B" and "C" positions

Extent to which all performance appraisals contain a specific, written development plan

Total compensation market percentile for "A" players

Firm salary/competitor salary ratio

Firm's target percentile for *total compensation* for "A" positions

Firm's target percentile for *total compensation* for "B" positions

Firm's target percentile for *total compensation* for "C" positions

Frequency and quality of employee survey and feedback

HR employees/total employment

Impact of workforce development initiatives on specific needed capabilities and behaviors

Incentive compensation differential (low versus high performers)

Job offers to "A" players rejected (or accepted)

Number and quality of cross-functional teams

Number and quality of performance appraisal discussions per year

Number and type of "special projects" to develop high-potential employees

Number of *exceptional* candidates for each *strategic* job opening

Number of hours of training typically received by a new employee in the *first year* of employment

Number of hours of training typically received by an experienced employee each year

Number of qualified applicants per hire for our most important hires

Number of suggestions for improvement made (or implemented) per employee

Number of suggestions generated and/or implemented

Percent of exempt and nonexempt employees eligible for annual cash or deferred incentive plans, or for profit sharing

Percent of all new hires selected based primarily on *validated* selection methods

Percent "A" players promoted per year

Percent "C" players promoted per year

Percent employee understanding of nonfinancial performance drivers

Percent employees whose pay is performance-contingent

Percent employees with development plans

Percent of "A" positions filled with "A" players

Percent of all employees involved in a 360-degree feedback process

Percent of communication budget spent on education of employees on strategic intent

Percent of employees in "A" positions with temporary (outsourced) contracts

Percent of employees in "C" positions with temporary (outsourced) contracts

Percent of employees willing to recommend our firm to friends as a great place to work

Percent of executive time spent on mentoring and coaching

Percent of new hires selected based on the results of a validated selection test (i.e., aptitude, skill, or work sample)

(continued)

TABLE 4-4

Measures for Right HR Practices (continued)

Percent of non-entry-level jobs that have been filled from within in recent (i.e., over the last five) years

Percent of positions filled by employees' referrals

Percent of the average employee's total compensation (wages + benefits) that is accounted for by all forms of variable pay

Percent of the workforce for which "A" and "C" performance evaluations have been accurately assessed

Percent of the workforce that has its *merit increase or incentive pay* determined by a performance appraisal

Percent of the workforce that is *eligible* for annual *cash or deferred* incentive pay plans, profit-sharing plans, and/or gain-sharing plans

Percent of the workforce that is included in a formal information-sharing program designed to communicate critical business and operational goals?

Percent of the workforce that is regularly (i.e., quarterly or annually) assessed via a formal performance appraisal

Percent of the workforce that owns shares of the company's stock

Percent of the workforce that receives formal feedback on job performance from multiple sources (e.g., superiors, subordinates, and customers)

Percent of merit pay that is determined by a formal performance appraisal

Percent employees with access to appropriate training and development opportunities

Percent employee development plans completed

Percent new material in training programs each year

Percent of employees making suggestions

Percent of employees with experience outside their current job responsibility or function

Percent of workforce that is promotable

Percent performance appraisals completed on time

Perception of consistent and equitable treatment of all employees

Performance of newly hired applicants

Planned development opportunities accomplished

Percent of the workforce that routinely performs its job as part of a self-managed, cross-functional, or project team

Percent of total compensation for your exempt and nonexempt employees represented by variable pay

Percent of training resources devoted to multiskilling

Percent of your HR budget that is spent on outsourced activities (e.g., recruiting and payroll)

Percent regrettable turnover

Percent retention of high-performing key employees

Percent total salary at risk

Percentage merit increase a *high-performing employee* normally could expect as a result of a performance review

Percentage merit increase a *low-performing employee* normally could expect as a result of a performance review

Proportion of absenteeism

Proportion of internal transfers

Quality of applicants provided by recruiting channel

Quality of coaching and mentoring activities

Quality of employee feedback systems

Range (distribution) of performance appraisal ratings

Range in merit increase granted by classification

Retention rate of "A" players in key positions

Retention rate of "A" players in noncore positions

Selection ratio: number of qualified applicants per hire

Senior manager and board member diversity

Success rate of external hires

Suggestion system and feedback process

Time to competence for new hires

Time to promotion for "A" players

Time to promotion for "C" players

Total compensation market percentile for "C" players

Turnover of high-potential minority candidates

Unemployment insurance experience rating

TABLE 4-5

Comparison of HR Systems by High and Low Levels of Strategic Capabilities

	Bottom 25% Strategic Capabilities	Top 25% Strategic Capabilities
For the five positions that your firm (or business unit) hires most frequently, how many qualified applicants does your recruiting process generate per position (on average)?	26.40	38.42
What proportion of all new hires have been selected based primarily on the results of a validated selection test (i.e., aptitude, skill, or work sample)?	12.99	14.79
How many hours of training are typically received by a new employee in the *first year* of employment?	38.72	122.32
How many hours of training per year are typically received by an experienced employee (i.e., someone employed more than one year)?	16.42	45.22
What proportion of the workforce is regularly (i.e., quarterly or annually) assessed via a formal performance appraisal?	72.22	87.07
What proportion of the workforce receives formal feedback on job performance from multiple sources (e.g., superiors, subordinates, customers)?	16.84	51.83
If the market rate for total compensation (wages + benefits) is considered to be the 50th percentile, what is your firm's target percentile for *total compensation?* (If you usually pay the market rate, enter 50.)	47.68	55.59
What proportion of the workforce is eligible for annual cash or deferred incentive pay plans, profit-sharing plans, and/or gain-sharing plans?	44.69	72.35
What proportion of the average employee's total compensation (wages + benefits) is accounted for by all forms of variable pay (merit pay and one-time bonuses)?	16.97	35.73
What proportion of the workforce is included in a formal information-sharing program (e.g., a newsletter or regular meetings) designed to communicate progress toward critical business and operational goals?	77.99	84.57
What proportion of the workforce owns shares of the company's stock?	13.82	44.07
What proportion of the workforce routinely performs its job as part of a self-managed, cross-functional, or project team?	9.03	44.88
What proportion of your HR budget is spent on outsourced activities (e.g., recruiting, payroll)?	8.90	14.97

aligned with firm strategy, has an important impact on firm performance via improving strategic capabilities. But world-class HR management systems don't just happen—they are developed specifically by HR professionals who have a deep understanding not only of the firm's strategy and goals, but also of the field of HRM and the allied social sciences. Thus, the questions that senior leaders need to ask are, Do our HR professionals have the skills they need to design and implement a world-class HR management system? How can we ensure that we have a cadre of HR processionals who know and understand the business, as well as understand the "HR basics" associated with the profession?

These are important issues: research has found that firms with more capable HR management professionals exhibit significantly better financial performance. Mark Huselid, Susan Jackson, and Randall Schuler examined the impact of what they called *technical HR effectiveness* (the ability to deliver the HR basics to the business) and *strategic HR effectiveness* (which involves designing and implementing an HR management system capable of executing firm strategy) on firm performance in a sample of 293 large publicly held firms.[8] What they found was that the HR managers in their sample were much more proficient on the technical than the strategic elements of their roles, but that it was strategic HRM effectiveness that had the greatest impact on employee productivity, firm cash flow, and market value. The impact of strategic HRM effectiveness was both statistically and economically significant.

The gap that Huselid, Jackson, and Schuler identified between strategic and technical HR manager proficiency (more than 35 percent) is largely driven by the capabilities of the HR managers themselves. A large proportion of this capability gap may be a knowledge gap. Sara Rynes, Amy Colbert, and Ken Brown studied the extent to which 959 HR professionals understood basic HR research findings.[9] These are the research foundations upon which the field of HRM is based, and would likely be covered in a college-level introductory HRM course. Their results were startling. Rynes and colleagues granted the average HR manager (who voluntarily participated in the research and who would thus presumably have greater insights into the answers than would nonrespondents) a "D" grade on knowledge of the thirty-five fundamental research findings in HRM. We show the questions that Rynes and her colleagues asked in table 4-6.

TABLE 4-6

Rynes, Colbert, and Brown (2002), HR Professionals' Knowledge of Basic Research Findings

	Answer (% correct)
Management Practices	
1. Leadership training is ineffective because good leaders are born, not made.	False (96%)
2. The most important requirement for an effective leader is to have an outgoing, enthusiastic personality.	False (82%)
3. Once employees have mastered a task, they perform better when they are told to "do their best" than when they are given specific, difficult performance goals.	False (82%)
4. Companies with vision statements perform better than those without them.	False (62%)
5. Companies with very low rates of professional turnover are less profitable than those with moderate turnover rates.	False (62%)
6. If a company feels it must downsize employees, the most profitable way to do it is through targeted cuts rather than attrition.	True (54%)
7. In order to be evaluated favorably by line managers, the most important competency for HR managers is the ability to manage change.	True (50%)
8. On average, encouraging employees to participate in decision making is more effective for improving organizational performance than setting performance goals.	False (18%)
General Employment Practices	
9. Most managers give employees lower performance appraisals than they objectively deserve.	False (94%)
10. Poor performers are generally more realistic about their performance than good performers are.	False (88%)
11. Teams with members from different functional areas are likely to reach better solutions to complex problems than teams from a single area.	True (88%)
12. Despite the popularity of drug testing, there is no clear evidence that applicants who score positive on drug tests are any less reliable or productive employees.	False (57%)
13. Most people overevaluate how well they perform on the job.	True (54%)
14. Most errors in performance appraisals can be eliminated by providing training that describes the kinds of errors managers tend to make and suggesting ways to avoid them.	False (25%)
Training and Employee Development	
15. Lecture-based training is generally superior to other forms of training delivery.	False (96%)
16. Older adults learn more from training than younger adults.	False (68%)
17. The most important determinants of how much training employees actually use on their jobs is how much they learned during training.	False (60%)
18. Training for simple skills will be more effective if it is presented in one concentrated session than if it is presented in several sessions over time.	False (59%)

(continued)

TABLE 4-6

Rynes, Colbert, and Brown (2002), HR Professionals' Knowledge of Basic Research Findings (continued)

	Answer (% correct)
Staffing	
19. The most valid employment interviews are designed around each candidate's unique background.	False (70%)
20. Although people use many different terms to describe personalities, there are really only four basic dimensions of personality, as captured by the Myers-Briggs Type Indicator (MBTI).	False (49%)
21. On average, applicants who answer job advertisements are likely to have higher turnover than those referred by other employees.	True (49%)
22. Being very intelligent is actually a disadvantage for performing well on a low-skilled job.	False (42%)
23. There is very little difference among personality inventories in terms of how well they predict an applicant's likely job performance.	False (42%)
24. Although there are "integrity tests" that try to predict whether someone will steal, be absent, or otherwise take advantage of an employer, they don't work well in practice, because so many people lie on them.	False (32%)
25. One problem with using integrity tests is that they have high degrees of adverse impact on racial minorities.	False (31%)
26. On average, conscientiousness is a better predictor of job performance than is intelligence.	False (18%)
27. Companies that screen job applicants for values have higher performance than those that screen for intelligence.	False (16%)
Compensation and Benefits	
28. When pay must be reduced or frozen, there is little a company can do or say to reduce employee dissatisfaction and dysfunctional behaviors.	False (72%)
29. Most employees prefer to be paid on the basis of individual performance rather than on team or organizational performance.	True (81%)
30. Merit pay systems cause so many problems that companies without them tend to have higher performance than companies with them.	False (66%)
31. There is a positive relationship between the proportion of managers receiving organizationally based pay incentives and company profitability.	True (62%)
32. New companies have a better chance of surviving if all employees receive incentives based on organizational-wide performance.	True (59%)
33. Talking about salary issues during performance appraisals tends to hurt morale and future performance.	False (51%)
34. Most employees prefer variable pay systems (e.g., incentive schemes, gain sharing, stock options) to fixed pay systems.	False (40%)
35. Surveys that directly ask employees how important pay is to them are likely to overestimate pay's true importance in actual decisions.	False (35%)

Source: Sara Rynes, Amy Colbert, and Kenneth Brown, "HR Professionals' Beliefs About Effective Human Resource Management Practices: Correspondence Between Research and Practice," *Human Resource Management* 41, no. 2 (2002): 149–174.

Why do we find these results? Part of the reason, no doubt, is linked to the poor quality with which academics have communicated their findings to managers. Nevertheless, it does point to a significant gap as well as a potential area of opportunity for HR leaders. While it would be highly unlikely for most firms to hire an accountant without training in accounting, or an engineer without training in engineering, or a marketer without training in marketing, HR professionals with graduate degrees or even undergraduate specializations in HRM are in the minority in this profession. There is a significant and increasing body of professional knowledge in the field of HRM, and ensuring that HR managers understand the latest developments in the field is an important opportunity for improvement for many firms. Example measures of HR workforce competencies can be found in table 4-7.

DESIGNING THE HR SCORECARD AT BIG PHARMA

We now turn to the design and implementation of an HR Scorecard at Big Pharma, the case example that that we introduced in chapter 3. Obviously, Big Pharma hopes to develop a highly competent workforce that is committed to helping to execute its strategy. The firm's

TABLE 4-7

Measures for HR Workforce Competencies

KEY QUESTION: DO OUR HR PROFESSIONALS HAVE THE SKILLS THEY NEED TO DESIGN AND IMPLEMENT A WORLD-CLASS HR MANAGEMENT SYSTEM?

Degree to which HR professionals are effective advocates for employees

Degree to which HR professionals are effective in facilitating change

Degree to which HR professionals are effective in providing operational excellence in HR

Degree to which HR professionals are effective strategic partners with line managers

HR manager ratings on validated 360-degree competency-assessment tool

HR workforce's level of understanding of criticalness of HR "tool kit" integration (survey response rate)

HR workforce's perception of HR's "tool kit" integration (practice by practice)

HR leadership bench strength

Individual recruiter productivity

Management satisfaction with HR contributions to organizational transformation efforts

Number of days of professional HR development per HR professional

Percent of HR budget devoted to "HR for HR"—professional development for HR staff

Percent of HR professionals with graduate degrees in HR

Percent of HR professionals with undergraduate degrees in HR

Percent of HR professionals with PHR or SPHR certification

overarching workforce strategy is to develop a high-performance culture by developing the measurement tools necessary to help exit poor performers and increase its investments in "A" players in "A" positions. Big Pharma's needed skill mix is changing as well. A new focus on genomics means that it will need more and better scientists with related skills, and fewer with the "old" skills. Knowledge capabilities in the pharmaceutical sciences, much as in engineering, have a half-life of no more than five to seven years. In addition, even the way in which R&D is performed is undergoing transformation at Big Pharma. Because of the development of what has come to be known as e-R&D (i.e., distributed and virtual teams work on compound development on a worldwide basis), Big Pharma has begun to seriously rethink its discovery model. As a result, R&D at Big Pharma is becoming increasingly global and distributed. Each of these elements highlights the need for an HR management system that is both flexible and closely aligned with the needs of the business.

Measuring Workforce Success at Big Pharma

As we described in chapter 3, Big Pharma's strategy requires it to shorten R&D cycle time to remain competitive. Big Pharma's management team has also been challenged to contain workforce spending in the current economic environment. The problem in executing this strategy is that there is a long lag between investment and return. When managers are under pressure to lower costs, they often respond by cutting funding for workforce development, which can have a significant and negative effect on Big Pharma's ability to deliver on its business model in the long run. For Big Pharma to win in the future, it must effectively invest in developing the right kinds of workforce skills today.

Big Pharma's leadership team members knew that they needed to strike a balance between information overload and the need to keep the workforce focused on the firm's key objectives, so they created indexes for each of their "A" positions that show the extent of goal attainment for each of the four elements on the Workforce Scorecard. As we describe in greater detail in chapter 5, the advantage of an index is that it can convert variables that can have very different scales to a format ranging from zero to one hundred. These data can then be averaged, or differentially weighted, as management feels best reflects the goals and needs of the firm. Big Pharma created the following indexes:

R&D success index. This measure consists of the average of the following standardized variables: (1) number of new compounds generated that progress to Phase I of clinical trials, (2) breadth and depth of therapeutic area knowledge, (3) introduction of new discovery and development technologies, and (4) cycle time from discovery to Phase I of clinical trials.

Manufacturing success index. This measure consists of the average of the following standardized variables: (1) quality index, (2) order fulfillment rate, (3) standard cost performance, (4) working capital ratios, (5) lost-time injuries, (6) work stoppages, and (7) productivity.

Sales success index. This measure consists of the average of the following standardized variables: (1) market share of therapeutic area or drug class, (2) new prescriptions versus total prescriptions versus quota, (3) comprehensiveness of product and competitor knowledge, (4) proportion of sales calls of greater than five minutes with physician, and (5) sample productivity.

Measuring Workforce Costs at Big Pharma

From the perspective of senior managers (and shareholders), the relevant workforce costs are the total costs, not just the costs associated with the HR function. This is an important distinction, because in most firms senior HR managers are held accountable to meeting a budget and are often rewarded if they can generate positive budget variances (i.e., save the company money). This can lead to significant and unintended consequences if the result is a lower-quality workforce. At a minimum, it may simply result in a false economy if the workforce costs are transferred from the HR function to line managers who must end up dealing with the costs associated with poor performance.

More than that, we need to ensure with our measures that we are encouraging managers to disproportionately invest in "A" players in "A" positions for "A" customers. At Big Pharma, this meant that it was important to measure the proportion of its training and development budget that was spent on high-potential or "A" players, as opposed to below-average or "C" players. They knew this was an important issue because exit interviews had identified that one of the key reasons that high potentials left the firm was because they did not feel they were being challenged or their skills were being developed quickly enough. Thus, Big Pharma collected the following workforce metrics:

Cost per "A" player hire. Many firms measure cost per hire, and indeed, it is often a key measure of the performance of the HR function. However, as we described earlier, this measure can be counterproductive because it can cause firms to focus on lowering costs without attending to new hire quality. Big Pharma's focus on cost per "A" player hire helps recruiting managers to managing their hiring budgets effectively while ensuring that they help select the very best new employees.

Total cost to competence for new hires. An extension of the cost per "A" player hire metric is reflected in Big Pharma's focus on total cost to competence for new hires. This measure includes not only cost per hire, but also the total costs needed to help the employee reach competence within his or her new position. These costs include the on-boarding and related assimilation costs, but more importantly, the direct and indirect costs of any on-the-job training needed to help new employees reach competence.

Percent of recruiting budget devoted to "A" positions. Big Pharma's managers realized that their increased focus on placing "A" players in "A" positions would require a reallocation of their recruiting expenditures and efforts as well. In the past, Big Pharma had allocated recruiting resources based on the level within the organization, as opposed to the strategic importance of the job.

Index of HR service quality. Big Pharma's HR leadership team developed two short surveys to measure customer satisfaction, one of which focused on the extent to which the workforce evaluated the HR function as helpful and responsive to their needs; the second, a similar survey, focused on the managerial population and the extent to which their needs were being met. Each survey was conducted via e-mail and sent to a random sample of the workforce once a month. Each employee was only surveyed once a year, but by collecting data on a monthly basis, Big Pharma was able to react to any problems and follow their progression much more effectively.

Percent of HR transactions that have been effectively shifted to self-service. Big Pharma's HR leadership team had identified eHR as a key source of savings, and closely tracked the extent to which common HR transactions (e.g., benefits administration) were automated.

Making the Pieces Fit Together— Measuring Alignment at Big Pharma

Big Pharma also knew that having the "right" HR policies and practices wouldn't ensure that they would automatically work together in an internally consistent manner that was aligned with firm strategy. Thus, Big Pharma created internal and external alignment indexes based on data collected from the key constituencies of HR's work— line and HR managers. Examples of these metrics are presented in figure 4-4.[10]

Figure 4-5 is an example of the external alignment measure. While the internal alignment index is based on data collected from all employees, data for the external alignment index are collected from managers. As described in the legend for each table, respondents (employees and managers) complete the form, the scores are summed for each form, and then the averages across forms are tallied to produce an alignment index. It is intended to reflect the extent to which the workforce has the requisite skills, motivation, and work environment (including culture and mind-set) to reach its specific strategic objectives.

Measuring HR Practices at Big Pharma

Effective strategy execution depends on having the right system of HR policies and practices in place to recruit, select, develop, appraise, compensate, and place, promote, or exit employees. Based on a careful analysis of the needs of the business, Big Pharma prioritized its

FIGURE 4-4

Diagnosing "Fit" Among HR Management Practices (Internal Alignment)

In the chart below please indicate your subjective estimate of the degree to which the various HR management subsystems work together harmoniously or "fit" together. Think of the degree of fit and internal consistency as a continuum from –100 to 100, and assign a value in that range to each relationship. Examples of the extremes and midpoints on the continuum are provided below:

–100	*The two subsystems work at cross-purposes.*
0	*The two subsystems have little or no effect on one another.*
+100	*Each subsystem is mutually reinforcing and internally consistent.*
DNK	*Don't know or have no opinion.*

	Recruiting and Selection	Training and Development	Performance Management and Appraisal	Compensation and Rewards	Mind-set and Culture
Recruiting and Selection	—				
Training and Development		—			
Performance Management and Appraisal			—		
Compensation and Rewards				—	
Mind-set and Culture					—

Source: Adapted from Brian E. Becker, Mark A. Huselid, and Dave Ulrich, The HR Scorecard (Boston: Harvard Business School Press, 2001), 137.

FIGURE 4-5

Diagnosing "Fit" Between HR Architecture and HR Deliverables (External Alignment)

The measurement process would ask each respondent to indicate the degree to which each HR deliverable would enable the appropriate strategic driver, on a scale of −100 to +100. Examples of the extremes and midpoints on the continuum are provided below:

−100   *This dimension is counterproductive for helping you to accomplish this goal.*
   0   *This dimension has little or no effect on your ability to accomplish this goal.*
+100   *This dimension significantly helps your firm to accomplish this goal.*
DNK   *Don't know or have no opinion.*

Strategic Goal	Employee Skills	Employee Motivation	Mind-set and Culture
1. Increase the new product pipeline by shortening R&D cycle time and effectively licensing external compound acquisitions			
2. Enhance sales force marketing competence and cross-selling			
3. Enhance the speed with which drugs go through the approval process			
4. Enhance manufacturing efficiencies— zero tolerance for defects			

Source: Adapted from Brian E. Becker, Mark A. Huselid, and Dave Ulrich, *The HR Scorecard* (Boston: Harvard Business School Press, 2001), 140.

strategic choices around workforce alignment for each of its three "A" jobs: sales force, manufacturing, and R&D scientist. Big Pharma translated these broad objectives into the following specific HR measures:

Percentage of the workforce hired using validated selection tools. Most firms make their selection decisions primarily as a result of resume screening and unstructured interviews by hiring managers. Yet, there is a substantial body of literature showing that this is a very ineffective way to make such decisions, and that the addition of relatively simple and validated selection tools can have a significant impact on workforce success and productivity.[11] Recognizing this, Big Pharma's HR leadership team developed a set of validated selection tests and structured interview guides, and then tracked the extent to which managers used them while making hiring and promotion decisions.

Percentage of managers with performance development plans.
Big Pharma's history with performance management had not
been particularly positive. While the firm's official policy was
that each employee was to be reviewed annually, managers generally perceived this to be an administrative exercise, and few took
it seriously or performed it well. Big Pharma's new approach was
to enhance its emphasis from performance appraisal to performance management, and to begin to hold managers accountable
for the extent to which they had effectively developed their subordinates. This measure was a first step in that process.

Percentage pay differential between "A" and "C" players. As a
result of Big Pharma's modest historical focus on performance
management, it isn't surprising that the firm didn't effectively
administer its incentive compensation plans as well. For midlevel
managers and above, Big Pharma's gap in incentive bonus payout
between low and high performers was only about 3 percent.
Going forward, Big Pharma's leadership team wanted the pay
differential to be much greater and based on an effective performance management system as well.

Percentage rollout of validated competency model. Big Pharma's
HR leadership team developed and validated a competency
model, and intends to use it as a basis for all of its job design,
selection, development, performance appraisal, and compensation decisions. This measure reflects the extent to which these
competencies have been effectively embedded in the firm's key
HR processes.

Measuring HR Manager Competence at Big Pharma

Finally, designing and implementing an effective HR management
system won't be possible without a competent and capable team of
HR professionals. Big Pharma's HR leadership team believed that
there was a minimum level of knowledge that everyone needed to
have, but also that specialists in a variety of areas were crucial to the
firm's ongoing success. Not everyone in the HR function could be a
successful change agent or strategic partner to line managers, and this
realization helped HR to be more effective in its development of HR

manager talent. Big Pharma developed the following metrics to assess HR manager competence:

HR manager rating on validated competency assessment tool. Big Pharma's HR leadership team developed and internally validated a 360-degree performance appraisal tool based on a set of HR manager competencies that were linked with the design and delivery of effective HR management processes. Big Pharma closely monitored these results and used them for development, compensation, and promotion/exit decisions.

HR leadership bench strength. Big Pharma also tracked the extent to which each of the key jobs in the HR function had one or more "ready replacements"—employees who were currently promotable to the next level.

Consolidating an HR Scorecard at Big Pharma

Figure 4-6 shows the consolidated HR Scorecard that Big Pharma's HR managers use to track the progress of strategy execution.[12] In addition to the specific objectives that managers are attempting to achieve and the associated metrics, Big Pharma sets specific targets for improvement and has designed specific initiatives for managers to use should the firm not achieve its objectives.

KEY LEARNINGS

The HR management policies and practices that a firm adopts represent one of the key levers it can use to execute its strategy and to achieve its desired financial results. Our evidence shows that firms that survive and prosper over the long run develop internally consistent systems of HR policies and practices that are specifically designed to execute strategy. Firms don't win by blindly adopting a series of "best practices" taken from other companies. They will also differ across the "A" positions within each firm. In contrast, lower-performing firms tend to use more generic HR management practices, and they tend to use the same HR practice for all employees throughout the business.

FIGURE 4-6

Big Pharma HR Scorecard

	Objective	Measure	Target	Initiative
Workforce Success	Has the workforce accomplished the key strategic objectives for the business?	• Workforce deliverables index • Strategic behavior index • Capability index • Mind-set index	• Average of indices at the 80th percentile or better • No index below the 50th percentile	
Right HR Costs	Is our total investment in the workforce (not just the HR function) appropriate (not just minimized)?	• % T&D for "A" versus "C" players • Cost per "A" player hire • Total cost to competence for new hires • % of recruiting budget for "A" positions • Index of HR service quality	• Average differential of > 25% • 5% reduction year over year • 5% reduction year over year • Greater than 45% • Average rating of at least 80%	
Right Types of Alignment	Are our HR practices aligned with the business strategy and differentiated across employee groups, where appropriate?	• % transactions shifted to self-service • Alignment index	• No negative ratings • Average rating of at least 80%	• Develop HR/line manager partnerships • Track progress of implementation
Right HR Practices	Have we designed and implemented world-class HR management policies and practices throughout the business?	• % selected with validated tools • % managers with PDPs • % rollout of competency-based training • Leadership capability evaluation • % pay differential between "A" and "C" players	• % above 90% • % above 90% • Number trained by deadline • 100% participation • Average differential of > 25%	• Competency model training • Design and roll out equity and bonus program • Develop and implement 360° feedback
Right HR Professionals	Do our HR professionals have the skills they need to design and implement a world-class HR management system?	• Rating on validated competency assessment tool (360° feedback) • HR leadership bench strength	• At least half of all criteria are rated at "A" player level	• Targeted in-house and external development programs • Special developmental

While the evidence on this point seems to us to be clear, this doesn't mean that designing and implementing effective systems of workforce management practices will be simple or easy. At Big Pharma, for example, one thing the leadership team learned was that it needed to radically rethink its workforce strategy, and it learned the importance of keeping the distinction between an HR philosophy and an HR practice clearly in mind.[13] An HR philosophy, for example, might say that we intend to reward people based on results. An HR practice, in contrast, is a specific tool for distributing rewards. Big Pharma's managers learned that they needed to continually push the key philosophies that they felt were important for business success while allowing local managers the latitude to design and implement the right HR practices consistent with the firm's broad goals.

Big Pharma also concluded that treating all categories of employees the same with respect to HR investments was neither fair nor equitable. Big Pharma learned, for example, that it was systematically overinvesting in "C" players. Detailed analyses within the firm showed that Big Pharma spent nearly 45 percent of its training budget trying to improve the performance of its lowest-performing employees, and only 20 percent of its budget on the "A" players. This might seem rational at the moment when a line manager is complaining about the poor performance of a specific employee. However, over the long run this can produce some unintended consequences, to the extent that it encourages low performers to stay with the firm, and high performers, in search of outstanding developmental opportunities, to leave.

Another conclusion that we drew from the experience at Big Pharma is that some of the HR practices are more directly influenced by HR managers than are others. We make this distinction because some of the HR practices are really the primary responsibility of line managers, while others are the primary responsibility of HR managers. The key point is that just as "one size doesn't fit all" for HR metrics across firms, this is also true within firms across key positions, and metrics need to be sensitive to this reality.

For alignment to work, the HR practices need to be strategically redundant. That is, it is not enough for the recruiting *or* the selection *or* the compensation practices to be aligned with the desired workforce outcomes—all of the HR programs and initiatives need to work together to shape the desired employee behaviors. The HR practices, as well as the message to the workforce, need to be internally consistent and supportive of the desired outcomes.

Identifying the metrics needed for the Workforce and HR Scorecards is an important step in the process of executing strategy with the workforce, but there is still more work to be done. The next challenge is to collect the data and begin to present them to the management team. In the next chapter, we show how to collect and analyze both Workforce and HR Scorecard data with an eye toward rapid strategy execution.

5

COLLECTING AND INTERPRETING WORKFORCE SCORECARD DATA

A KEY THEME up to this point has been that line managers and HR professionals need to adopt a new perspective on what constitutes workforce success. Senior executives and line managers must understand that for most companies, workforce success is required for organizational success. Workforce success means effectively delivering the business outcomes required to execute the firm's strategy. This new perspective poses a new challenge requiring new measures that accurately reflect the contribution of the workforce to firm success. By now it should be clear that these new measures are not just the warmed-over efficiency measures from the past. Efforts to reconfigure existing accounting and efficiency measures (e.g., revenue per employee) under rubrics like "human capital value added" are largely an attempt at "HR alchemy." The challenge is not to find new ways to combine old measures. New measures mean different measures.

New and different measures pose at least two challenges. Where do we find them and what do we do with them? You will not generally find them in off-the-shelf ERP systems. These programs typically define workforce success in terms of employee stocks (How many do we have?), employee flows (What happened to our head-count over the past year?), and costs. In contrast, what are needed are measures that reflect whether the workforce is delivering the kind of performance results required by your firm's strategy. Likewise, you cannot expect to interpret these new workforce measures in the same way you might traditional efficiency measures. As we described earlier, measures are answers to questions. If the question is, How does the efficiency of our HR operations compare with other firms in our industry? then perhaps measures like "cost per hire" provide the answer. It's not so much that "cost per hire" is the wrong measure—the problem is with the question being asked. Instead, CEOs need answers to questions like, How does the workforce make a difference? How does the workforce contribute to firm performance? Questions like these cannot be answered by relying on HR benchmarks. Nor will you find the answer in a list of "Ten Best Measures for Measuring HR Performance." Instead, these new questions require success measures that demonstrate how the workforce contributes to strategy execution, as well as measures that track the drivers of that success.

In chapter 3 we described how measures of workforce success can be both leading and lagging indicators of firm success. They are a leading indicator of successful strategy execution and ultimately of firm performance, but they are also a lagging indicator of the strategic content and focus of the HR management system and the human capital investment decisions by line managers and HR professionals. They are the *deliverables* for the HR professional, but they are strategy *drivers* for line managers. This perspective recognizes workforce success as part of the causal flow of value creation in the firm. Instead of measuring workforce success primarily in terms of how few resources we use, the focus is foremost on how much value we are creating with our workforce. This perspective will guide both how the measures are collected and how they are interpreted.

Chapters 3 and 4 outline the Workforce and HR Scorecards. The measures in these scorecards range from business outcomes that drive strategy to elements of the HR function. In our experience HR managers are reasonably good at measuring operational performance of HR activities. However, they have a much more difficult time demonstrating how these measures are related to workforce success. Measures that describe HR activities and how little they cost might describe what HR is doing, but they don't describe how those activities contribute to firm success. Therefore, in this chapter we discuss how you go about collecting the kinds of measures discussed in chapters 3 and 4 and some of the decisions you will have to make. Our focus will be on those measures of workforce success that senior executives are most interested in but also the leading indicators of workforce success that are largely the responsibility of the firm's HR professionals.

We begin by highlighting five key principles for developing these new workforce measures. Performance measurement can sometimes be an arcane subject, but these are the five measurement elements that line managers and HR professionals should keep in mind as they begin to develop a Workforce Scorecard. Sometimes, however, we find that organizations are overwhelmed by the scope of change required to fully implement the measurement system. They would like to move in the direction of measuring strategic workforce success but may not be ready for the comprehensive changes we describe. Therefore, in the spirit of software manuals that begin with "Getting Started Quickly," in the last half of this chapter we suggest how your firm might get an initial measurement system up and running in relatively short order.

FIVE KEY PRINCIPLES FOR DEVELOPING WORKFORCE MEASURES

These principles focus largely on implementation issues, but they are important because they are directly related to the ultimate interpretation and management value of these measures. Unfortunately, one of the first lessons of performance measurement is that the value of the measure tends to be inversely related to the ease and cost of implementation. The best example is the widespread use of benchmarked measures of HR performance that rely on currently available efficiency and activity measures. These measurement systems are very easy to implement but have very little value as measures of workforce success.[1]

Principle 1: The Measures Must Answer an Important Strategic Question

The most important principle for developing valuable measures of workforce success is to remember that you don't start with the measure. Too often managers begin the search for measures based on their characteristics. Are they objective? Can they be expressed in financial terms? But this misses the point of strategic performance measurement, which is to answer important management questions. We believe those important questions should focus on how the workforce is contributing to successful strategy implementation. If there is a choice between objective and dollar-denominated measures that answer the wrong question, and measures that are based on more subjective data but answer the right question, we strongly recommend the latter. We believe in the maxim that it is better to be approximately right than precisely wrong.

In effect, we argue that the first principle of effective workforce performance measurement is that these measures be strategically valid. The concept of validity is simply that a measure should measure all of what it is supposed to measure and none of what it's not supposed to measure. Measures of workforce success are supposed to measure the contribution of the workforce to successful strategy execution. If we think of successful strategy execution as the combined influence of a number of performance drivers, workforce success measures should give the CEO and senior executives an accurate and meaningful summary of the human capital dimension of those performance drivers. For senior HR professionals, they also represent the answer to the question, How is HR contributing to firm performance?

The principle of strategic validity can be illustrated with the retail industry example introduced in chapter 1. That example demonstrated that while there is a wide range of measures of workforce success that *might* be selected, some do a much better job answering an important question than others. The important question posed by the CEO was, How do we drive sales growth? The specific question to the senior HR leadership team is, What is HR's contribution to this strategic goal? HR leaders could respond with measures of sales training activities or cost per trainee compared with industry standards. But those measures really don't reflect the concept of workforce success described in chapter 3. Nor do they answer the questions posed by the CEO or by line managers charged with driving sales growth. Instead, let's begin with the notion of strategic validity and focus on the firm's strategy drivers and how the workforce will contribute to the performance of those drivers. Recall that one of the drivers of future sales growth is improved customer satisfaction, which is in part driven by the quality of the buying experience. One of the answers to the CEO's question about how to drive sales growth is to improve the quality of the buying experience. In this industry, the buying experience is in part driven by frontline staff who are knowledgeable, timely, helpful, and courteous. Those performance behaviors represent workforce success because of their impact on the performance drivers (customer buying experience, customer satisfaction, wallet share) that ultimately drive revenues.

Figure 5-1 is an abridged illustration of the human capital value creation process described in figure 1-1. It highlights several points in that value creation process that are often the focus of HR or workforce measurement. We also give examples of right and wrong measures that might be used in this particular example, and we will discuss the basis of those choices throughout the chapter. The most fundamental lesson is that the workforce success measures are selected based on the unique demands of the firm's strategy, not a generic list of benchmarking measures. In other words, they are strategically valid. There is a compelling business case, understood by senior executives and the CEO, for the value of these measures of workforce success. Improving those measures, or maintaining them at high levels, is equivalent to optimizing the human capital dimension of one of the firm's key strategy drivers.

Principle 2: Be Very Careful with the Feasibility-Validity Trade-off

Strategic validity is simply a way of characterizing the value of the measure of workforce success. At the same time, managers don't have time to let the perfect be the enemy of the possible. Except in the case of the proverbial low-hanging fruit, there is typically a trade-off between feasibility and strategic validity. Unfortunately, when it comes to workforce measurement, feasibility seems to be the overriding concern in many businesses. The most feasible solution to workforce measures is outsourcing, relying on outside vendors with benchmark data from other firms. Your firm provides efficiency and activity data and in return gets benchmark comparisons to industry standards. The comparisons create an aura of value since your organization can be compared with the "performance" of other firms on an objective basis. Even if most managers aren't sure exactly what these measures mean or how they drive value, there is some comfort (and cover) in being

FIGURE 5-1

Measuring Value Creation from HR Through Workforce Success

SIMPLE RETAIL EXAMPLE

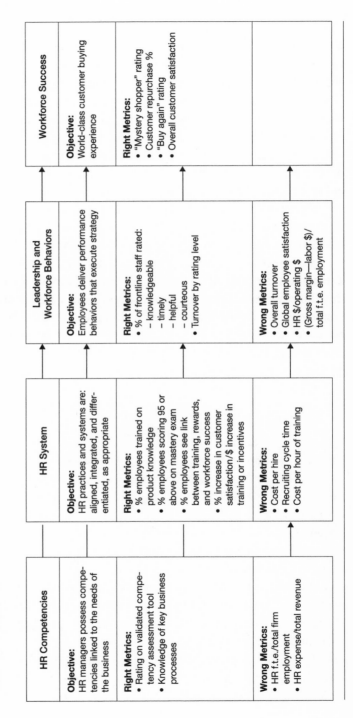

HR Competencies	HR System	Leadership and Workforce Behaviors	Workforce Success
Objective: HR managers possess competencies linked to the needs of the business	**Objective:** HR practices and systems are: aligned, integrated, and differentiated, as appropriate	**Objective:** Employees deliver performance behaviors that execute strategy	**Objective:** World-class customer buying experience

Right Metrics:
• Rating on validated competency assessment tool
• Knowledge of key business processes
	Right Metrics:
	• % employees trained on product knowledge
	• % employees scoring 95 or above on mastery exam
	• % employees see link between training, rewards, and workforce success
	• % increase in customer satisfaction/$ increase in training or incentives
		Right Metrics:
		• % of frontline staff rated:
		  – knowledgeable
		  – timely
		  – helpful
		  – courteous
		• Turnover by rating level
			Right Metrics:
			• "Mystery shopper" rating
			• Customer repurchase %
			• "Buy again" rating
			• Overall customer satisfaction

Wrong Metrics: • HR f.t.e./total firm employment • HR expense/total revenue	**Wrong Metrics:** • Cost per hire • Recruiting cycle time • Cost per hour of training	**Wrong Metrics:** • Overall turnover • Global employee satisfaction • HR $/operating $ • (Gross margin—labor $)/ total f.t.e. employment	

able to show that your firm is 6 percent below the industry standard on a particular cost. But of course this is completely at odds with principle 1. These measures can't be strategically valid unless your organization is pursuing the same strategy as other firms in the benchmark comparison. This is unlikely unless you are producing undifferentiated commodities that compete entirely on price.

Another feasible set of measures is employee surveys. Again, an outside vendor can provide a set of common measures so your organization can compare its own employee responses to those in other organizations. Over time, if you use the same measures, managers might gain additional insight by comparing how these responses vary from period to period. It's nice to know that there has been a 15 percent gain in workforce commitment, or perhaps you will be concerned by a 10 percent decline, but what does it mean? What important management question does it answer? Is there a compelling business case that links these results to bottom-line performance? The problem with employee surveys is not the *form* of the measure; it's the *motivation* for the measure. Organizations too often rely on employee surveys for workforce measures because they are often the most feasible method of measurement. What makes them most feasible (outside vendors develop and administer the measures), however, is also what makes them least useful as measures of workforce success.

The feasibility–strategic validity trade-off is a particular challenge now because some managers and HR professionals don't feel they have the competency to develop measures of workforce success on their own, nor does their firm have the IT capability or software to easily implement the measures. This is gradually changing. The trade-off is slowly becoming less severe as software options improve and knowledge of workforce measurement becomes more widespread. For now, however, developing and implementing a set of workforce measures that truly have value to both the CEO and HR professionals remains a challenge. That's why so few firms do it well. It requires a new perspective. Instead of trying to find nuggets of value among the most feasible set of measures, they need to find the most feasible way to implement a set of strategically valid measures.

Consider the measurement decisions represented in figure 5-1. There are two dimensions to selecting the appropriate measures of workforce success. They both follow from the perspective that workforce success is a lagging indicator of prior HR initiatives, investments, and practices. First, you want to measure workforce success as late in the value creation process as possible. The primary focus should be on the actual workforce performance behaviors and the immediate performance drivers that execute the strategy rather than the earlier HR initiatives that potentially drive those behaviors. If there were a one-to-one correspondence between implementing a sales training program and subsequent employee sales behavior, this wouldn't be a problem. Unfortunately, this isn't the case. Second, at any stage in this value creation process, it is important to focus on the *drivers* in that process. For example, the characteristics of the HR management system that really drive value are the extent to which they are delivering competencies that are the basis for the performance behaviors required to execute strategy. Too often, however, the organizations simply measure the efficiency of those systems. Those efficiency measures don't tell you anything about whether your firm is creating the foundation for workforce success. In this case, HR professionals become program managers instead of strategy managers.

We recommend that managers first determine what strategically valid measures might look like, and then develop several feasible alternatives for actually collecting those measures. In the retail example, there are several options. One is to work with the marketing group and piggyback workforce success measures onto their customer satisfaction surveys. They key is for HR and marketing to have a shared responsibility for delivering an improved buying experience (and subsequent sales growth). This will mean that whoever is responsible for workforce measurement needs to be involved in the development of those customer satisfaction surveys, from the beginning of their development. An alternative might be supervisory appraisals or 180-degree feedback. The key issue would be whether supervisors or peers are in a position to regularly observe these behaviors.

Principle 3: Think in Terms of Relationships Among Metrics Before You Think About the Levels of the Metrics

One of the distinguishing features of our approach to workforce measurement is that it is grounded in a firm-specific business case. We believe that just as strategies are successful because they create unique and differentiated sources of competitive advantage, workforce success will mirror this differentiation. Benchmarking, by contrast, offers a much more limited measurement solution because it focuses only on workforce commonalities and ignores the more important workforce differentiators. The key element of this differentiation is the network of causal relationships that uniquely drive your firm's strategy. Your choice of measures should follow directly from your understanding of how the workforce contributes to this value creation process in your specific firm.

Thinking in terms of levels, or appropriate targets, follows from this understanding of relationships, because it is those relationships that give you a context for understanding what the appropriate measurement target ought to be. For example, consider the measures in figure 5-1. The measures earlier in the value creation process (e.g., HR management systems) should be selected because of their expected causal influence on workforce success (e.g., improved buying experience), not because they can be compared with HR efficiency in other firms. Training measures should describe success in developing the competencies or skills required for strategic performance behaviors. Recruiting and selection measures should describe the extent to which those hiring practices are aligned with those behavioral requirements. Or they might measure how new hires scored on work sampling tests designed to predict the strategic performance behaviors. The target levels for these workforce drivers depend on the anticipated relationship between those practices and the required behavioral outcomes. While the magnitude of this relationship might be quantitatively estimated in some cases, in most situations it's a judgment call. But at least it's a judgment that's guided by your firm's strategy. Compare this with a benchmarking result where levels are the only measurement focus, and those levels tell you nothing about your success in driving your own firm's strategy.

We have emphasized the importance of new perspectives when thinking about workforce measurement. This is another example. Traditional workforce measurement, with its emphasis on accounting and efficiency measures, has taken the form of disaggregated measures based in the functional areas, or "silos," of the HR function (e.g., recruiting and selection). These measures begin with an organizational strategic goal like cost reduction and attempt to measure work groups, teams, or even employees on some aspect of that goal. The idea is that each subunit in the organization contributes in the aggregate to cost reduction, and the larger strategic goal can be parceled out, with each "unit" receiving an appropriate disaggregated target. Our approach is different. The important perspective is not drilling down within one strategic metric, but rather managing across the system of strategy activities that constitute successful strategy execution. Managers need to think in terms of relationships if they hope to manage this system successfully.

This often requires a new mind-set for line managers and HR professionals who are accustomed to thinking in terms of functional silos. It means that line managers need to think about workforce success as a strategy driver and understand exactly what that means for their firm's success. For HR professionals it means that HR's contribution to firm performance is going to be more strongly linked to how the respective HR functions (e.g., compensation and staffing) are integrated to make the workforce a strategy driver, and not just how efficiently each of these functions operates as unit.

Principle 4: Workforce Measurement Is Not Just HR's Responsibility

Principle 4 follows from the first three principles. We've already touched on the problem of how effective implementation requires the elimination of measurement silos. This point needs to be emphasized because it is a major barrier to successful implementation of an effective workforce measurement system. Too often we find that workforce measurement is seen as HR function measurement, and hence largely the responsibility of HR professionals. The problem is that even if HR professionals take the lead in this area, they don't typically have access to the breadth of measures required to do the job effectively. It's no wonder there is such a reliance on external benchmarking. It's often easier to collect low-value efficiency measures from the same functional areas in other firms than to get useful measures from other functional areas in your own firm!

An integrated approach to workforce measurement directly affects the management value of those measures. It is not only important to understand that workforce success measures require a new focus on what to measure, but equally important is understanding *when* to measure. This follows from our emphasis on relationships and understanding that workforce success is both a leading and lagging indicator. Remember, workforce measurement is not just about accountability and is not an end in itself. Because workforce success is such a key intermediate link in the system of strategy execution, workforce measurement should also play a key role in management decision making. But to usefully inform those decisions, workforce measures must reflect the cause-and-effect relationships inherent in the role of workforce success as a strategy driver. Specifically, this means workforce measures are more useful when they are collected and analyzed in a way that reflects that cause-and-effect logic.

Following principle 3, this means thinking in terms of relationships when considering when to collect these measures. At a minimum, you don't want to measure leading indicators at a point in time after the lagging indicators. In others words, don't measure the cause after the result. Ideally, information on leading indicators can be used to predict future results or at least indicate when a problem might be anticipated so that remedial action can be taken. Consider the example in figure 5-1 again. The strategic question that should be equally important to line managers and HR professionals is, Are we meeting our goals on workforce success and thereby optimizing the workforce dimension of sales growth? An additional question, particularly for HR professionals, is, Are we achieving our goals on the various HR drivers of workforce success? If not, what are the future consequences for workforce success, and what initiatives are required to improve these results?

In figure 5-1 we can see that there might be several HR drivers of workforce success. For example, the firm might select new hires based on a battery of tests designed to measure personality traits linked to the desired sales behaviors. Similarly, training and development focuses on those same dimensions of employee performance. What if selection test scores begin to fall for new hires? This might predict a decline in customer buying experience in six months as these new hires come online in significant numbers. Timing is an issue because sales won't decline immediately, but we should expect to see missed sales targets as these new hires become an increasing percentage of the workforce. To accurately understand the significance of this lagged effect, however, the firm will need to have measures at two points in time. There is no way to answer the questions posed earlier if workforce success is measured in a one-shot effort where new hire test results are collected at the same time that workforce success measures are collected on current workers. One is a harbinger of future results; the latter is the result of past decisions.

This more strategic management of workforce success also highlights the importance of an integrated approach to workforce measurement. For example, what if the solution to falling applicant test scores was more extensive training? Thinking in terms of relationships, training and selection are considered alternative HR drivers with the same strategic goal: workforce success. Additional training costs might appear to be inefficient when compared with an industry benchmark on training costs, but for this firm they are a wise strategic investment. Both line managers and HR professionals would have a shared interest in the greater training investment given the line of sight to workforce success. It's numerator management (i.e., focusing on the value created) instead of denominator management (i.e., focusing solely on the costs incurred).

Measures are more valuable when they can be analyzed in a way that provides meaningful input to decision making for both line managers and HR professionals. Workforce measurement systems that are well integrated with HR and across other functions in the business significantly increase the value of this analysis. For example, if the measures in figure 5-1 are part of an integrated measurement system, measurement can be transformed into a valuable management tool. How would this work? Workforce success measures, either from mystery shoppers or peer appraisals, are collected for a sample of the sales staff. At the same time, applicant test scores and training performance for these same employees are merged with the workforce success measures. This of course assumes that the need for these measures has been anticipated and that they were collected at an earlier point in time. A straightforward statistical analysis can indicate how changes in applicant test scores and training performance predict future workforce success. It would also be possible to determine the relationship between employee performance behaviors and ratings of customer buying experience (See "The Value of Estimating Quantitative Relationships"). What does this extra analysis tell you? It confirms for line managers whether or not workforce success is a key strategic driver and how important it is. It also gives both line managers and HR professionals important insight into the effectiveness of key HR initiatives designed to drive workforce success. It also changes the conversations between line managers and HR professionals. These conversations can now be focused on strategy execution instead of budget variance and cost control.

THE VALUE OF ESTIMATING QUANTITATIVE RELATIONSHIPS

Thinking in terms of relationships means going the next step and measuring those relationships. This focus on workforce performance or human capital is a relatively new concept for both line managers and HR professionals. It is, however, increasingly a feature of the larger effort to measure the performance of intangible assets. A recent study by Christopher D. Ittner and David F. Larcker demonstrates that whereas less than a quarter of companies in their survey engaged in "extensive causal modeling" of intangibles, those companies reported higher return on assets and return on equity.[a] The well-chronicled experience at Sears was one of the earliest, and most comprehensive, efforts to measure the relationships between workforce behaviors and business outcomes.[b] In a more recent example, IBM has examined the influence of workplace climate on employee retention, customer satisfaction relative to competition, and ultimately business performance (market share). The measure of workforce climate is a very broad concept and includes employee perceptions of IBM's strategy execution and leadership practices. Based on data collected from 1997 to 2003, they find that workforce climate is a good predictor of future customer satisfaction, which is a good predictor of future market share. Finally, recall our retail example. If measures are answers to questions, how much more compelling would those "answers" be if we could determine the relationship between the measures of strategic performance behaviors and customer buying experience? Both the line managers and the SVPHR would be able get more specific answers, like "a 15 percent improvement in performance behaviors has increased customer buying experience by 25 percent, which in turn has increased sales growth by 6 percent."

[a]Christopher D. Ittner and David F. Larker, "Coming Up Short on Nonfinancial Performance Measurement," *Harvard Business Review* (November 2003): 91.

[b]Anthony J. Rucci, Steven P. Kirn, and Richard T. Quinn, "The Employee-Customer-Profit Chain at Sears," *Harvard Business Review* (January–February 1998): 76.

Principle 5: Focus on the Vital Few

Sometimes one of the most difficult measurement challenges is to sort through the range of available measures and decide which should actually be reported and to whom. For the CEO and senior executives, the emphasis should be on those measures with strategic importance—namely, those that reflect how well the workforce is successfully implementing the firm's strategy. Figure 3-1 in chapter 3 identifies four dimensions of the Workforce Scorecard:

- Workforce success

- Leadership and workforce behaviors

- Workforce competencies

- Workforce mind-set and culture

In the simple retail example in figure 5-1, workforce success focused on the customer buying experience. Essential workforce behaviors for those outcomes required that employees be knowledgeable, courteous, timely, and helpful. Each of these four dimensions of the Workforce Scorecard could in turn be measured for each strategy driver.

Most firms might have ten to twenty such strategy drivers, all of which are required to successfully execute the firm's strategy. A useful set of summary measures needs to capture workforce success across all of those strategy drivers. Does that mean $5 \times 20 = 100$ workforce measures for the CEO to monitor? No. At the level of a corporate dashboard, workforce measures should be aggregated along the four dimensions of the Workforce Scorecard. In order to combine disparate activities like customer buying experience and R&D, a performance index should be constructed for each of the four dimensions. For example, performance targets could be constructed for each dimension within a category of workforce outcome. In the retail example, the target for essential workforce behaviors might be 90 percent of the employees rated "above average" or "excellent." For the workforce success target, customer ratings of the buying experience might be 75 percent or more rating the experience as "above average" or "excellent" on product knowledge, courtesy, and so on. Once the targets have been established, summary measures are easily calculated to reflect progress toward those targets and variation in success. A typical summary measure might include "percent of performance targets achieved" for each of the four dimensions of the Workforce Scorecard.

The measures can be reported in a reasonably simple format because of the effort and analysis that went into the development of the measures and their clear link to the execution of the firm's strategy. This is in contrast to the traditional approach to workforce measurement, where hundreds of measures might be available and managers pore over them hoping to glean useful insights after the fact. With the Workforce Scorecard, both line managers and HR professionals already know exactly why those measures are being reported and what they mean, because they've been developed with the larger value creation relationships in mind. At this point, the only question is, What is the performance on those measures?

An example of the systematic metrics selection process can be seen at IBM, which is currently reviewing the HR measures that are shared with the top management team and business leaders, and reducing this number from 110 to less than 30. The goal is a single-page report that summarizes HR and workforce performance. In doing this work, the team at IBM interviewed more than sixty key executives both within as well as more broadly throughout the business (e.g., marketing, strategic planning, finance, and operations). The goal was to select a mix of approximately 35 metrics representing both leading and lagging indicators. They began by developing strategy maps for both key businesses within IBM as well as for the global HR function. IBM hoped to achieve a manageable set of measures that were linked to quantitative measures of business success and that could demonstrate, to both line managers and HR professionals, the relationship between HR activities and business value. IBM uses decision rules shown in figure 5-2 to help them select the vital few measures.

This isn't to suggest that these measures would *only* be used in this highly aggregated form, but this provides a useful strategic overview of workforce performance. When performance on workforce outcomes fails to meet targets, managers can drill down to leading indicators that are driving those results. Given the importance of relationships in strategic workforce management, the flexibility to analyze

FIGURE 5-2

IBM Eliminated Any Metrics That Did Not Meet "Must-Have" and "Absolute" Criteria, and Then Rated the Remaining Metrics on the "Desired Characteristics"

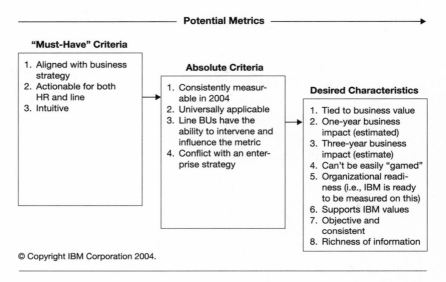

© Copyright IBM Corporation 2004.

various points in this relationship is a more important design feature than the number of measures. The CEO dashboard should represent the tip of the iceberg, but it should be clear that there is an iceberg and that its structure can be probed and understood. The problem with traditional workforce measures is that what might appear to be the tip of the iceberg is in reality just chunks of data floating aimlessly on a sea of information.

A FIRST STEP TOWARD MEETING THE IMPLEMENTATION CHALLENGE

Just as there is no one list of workforce measures that can be applied to all companies, there also is not one implementation solution that is right for all firms. The problem gets particularly unwieldy when managers try to integrate disparate measures collected for other purposes, residing in different software systems. For example, you might have useful employee survey data, but these measures have been collected by an outside vendor, often anonymously so they cannot be linked to other measures or disaggregated to meaningful units of analysis. Or we often find firms with excellent 360-degree feedback systems that are solely under the control of leaders being rated, in order to retain their developmental focus. These measures would fit perfectly as pieces in the larger strategic measurement system, but they aren't available. So sometimes even though organizations collect workforce measures in the right form, they are not useful because of the way or the reason they are being collected.

These examples reflect the feasibility-validity trade-off in practice. So where do we start if we want to overcome those hurdles? Typically, the implementation solution should be available at a reasonable cost and over a reasonable time frame. Ideally, it would have a limited reliance on other software but would also reflect the measurement principles described earlier. Benchmarking, of course, excels at meeting the first three criteria but fails miserably on the fourth.

There are several design features that need to be kept in mind as you try to implement the measurement principles described earlier. First, you need to collect workforce measures along the value creation process from workforce success back to workforce mind-set and culture (figure 3-1). That doesn't necessarily mean every point in that process, but you need enough coverage so that you can manage the process. Second, in order to meaningfully interpret the measures, you will need to collect measures at the same level of analysis. This makes it much easier to interpret the relationship between the leading and lagging indicators in a way that the measures can be effective guides to management decisions. Ideally, as many measures as possible will be collected at the level of the individual employee. You can always aggregate up to higher levels of analysis, but if you only have unit-level performance, there is no way to reconstruct individual performance.

THE WORKFORCE SCORECARD

There are several approaches an organization might use to bring a more strategic perspective to its workforce measurement system. In this section, we illustrate one example of how you might begin.

Measuring Workforce Success

What distinguishes our approach to workforce measurement is the definition of workforce success as the contribution to strategy execution rather than measuring only HR activities and workforce potential (competencies). The key implementation challenge is how to measure those varied workforce outcomes. Figure 5-1 illustrates just one example of workforce success, but in most firms there are likely to be ten to twenty strategy drivers that will be the focus for these workforce outcomes.

In figure 5-1 we saw the value in having direct measures of both workforce performance behaviors (frontline sales staff behaviors) and workforce success (improved buying experience). Those separate measures may not initially be available in many firms. An alternative approach is to use individual performance goals for "A" players as an approximation of these two separate measures. The essential requirement is that the organization has established a set of performance goals that are tied directly to one or more of those ten to twenty strategy drivers. This implies that the organization has made some progress in developing a differentiated workforce strategy and been able to identify its "A" positions. Progress on these performance goals for all employees in these "A" positions then becomes the summary measure of strategic workforce success. A simple refinement of this measure would be to assign differential importance to the ten to twenty strategy drivers and thereby assign differential weights to workforce performance in different positions. In other words, in order to create an overall measure of workforce success, the organization can weight each of the ten to twenty strategy drivers by its relative importance and also weight the relative importance of each "A" player's performance goals.

The linchpin of this approach is that the performance management system for "A" positions be directly linked to the key drivers of successful strategy execution. It puts the implementation burden on the design and alignment of the performance management system rather than on the development of new workforce measures. The result should be a strategically valid set of performance goals that enable the CEO to be confident that if those goals have been met, the strategy is being executed successfully.

Workforce Competencies

Workforce success is the key lagging indicator for the Workforce Scorecard, and is the most essential workforce measure because those workforce outcomes are required to execute your strategy. What is the next measure that meets our implementation criteria? In this "quick start" example, we would use the performance goals as a composite measure for both workforce success and workforce behaviors because behavioral measures are likely to require more significant investment in measurement infrastructure. Therefore, the first leading indicator that would be measured would be workforce competencies. Competencies only represent potential performance, but they are a key driver for managing actual performance. Here we would look to three possible sources of measures. The first might be self-reporting measures from employee surveys in which employees are asked to evaluate whether they have the competencies necessary to meet their performance goals. The second could be the results from any training and development efforts. Ideally, these measures would include some measure of actual performance in these programs, but at a minimum would indicate participation, completion, and currency of program content. Development measures might also include assessments of career and promotion potential based on previous developmental assignments. Third, HR could include the results of various assessment tests at the point of hire. The choice among these measures depends upon the firm's workforce development strategy and the particular HR initiatives designed to support that strategy. The bottom line is that you want one or two measures that capture the current level of the workforce competencies required to produce the essential workforce outcomes. Once again, thinking about relationships is the key. These leading indicators are only important to the extent that they are considered to be key drivers of strategic workforce success.

Workforce Mind-set and Culture

Culture is a term that means many things to many people. At its most basic level, culture reflects what's important and what's appropriate in a social context. Employment cultures vary and arguably serve many purposes in the organization. Our interest is in how the culture supports performance. Therefore, we look for evidence that the firm has a high-performance culture. A key dimension of a high-performance culture requires that "A" players accept and understand the prominence of strategy execution in their work. They understand how their job contributes to the firm's strategic goals, and all of the organizational signals reinforce that same high-performance message. We call this central cultural attribute *employee strategic focus*. In one of our studies, we found that employee strategic focus had a powerful influence on strategy execution, and as a result, on a firm's financial performance.[2] It's just one more example of how execution separates the winners and the losers.

Employee strategic focus can be measured with an employee survey. The intent is to measure how well employees, particularly those in "A" positions, understand how their position contributes to the successful execution of the firm's strategy. Where the workforce strategy is differentiated, it would be useful to evaluate how their understanding of how specific strategy drivers relevant to their job influenced firm performance. In the retail example in figure 5-1, frontline sales staff (and their leaders) would be asked to rate the extent to which they understand how their performance affects customer buying experience and/or customer satisfaction.

THE HR SCORECARD

The HR Scorecard is designed to guide the management of the HR function, but the elements in the HR Scorecard are key leading indicators for workforce success. Therefore, it is appropriate that several summary measures from the HR Scorecard be highlighted in the larger workforce dashboard as possible explanations for the workforce outcomes. In this "quick start" measurement effort, we would focus on two dimensions of the HR Scorecard: the HR management system and HR workforce competencies.

The HR Management System

There are two key strategic drivers here. The first is whether the HR management system is aligned with the requirements of effective strategy execution. This is related to how well the firm has clarified strategic and core HR activities. The HR management system sends a complex set of signals about what's important and what's valued in the firm. An HR management system that is strategically aligned will send a uniform signal that strategy execution is valued. If the HR management system is largely generic, "A" players may find that training has little relationship to the strategic dimension of their job. Or they may find that training is considered a remedial activity to improve the performance of employees who never should have been hired in the first place or who should be exited for poor performance. It might also reveal that performance management systems provide little motivation to execute strategy. Any of these misalignments will make it more difficult to create the workforce outcomes required by the firm's strategy.

Alignment is in the eye of the beholder—in this case, the "A" employees. Employee surveys can be used to measure the second driver—the extent to which "A" players see the various elements of the HR management system as supporting and reinforcing the performance goals (workforce outcomes) required of them. A similar survey of the HR professionals on these same questions would provide a useful source of comparison. For example, low levels of alignment, where both groups agree, provide one basis for action, while a result where employees find little alignment, but HR professionals rate the alignment as high, suggests a different problem. It would also be appropriate to include line managers charged with managing the key strategy drivers in this alignment survey, since the nature of the alignment will have such a significant effect on workforce success in "A" positions.

HR Workforce Competencies

HR professionals have several roles, and only one of them is strategic partner. However, this is the key role for driving workforce success. Unfortunately, it is often the least developed competency because of the continuing pressure for operational excellence and administrative efficiency in the HR function—demands that can work at cross-purposes with the strategic role of HR professionals. For the purposes of this initial measurement system, it is not as important to measure the level of the underlying competency as it is to measure role performance. This assessment can be made as part of an employee survey and include the perspective of line managers and "A" players as well as self-assessments by HR professionals. It would also be useful to collect estimates from HR professionals of the percent of their work time focused on the role of strategic partner, and collect similar estimates from line managers. This measurement system is summarized in table 5-1.

INTERPRETING THE MEASURES

We've said that measures are answers to questions, so what important questions can we answer with this relatively modest workforce measurement system? Let's start with senior executives and move to the HR professional.

The CEO

Questions the CEO might have about the workforce could include the following: Is the workforce contribution to strategy execution on track? If not, where is it falling short? Which strategy drivers are most likely suffering from subpar workforce success? All of these questions can be answered by the proposed system. Since the "A" position performance goals correspond directly to successful execution (i.e., strategic validity) of the firm's ten to fifteen strategy drivers, the workforce success index accurately describes whether the workforce dimension of strategy execution is on track. Since this measure was collected at the individual employee level, it can be aggregated to the level of the firm as well as to the individual strategy driver. This means the CEO can quickly determine overall workforce success, but also identify how workforce success varies by strategy driver and which line managers are responsible for that workforce success.

Senior Executives

Senior executives and heads of business units, will want to focus on workforce success in the strategy drivers for which they share responsibility. As importantly, they should ask questions about the drivers of this workforce success. If there are shortfalls, what are the likely explanations? Similarly, if leading indicators of future workforce success are falling short of targets, senior executives need to be forewarned of

TABLE 5-1

Summary of Measurement Implementation Example and Data Sources

Scorecard Category	Measure(s)	Level of Analysis	Data Source
Workforce Success	• % employees in "A" positions at or above performance target • % of strategy drivers with employees at or above target	• Individual employee aggregated to higher levels as needed	• Web-based goal management program
Workforce Capabilities	• % "A" players self-report required strategic competencies • Development ratings for "A" players	• Individual employee aggregated to higher levels as needed • Individual employee aggregated to higher levels as needed	• Employee survey • HR information system

Workforce Mind-set and Culture	• "A" player strategic focus
	  – Overall
	  – By strategy driver
		• Individual employee aggregated to higher levels as needed	• Employee survey

HR System	• "A" player perspective on HR system alignment • HR perspective on HR system alignment	• Individual • Individual	• Employee survey • Employee survey
HR Workforce Competencies	• Line manager assessment of strategic role performance • Employee assessment of strategic role performance • HR self-assessment of strategic role performance • HR estimate of time % allocated to strategic role • Line manager estimate of % of HR time allocated to strategic role	• All individual, but can be aggregated to higher units of analysis	• Employee survey

potential problems. These are all questions that can be answered with this simple system. The system includes measures of workforce culture and competencies that should be leading indicators of workforce success. Senior executives can not only identify the overall levels of workforce competency and culture within their area of responsibility, but can also identify those subunits or managers that have problems on these dimensions. In short, both the source (which dimension of the Workforce Scorecard) of the workforce problem and the location (employee group) of the problem can be identified.

For example, workforce success may be 5 percent below target for a particular strategy driver, and the problem may be linked to a particular employee group. Further evaluation might reveal that the culture measure (employee strategic focus) is well below target for the firm. Why this is occurring requires further investigation, but the nature of the problem has been identified. Perhaps the employees are getting mixed signals from different levels of organizational leadership. It might also be due to inconsistent HR policies and rewards that work at cross-purposes with the stated strategy.

Senior HR Leaders

Using this simple measurement system, senior HR professionals are in a position to both validate HR's strategic contribution and identify potential HR "solutions" where workforce success problems might be encountered. First, let's take the other side of the CEO's question about workforce success. Often this is phrased more directly in terms of what is HR's contribution to firm performance? Instead of relying on activity measures, efficiency benchmarks, or other accounting-based measures, this system provides HR leaders with a very clear and compelling answer. HR has a shared responsibility for implementing the firm's strategy, and the progress toward that goal is reflected in the workforce success index. At the same time, using leading indicators in the Workforce Scorecard and the HR Scorecard, senior HR professionals are in a position to identify leading indicators that could explain workforce problems and target solutions.

Of particular interest to HR leaders will be how the firm's workforce and line managers evaluate the strategic alignment of the HR management system and the strategic competencies of the HR professionals with whom they interact. Because the measures focus on individual HR functions, functional misalignments can be identified and remedied as required. One of the most revealing measures will be how line managers and HR professionals evaluate the time spent by HR professionals on strategic issues. The very presence of this measure will encourage more conversation between line managers and HR professionals about what really is strategic (i.e., what's important) and what's not.

It would also be possible to analyze the actual impact of the leading indicators on workforce success. For example, given that the measures are collected at the level of the individual, HR professionals could statistically analyze how changes in workforce culture and competencies affect workforce success. This would allow HR professionals and line managers to predict future changes in workforce success, based on current levels of workforce culture and competencies as well as the magnitude of the lag.

PART THREE

The Execution Challenge

6

STRATEGY EXECUTION I

The Roles of the CEO, Executive Team, and Workforce Metrics

THIS IS THE FIRST of three chapters addressing the *execution challenge*—ensuring that managers have the access, capability, and motivation to use workforce metrics to drive strategy execution. While we described the importance of aligning clear strategic priorities with workforce metrics in the first chapters of this book, in this chapter we return to these concepts and describe the specific roles and responsibilities for business leaders wishing to implement workforce measurement systems effectively in their own firms. We will attempt to provide insights into the execution challenge with examples of how firms have developed workforce and HR strategies to drive strategy execution efforts, and offer suggestions about workforce metrics that might enhance your firm's success in strategy execution. As we've stated previously, we believe effective strategy execution requires a new partnership between leaders, the workforce, and a firm's HR function. When working in concert, these three components enhance strategy execution substantially and leverage a firm's competitive advantage. The theory may be obvious, but, in our experience, the practice is not. When these components are not working harmoniously, firms underperform. No one believes that the CFO and finance function can execute effectively without a philosophy, a budget, and financial controls. Shouldn't the same approach apply to a firm's workforce?

By analogy, we believe that successful execution of a firm's strategy requires a clear business strategy, a workforce strategy, and a strategy for the HR function. We also need metrics to assess the progress of the workforce as it pursues the firm's business strategy. These metrics are reflected in the firm's Balanced Scorecard, Workforce Scorecard, and HR Scorecard, respectively. We believe that firms must understand and articulate these three facets of the business to be strategically successful. While most firms have focused on developing a clear business strategy, few have focused on developing a workforce strategy. The thrust of this chapter is to describe why and how the CEO and the executive team can develop workforce strategies to execute a firm's business strategy.

A firm's business strategy should describe how it intends to win in the markets it targets—its intended competitive advantage. Developing business strategy requires a clear statement about how the firm will differentiate itself externally in the marketplace. This is clearly a significant decision for any firm, which requires clear strategic choices, or the firm becomes unfocused and confused and risks underperformance.[1]

The logical next step after external differentiation is differentiating the firm's resources internally. Differentiating on the inside requires aligning all of the firm's resources, especially its workforce, with the firm's intended, differentiated competitive advantage on the outside. For us, this issue is paramount. It is the major theme of this book—the workforce executes strategy and therefore firms must differentiate resources internally to align them with the firm's external competitive advantage to ensure effective execution. To achieve this internal differentiation and alignment, we believe, requires what we call a workforce strategy.

What does a workforce strategy entail? The objective is to introduce workforce considerations into the firm's strategic decision-making processes and ensuring that they are acted upon. The process begins with an analysis of the firm's business strategy, culture, and brand and a determination of the strategic capabilities (or core competencies) that create the firm's competitive advantage (i.e., bundles of information, technology, and people).[2] Such an analysis also looks at whether the firm's culture is aligned with its strategy; identifies the firm's strategic capabilities, "A" positions within those capabilities, and "A" players; and, most importantly, develops a workforce philosophy to serve as a system of governance for the CEO, executive team members, line managers, and the HR function in making strategic workforce decisions. The approach is dynamic. As firm strategy changes to adapt to a changing marketplace, the workforce strategy must change internally in order to stay in alignment. New games require new rules.

ACCOUNTABILITY AS A CAPABILITY

For strategy execution to be successful, leaders and employees must be held accountable for the allocation and use of resources; accountability must become a firm capability. Accountability for a workforce—its culture, its capabilities, and assurance that it delivers the firm's strategy—is also critical. This is a joint challenge for the firm's leadership and its HR function; both must be accountable for delivering the workforce that delivers business results. While leaders have far more day-to-day influence on a workforce than does HR, HR's primary contribution is helping line managers to see the "big picture" and differentiating among present and potential employees. Therefore, both leadership and HR must be responsible for the delivery of the workforce necessary to successfully execute the firm's strategy.

The essence of strategy execution is making the strategy a reality. It is the job of leaders to clarify and communicate the firm's strategy, the metrics indicative of strategic success, and workforce consequences (especially rewards). This is the first step to making accountability a capability—a central part of the firm's culture.

We will now focus on workforce processes for strategy execution through which a firm builds a system of strategic accountability—a performance system based on employee accountability that is strategically aligned and integrated, with consequences for contributors (as well as noncontributors) to strategic success.

Our model for strategy execution is simple. It consists of three major components: strategy, measurement, and consequences. We believe strategy should dictate the metrics indicative of strategic progress, and success on these metrics should dictate consequences for individuals. Very often these critical components are not aligned or well managed, causing firms to perform well below their true potential.

Accountability Is "What?"

Clearly, strategy is important. Strategic choice—choosing a value proposition that targets a specific way to win customers (i.e., differentiating on the outside)—is critical. The role of the CEO and all line managers is to select a strategy and constantly communicate it so that the workforce understands how the firm intends to win a disproportionate share of its market. This understanding shapes the mind-set and culture, and dictates the capabilities necessary for strategic success. It distinguishes between employees making a contribution and "having a job."

Accountability Is "How Well?"

The second component of building an accountability capability is measurement—strategic success metrics. This requires specific measures within the business model, not only financial, but also customer, business processes, and, as we emphasize here, workforce metrics. Thus, the job of executives and leaders at all levels is to constantly articulate where the firm stands relative to its intended strategy: financially, with customers, with business processes, and with the workforce. These metrics should be "online, real time," enabling midcourse corrections to bring about strategic change and deliver results.

Accountability Is "What's in It for Me?"

Finally, consequences for strategic success, the rewards that exist for significant results, are essential. Strategic metrics can be provided at three levels of analysis—the entire organization, groups and teams, and individuals—but rewards are allocated only to individuals, despite the level of measurement. This creates a performance paradox in strategy execution that can cause dysfunctional outcomes. The paradox is that motivational impact is greatest at the individual level of accountability, yet trust in measurement is low, as has often been argued by many employees and unions. More strategic, trusted metrics, including trustworthy workforce metrics, are needed to increase employee motivation and provide equitable consequences to build greater accountability. Individual, team, and organizationwide rewards all can be powerful depending on the circumstances, but rewards must be triggered by success on the "strategic metrics" and directed to contributors—those who have changed their behaviors, leading to higher levels of strategic contributions.

Assessing the readiness of a firm to execute its strategy establishes an important baseline for executives. Executives who know their firm's readiness are better prepared to take on the daunting challenge of strategy execution. A sample survey from a firm concerned about its strategy execution readiness is shown in figure 6-1.

FIGURE 6-1

Strategy Execution Readiness Survey

The goal of this survey is to help identify team/individual progress in strategy execution. Please read each statement and select the most appropriate response.

Strongly disagree	Disagree	Neither agree or disagree	Agree	Strongly agree	Not applicable or cannot respond
1	2	3	4	5	N/A

Setting Strategic Goals and Priorities
1. My manager has clearly communicated our firm's business strategy and the priorities for the group.
2. My team has three or fewer clearly defined priorities.
3. I have three or fewer clearly defined individual priorities.
4. I have a clear understanding of my priorities and deliverables.
5. In my team we are clear on who is accountable for what.

Following Through
6. At least once a month our team evaluates our progress against our priorities (goals).
7. I provide an update to the team at least once a month on my progress against my priorities/goals.
8. My manager checks with us frequently to see how we are tracking against our priorities.

Being Realistic
9. I have challenging but realistic individual objectives.
10. We question the goals/priorities set for the team to see if they are achievable.
11. I question the goals/priorities set for the team to check if they are achievable.

Project Planning
12. We set milestones in our team to track our progress against our priorities.
13. We set timelines in our team to track our progress against our priorities.

Being Decisive
14. As a team we make decisions quickly even on tough issues.
15. I make decisions quickly even on tough issues.

Emotional Fortitude
16. My manager directly addresses performance concerns with team members in a timely manner.
17. I have the courage to address performance concerns with team members.

Rewarding the Doers
18. In my team we consistently reward/acknowledge achievements of team members.
19. We celebrate the achievement of project milestones.

Open-Ended Questions
1. How good are we at strategy execution?
2. What are some of the key reasons we are or are not good at strategy execution?
3. What are three areas we should focus on to get better at strategy execution?

THE STRATEGY EXECUTION PROCESS

A major challenge of strategy execution is to ensure that firms have a workforce strategy and mandate leadership accountability for the success of the workforce in delivering business results. We believe that this is a shared responsibility among the CEO, the executive team, line managers, and HR. Strategy execution requires strategy clarity *and* accountability by leadership and the workforce to ensure that the strategy becomes a reality. Much of what follows is built around this simple model—of the roles of the leadership, the workforce, and HR in the execution of the strategy of the firm.

We cannot emphasize enough the importance of accountability in strategy execution. It has often been said that "the problem for our firm is not the strategy, but its execution."[3] Holding work units and individuals accountable for business results *is* strategy execution. Firms need direction, and they need measurement to track progress. Individuals also require consequences that reinforce when they have been successful and when they have not, based on the considerable literature demonstrating the power of consequences in influencing firm performance.[4] The challenge for leadership is building a culture of accountability.

How Should a Firm Execute Its Workforce Strategy?

An important determinant of successful strategy execution is the extent to which the firm can create a culture of accountability within the firm. The tasks shown in figure 6-2 describe the process to execute workforce strategy, the CEO and executive team's workforce responsibilities, the business leader's/line manager's workforce responsibilities, and the responsibilities of the HR function.

Expectations of the CEO and the Executive Team

The CEO has specific responsibilities that are essential for the direction and focus of a workforce. That is, the CEO and the executive team must decide the strategy of the firm, the brand message, and how the firm and its products are to be represented in the market. From these, the firm's culture needs to be determined. Again, we believe that culture should be by choice rather than by accident. Different strategies

FIGURE 6-2

Executing Workforce Strategy: The Process

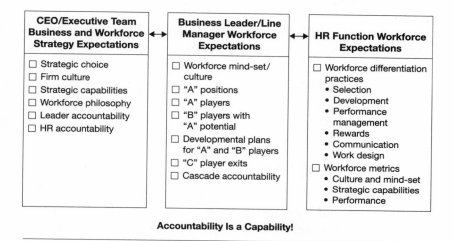

CEO/Executive Team Business and Workforce Strategy Expectations	Business Leader/Line Manager Workforce Expectations	HR Function Workforce Expectations

☐ Strategic choice
☐ Firm culture
☐ Strategic capabilities
☐ Workforce philosophy
☐ Leader accountability
☐ HR accountability
	☐ Workforce mind-set/
	   culture
	☐ "A" positions
	☐ "A" players
	☐ "B" players with
	   "A" potential
	☐ Developmental plans
	   for "A" and "B" players
	☐ "C" player exits
	☐ Cascade accountability
		☐ Workforce differentiation
		   practices
		  • Selection
		  • Development
		  • Performance
		    management
		  • Rewards
		  • Communication
		  • Work design
		☐ Workforce metrics
		  • Culture and mind-set
		  • Strategic capabilities
		  • Performance

Accountability Is a Capability!

require different cultures in order for firms to be successful. An operational excellence strategy, where firms attempt to eliminate all process variance, requires a much more rigid approach to the workforce as opposed to the approach required by the creative or R&D group within an advertising agency or a pharmaceutical firm. Therefore, the identification of the cultural pillars of the firm consistent with its strategy and market image (i.e., how it is to be viewed in the "hearts and minds" of its future customers/consumers) should be major dictates of the firm's culture. But as we described in chapter 2, this type of "core differentiation" needs to be expanded as well to reflect the extent to which different strategy drivers or areas in the business will require different cultures. Effectively managing strategy execution requires a careful balance of these core and differentiated dimensions of firm culture.

As we also described in chapter 2 in our discussion of "employer-of-choice" and "employee-of-choice" workforce branding strategies, the differentiation process can begin even before candidates apply. Like the marines' recruiting motto—"a few good people," not all employees fit all organizations. Such an approach discourages applicants the marines do not seek and encourages those who see themselves as fitting the culture that the marines view as essential to successfully executing their strategy.

The CEO and the executive team also need to consider the responsibility and accountability requirements of leaders (at all levels) for implementing the firm's strategy. The accountability of the HR function also must be clarified and specific expectations created by the CEO whereby the senior HR leader, as well as the HR function, can be held accountable (with specific metrics) for the delivery of the workforce, by making the firm's workforce strategy operational through line managers and executives.

Expectations of Business Leaders and Line Managers

The second box of figure 6-2 describes the workforce expectations of business leaders and line managers, including how they are to manage their workforces in executing strategy. Each line manager should be responsible for the culture and mind-set of the workforce that reports to him or her. That is, the workforce should understand why their unit is a part of the firm, what it contributes, how well it is doing, how it relates to customers, what obstacles it faces, what it needs to do to overcome these obstacles, how it might accelerate its performance, and the consequences for successful performance. These are the major messages that leaders at all levels must continually communicate.

In addition, the business leaders and line managers need to identify the "A" positions within the business unit as well as assess (and track) their "A" players and "B" players with "A" potential. Business leaders and line managers must also provide an exit strategy for "C" players (employees who are not meeting performance expectations and, after unsuccessful coaching, may need to leave the organization) as well as clarify that line managers who report to *them* are accountable for the identification and removal of "C" players now and in the future. Finally, business leaders and line managers must cascade the firm's workforce philosophy and hold their managerial direct reports accountable for the performance of their workforce. Thus, strategy execution requires all managers to be accountable for the mind-set and culture of their workforce, to identify their "A" players and have developmental plans in place for them, and to have a plan to address, if not exit, individuals who continue to perform less than successfully.

Expectations of the HR Function

The third box in figure 6-2 describes the responsibilities of the HR function. The CEO and the executive team are to set the strategic direction and workforce strategy, and business leaders and line managers are to manage the workforce to ensure that it is achieved. The role of the HR function is to provide enabling tools and techniques to create the workforce that executes the firm's strategy. The HR function must impact the creation of the firm's workforce and be held accountable for the same workforce metrics as line managers (i.e., the accountability for the culture and mind-set of the workforce, the strategic capabilities, and employee performance). Again, the execution of the workforce strategy is a joint responsibility between HR and line executives.

ESSENTIAL ROLES FOR EXECUTING WORKFORCE STRATEGY

Effectively executing the workforce accountabilities of a firm's strategy involves a new set of roles and responsibilities at all levels. Here we intend to further define these roles and provide examples of how these might be more successfully enacted. Figure 6-3 describes what the roles and actions might look like for major contributors to effective strategy execution, as well as the associated metrics. The actions we explore under each of five major constituencies (CEO, executive team members, line managers, the workforce, and HR) are needed to better ensure that strategy is executed. These are suggestions with a few examples provided to demonstrate how your strategy execution efforts with your workforce might be enhanced. There are possibly many more actions that you have developed through your own experience that lead to heightened strategy execution, perhaps many better than those described here. What we have provided are ideas and examples of how strategy execution can be accomplished through an explicit workforce strategy and workforce metrics and by holding leaders accountable for their workforces. These roles and responsibilities are described here for the CEO and the executive team, while in the next chapter we provide a similar discussion for line managers and the HR function.

FIGURE 6-3

Strategy Execution and Workforce Metrics

CEO

- Conduct strategy review meetings that include discussions of business strategy and workforce strategy
- Negotiate performance expectations, including workforce accountabilities, with each member of the executive team
- Negotiate with senior HR leadership concerning the HR function's workforce deliverables

Executive Team Members

- Participate in crafting business strategy, workforce philosophy, and workforce strategy
- Participate in discussions determining desired firm culture, strategic capabilities, and leader behavior metrics
- Identify the firm's "A" positions
- Identify "A" players and "B" players with "A" potential in "A" positions
- Create developmental plans for "A" and "B" players (in "A" positions)
- Detail performance expectations for direct reports

Sample Workforce Decision Metrics

- Leadership and Workforce Behaviors
  - Effectiveness of executive team members in leading strategy execution (180° feedback) survey
  - Effectiveness of workforce behaviors in delivering firm's strategy (e.g., strategic workforce success surveys)
- Workforce Competencies
  - Number/percent of viable successors
  - Unwanted turnover of strategic talent ("A" players in "A" positions)
  - Capability of leadership talent on executive team (percent "rotation ready now")
  - Growth/development of strategic talent ("B" players with "A" potential in "A" positions, etc.)
- Workforce Mind-set and Culture
  - Percent of workforce understanding the firm's strategy and goals
  - Percent understanding firm's status on firm's "success metrics"

- Leadership and Workforce Behaviors
  - Effectiveness of line managers in leading strategy execution (180° feedback)
  - Effectiveness of workforce behaviors in delivering unit's strategy (e.g., key customer success metrics)
- Workforce Competencies
  - Number/percent of viable successors
  - Turnover of talent key to unit's strategic success ("A" players in "A" positions)
  - Capability of line managers (percent "ready now")
  - Growth/development of talent key to unit's success ("B" players with "A" potential in unit's "A" positions)
- Workforce Mind-set and Culture
  - Percent of business unit understanding unit's strategy and goals
  - Percent understanding unit's status on its "success metrics"

Human Resources

- Work with HR and the executive team to shape the firm's business strategy and workforce philosophy
- Finalize workforce philosophy and strategy and communicate them to management

- Design performance measurement and reward tools
- Design "A," "B," and "C" tracking systems
- Build a 180° strategy execution leadership feedback system

Line Managers

- Acknowledge responsibility for work unit culture, capabilities, and performance
- Acknowledge responsibility for their own leadership behavior
- Detail performance expectations of direct reports
- Execute workforce differentiation decisions

Workforce

- Seek to understand the business from the outside in
- Acknowledge that they must constantly grow their capabilities and add new capabilities
- Acknowledge that they must own/be accountable for their own performance/behavior

---

- Supervisory and Workforce Behaviors
  - Effectiveness of supervisors in leading strategy execution (180° feedback)
  - Effectiveness of workforce behaviors in meeting group's customer and service goals (e.g., customer surveys)
- Workforce Competencies
  - Number/percent of viable successors
  - Turnover of talent essential to group's success
  - Capability of supervisors (percent "ready now")
  - Growth/development of talent essential to group's success
- Workforce Mind-set and Culture
  - Percent of work unit understanding work unit's goals
  - Percent understanding status on unit's "success metrics"

- Workforce Behaviors
  - Effectiveness in meeting workforce success metrics
- Workforce Competencies
  - Percent understanding importance of meeting performance expectations
  - Percent understanding the need to grow their competencies
  - Percent improving their capabilities
- Workforce Mind-set and Culture
  - Percent understanding firm's competitive position/competitive advantage
  - Percent understanding firm's workforce philosophy

- Provide workforce differentiation guidelines
- Provide processes to exit "C" players
- Provide mind-set/culture survey process

- Provide competency growth guidelines
- Distribute mind-set/culture surveys

THE ROLE OF THE CEO

What are the roles and responsibilities of the CEO with respect to strategy execution? Following are those details we regard as crucial.

Conduct Strategy Review Meetings That Include Discussions of Business Strategy and Workforce Strategy

In theory, the CEO is expected to conduct strategy discussions with the executive team and, with the board, decide the firm's growth strategy and the performance targets for which the executive board will be held accountable. But too often, the focus of executive team and board meetings is tactics, not strategy, as we have witnessed far too many times. In fact, 44 percent of company directors say they "do not understand the key value drivers of the firm."[5] But strategy is not a hope, a prayer, a number, or an elongated budget. It requires a much richer discussion about firm capabilities and strategic intent, and clear statements about how the firm will differentiate itself both internally and externally.

Thus, the CEO should engage the executive team (and often the board) in determining the strategy of the business. These are often long and painstaking discussions. The meetings may venture into highly contentious areas, because determining where the firm is and where it may need to go can have dramatic ramifications for current leaders, especially when the firm's strategy will impact the metrics by which leaders are evaluated. For some, the new metrics may be terrifying and may severely threaten current leaders. For others, new metrics may be seen as challenging and exciting new opportunities.

These issues are complex, and yet the CEO must not only remain focused on strategy, but also honestly assess how the firm's culture and capabilities fit with alternative strategies. Because the strategy selected will have a profound impact on the expectations, behaviors, and rewards of leadership at all levels, going forward in a different, hopefully more competitively advantaged direction requires a determined CEO. The goal of these meetings is a strategy that creates a competitive advantage, which enables the firm to win a disproportionate share of future markets.

An example is a firm in the roofing business that significantly transformed itself through its strategy discussions. Its previous strategy was simply elongated budgeting combined with marketing and pricing plans to increase the sale of "black line," the roofing product used for many industrial buildings. This market is highly competitive and margins were small. But in strategy discussions, executives kept asking questions about the future and what the customer would be interested in buying in the future. The executive team hit upon the idea of "roofing peace of mind" as something for which customers would pay a premium. Thus, the firm began to sell roofing products with warranties of ten, twenty, or thirty years with different pricing. Customers were very pleased, and of course the margins were substantially greater.

In subsequent strategy meetings, executives continued to reexamine the firm's strategy and explore additional possibilities. What was key was to focus on not what they were selling, but what customers were willing to buy in the future. The what-we-are-selling versus what-future-customers-are-willing-to-buy framework was very effective. In fact, the firm began to help its customers think more about their strategy and what they would "not like to have to worry about." From this, the roofing company decided since it was already at its clients' workspace, it could also begin to provide facilities maintenance. Thus, the firm transitioned from the roofing business to the insurance business to the facilities maintenance business by consciously engaging in strategy review meetings that were not constrained by definitions of its industry or how it was to compete against existing competitors. Instead, it was constantly asking how it might differentiate itself in the eyes of its potential customers. The firm was trying to gain a larger share of its customer's wallet through new offerings for which customers were willing to pay a premium. Certainly, these changes challenged the traditional leadership of the business as well as its culture and strategic capabilities. Again, new games require new rules, and hopefully leadership will be leading the change or can quickly adapt. At least we hope it does not oppose new business models and future sources of competitive advantage.

Negotiate Performance Expectations, Including Workforce Accountability, with Each Member of the Executive Team

Once the strategy is determined, the CEO needs to ensure that it is executed; new strategy requires new performance metrics, including workforce metrics. Often, the "performance promises" of a CEO's direct reports concern only financial expectations. To effectively execute strategy, performance agreements and strategic success metrics must go beyond financial expectations. That is, all executives and managers are expected to meet financial expectations, customer expectations, business process expectations, *and* workforce expectations.

Certainly, the financial expectations are the most common, yet for many firms, there is an emerging set of expectations around customer and consumer metrics. Customer metrics are important for understanding what makes a firm successful with its customers and consumers (those who use the product). We are not advocates of undifferentiated customer satisfaction metrics in the traditional sense, for a firm can go out of business satisfying unprofitable customers (as well as satisfying low-performing employees). The issue is how firms can make customers successful in their experience with the firm—that is, having their expectations met in all aspects of the firm-customer interaction—at a profitable level for the firm. Hopefully, these experiences will subsequently result in customer retention, referrals, and expanded business with the client.

John Chambers of Cisco Systems provides a good example of the importance of customer metrics and how to hold managers accountable for meeting customer expectations. He constantly discusses customers with his managers and demands that they focus on customers. In fact, in attending meetings with other firms, he often notes that the word *customer* is seldom mentioned, and he believes this is a major source of these firms' underperformance. At Cisco, workforce awareness of the customer's perspective is mandated as essential to effective strategy execution.[6]

The importance of customer success is reinforced at Cisco because managers must hit customer targets before incentive payouts are triggered. That is, irrespective of a manager's success in achieving revenue targets, if customer targets are not met, the incentive targets are reduced. It is a hurdle that executives responsible for revenue must meet and reinforces accountability for customer metrics. Thus, negotiating customer expectations between the CEO and line-of-business executives is critical to strategy execution and sends a message to executives and the workforce about the firm's commitment to customer success.[7]

Negotiations also concern business process expectations. A firm pursuing an operational excellence strategy must improve its productivity year after year as its employees become more experienced (and more capable) of devising new and better ways of reducing operating costs. Instead of demanding cost reductions year over year, as many firms do on the assumption they can "save their way to prosperity," we prefer the firm to use productivity measures and hold leaders accountable for the delivery of annual productivity improvements. Many firms, including General Electric, Wal-Mart, AlliedSignal, and those that engage in profit sharing, demand that productivity continually improve. For example, they may demand 3 to 5 percent productivity improvements annually, which also makes workforce rewards possible without adding to the relative cost of doing business, and avoids passing wage increases on to customers. The simple productivity metrics that are often used include "total cost productivity," such that as revenues go up, costs may go up but at a decreasing rate. Of course, in the obverse, when revenues go down, costs must go down at an increasing rate. In any case, with these systems, leaders are held accountable for improved productivity.

The CEO must also have data for decision making in terms of workforce success. As is seen in figure 6-3, this could include data about the CEO, his direct reports (executive team), and the workforce as a whole. The CEO's leadership behavior and the behaviors of the workforce, especially in delivering a firm's strategy to its customers, can be assessed with surveys and focus groups. Certainly, feedback from direct reports or from even further down in the organization can be valuable input for the CEO to use to change/improve their behavior just as customer feedback can have a positive influence in changing the behavior of employees in customer-facing positions. Consider how much strategy execution could be impacted if the CEO had the data shown in the center of figure 6-3 and acted upon such data if it did not meet performance expectations.

Consistent placement of "A" players in "A" positions should also be of interest to the CEO with metrics such as unwanted turnover, "ready-now" depth, and "B" players with "A" potential. These measures are indicative of the quality and depth of strategic talent within each of the firm's strategic capabilities (e.g., leadership, research and development, supply chain management, mergers and acquisitions, consumer insight). Finding talent deficits in strategic capabilities should focus the CEO's attention on remedying these deficiencies, as well as fixing accountability with those responsible—whether HR or line managers. The CEO should also demand mind-set data about the firm's workforce, which can also be collected by surveys and/or focus groups. These are also data for decision making in that they should provide information about the workforce's culture, focus, and understanding of the firm's strategy. Some firms, such as American Century Investments, have gone to great lengths to assess the culture/knowledge/business acumen of their workforce. American Century believes that all employees should know the business well, and gives them a quiz on this (see figure 6-4). After the "exam," employees are given

---

FIGURE 6-4

American Century Investments Core Business Knowledge Test

SELECTED SAMPLE QUESTIONS

American Century Investment's business strategy specifically requires that we continually invest in the skills and knowledge of our people. The company's core business knowledge assessment measures the baseline level of broad-based knowledge about our company, industry and business strategy.

The business knowledge assessment is administered twice each year and is supported by focused learning activities that address gaps identified in the assessment. The company's scorecard includes a metric which targets a 10% improvement for the company as a whole.

Sample categories and questions are noted below:

Category: Our Company

Which of the following statements does NOT characterize American Century Investments as a Premier Investment Manager?
a. We practice active money management
b. We build long-term customer relationships
c. We invest in our people and our culture
d. We invest in only top-tier securities
e. We focus on our value proposition

Our public position, *Putting Investors First,* summarizes our stance on significant industry issues. Specifically, it addresses:
a. Late trading
b. Best execution and soft dollars
c. Position on socially conscious funds
d. A and B
e. All of the above

Category: Investment Management

At American Century Investments we take pride in being active money managers. Which of the following statements BEST describes what we mean by the term "actively managed"?
a. We look for investments within the framework of a disciplined process to construct a portfolio that will beat a benchmark over time
b. We build our portfolios to match specific indices and make decisions on a predetermined, proven timetable
c. We shift our portfolio assets from one sector or industry of the economy to another in anticipation of broad-based economic development
d. We empower our Portfolio Managers to make decisions by following their instincts

True or False:
The following statement describes the Value Investment Discipline: Wealth protection strategies designed to preserve investments and/or provide monthly income.

their score, and the ten most commonly missed questions are posted on the firm's Web site, with answers and explanations. Some employees are asked to meet with their manager, who provides the "correct" answers and discusses the reason for each answer. This is merely one way among many of obtaining and measuring the strategic focus of a firm. However, it provides insight about the workforce and how well leaders are discharging their workforce responsibilities in shaping the strategic mind-set of their workforce.

Underperforming firms facing significant competitive challenges must often tackle financial, customer, business process, and workforce objectives simultaneously, as recently illustrated by General Motors. GM has now become North America's most financially successful

---

Category: Product Management

When do you pay a mutual fund's load?
a. When you buy the fund
b. When you sell the fund
c. It depends on the load structure

Which of the following is TRUE with respect to the Learning Quest 529 Education Savings Plan?
a. It was named after Section 529 of the Internal Revenue Code
b. Earnings in the account grow tax-deferred
c. Anyone can open or contribute to a Learning Quest account
d. Parents can use the money for their own educational opportunities
e. All of the above

Category: Product Distribution

Which of the following choices BEST represents the products distributed through the Third Party channel?
a. Separate accounts and sub-advisory services
b. Variable portfolios and adviser funds
c. Separate accounts and no-load, investor class mutual funds

The investment consultant in the institutional industry is NOT responsible for which of the following:
a. Managing money
b. Asset allocation
c. Performance analysis
d. Investment manager selection

Category: Our Customers

Which of the following is NOT a true statement with regards to how our customers from different markets evaluate performance differently?
a. Institutional customers primarily focus on our adherence to a disciplined process over time
b. Third-party customers evaluate our products based on relative returns as reported by external rating agencies
c. Direct customers rely on style-box consistency

True or False:
Morningstar and Lipper are external rating agencies used predominantly by Institutional customers to evaluate investment performance.

Category: Our Industry

What is the one major difference between the Dow Jones Industrial Average and most other market indices such as the S&P 500?
a. It is calculated by the U.S. government
b. It includes primarily large-cap stocks
c. It is not market-cap weighted

What can happen to interest rates to cause an investor to sell his bond at a discount?
a. Interest rates can rise
b. Interest rates can fall
c. Interest rates stay the same

Source: American Century Investments. Used with permission.

automotive firm and ranks third in quality among its global competitors. Such gains clearly required substantial improvements in all aspects of its business model, especially the strategic perspective of its leadership, engineering, and line workforces in producing quality vehicles.[8]

Negotiate with Senior HR Leadership Team Concerning the HR Function's Workforce Deliverables

Another issue for the CEO is executing workforce strategy, which requires negotiation with the senior HR leadership team concerning the HR function's "workforce deliverables." Efforts in this area are often misdirected, with unintended consequences. In the rush to HR metrics, some CEOs have demanded reducing the cost of the workforce (and consequently the cost of the HR function). But as we noted earlier, the costs of the HR function are less than 1 percent of firm revenues, while the cost of the workforce is around 70 percent of a firm's total expenditures. Reducing the cost of the HR function, which is minuscule compared with the cost of the workforce, has little upside potential relative to increasing the performance of the workforce or the firm's financials. However, maximizing a firm's workforce performance can have an immense strategic and financial impact—the major theme of this book. Not only must the firm have the right strategy, but the CEO must clearly communicate to the senior HR leader that the deliverable of HR is the workforce to execute the firm's strategy.

Thus, the CEO, with the senior HR leader, must clarify workforce expectations based in part on input from the senior HR leader concerning the current workforce, future workforce requirements, and labor market availability. It is important to clarify that the major objective, the major deliverable of the HR function, is a workforce that can deliver the firm's strategy and the ability to flex as the business strategy changes. Thus, the senior HR leader, the executive team, and the HR function need to participate in the identification of the firm's strategic capabilities and identify "A" positions that significantly impact the firm's strategic success. The HR function and leaders need to ensure that these "A" positions have sufficient "A" players and that HR is disproportionately investing in the selection, development, measurement, reward, retention, and so on of these "A" players. This is an opportunity for HR to directly influence the firm's strategy execution and impact its competitive advantage. The CEO should remember that a strategically aligned HR function that differentially invests in "A" positions can be a source of the firm's competitive advantage.

As we noted earlier, the workforce strategy also encompasses a workforce philosophy, which addresses the firm's relationship to its workforce as well as how the workforce is expected to behave, including the corporate governance/ethics issues expected of each employee. Thus, the firm's workforce philosophy not only includes how it will differentiate its capabilities through workforce practices but also how it expects every employee to behave in pursuit of the firm's strategic success.

EXECUTIVE TEAM MEMBERS

In addition to the CEO, executive team members are expected to play a significant role in strategy execution through the development and implementation of a firm's workforce strategy. How a firm chooses to manage its workforce should be rooted in a common set of agreements about the firm's workforce philosophy and how leaders are to act in discharging their workforce responsibilities.[9]

The firm's workforce philosophy concerns issues we have previously discussed, such as the leader's responsibility to clarify the firm's strategy to the workforce and the executives' responsibility to invest differentially in their workforce based on the position's strategic value to the firm and level of performance. Therefore, workforce success metrics for all leaders could and should have many common areas (e.g., strategic focus and "A" players in "A" positions). The role of members of the executive team relative to these issues is discussed next.

Participate in Crafting Business Strategy, Workforce Philosophy, and Workforce Strategy

One discussion that may need to be expanded at the executive team level concerns the workforce implications of a business strategy, in addition to discussions about a workforce strategy and how it will be made operational. The need for a workforce strategy is critical because many executive team members view the workforce as a commodity that can be bought and sold—on-boarded and off-boarded easily and readily with little consequence on the firm's performance. Of course, this is changing as firms recognize that "brainware" is a source of competitive advantage. Thus, executive team members need to consider sending a message to all managers that they are responsible for the extent to which the workforce understands and embraces the strategy, and that they are in addition expected to effectively manage talent critical to the firm's strategic success. They will also need to be informed that they are accountable for the success of their workforce and that part of their evaluation will be on workforce metrics.

To help executives and line leaders effectively manage their workforces, a statement of the firm's relationship with its workforce may be necessary. This requires that the CEO, senior HR leaders, and the executive team make difficult decisions about the firm's workforce philosophy. The philosophy comprises statements about the firm's covenant with its workforce and provides concepts of workforce governance, as well as decision guidelines for executives and line managers. In figure 6-5 are examples of what firms have considered or are using to craft a workforce philosophy. Note that it involves difficult choices that attempt to focus the executive team on the relationship the team members want the firm to have with its workforce. They also provide guidelines to managers as to how they can make the firm's workforce philosophy a decision tool and eventually a practice that becomes a part of the firm's culture. Notice too that some of the items listed may be an existing practice within your firm. If so, do you wish to continue it, given your strategy? Why or why not?

Note in figure 6-5 that for each item there are two responses to select—what your firm's current workforce position is on the issue *and* where you believe it should be in the future. Once these decisions about the present and the future have been made, the firm can elect the time frame for it to implement the "future" items it indicated are necessary. However, what is most important is to use the items selected as workforce governance precepts to guide workforce decision making by line managers and HR. Holding both accountable for operating within this workforce governance system is critical; thereby workforce accountability can become a capability.

Some of the items may be threatening for some firms, yet depending on their strategy, they may find a very challenging item critical to the firm's strategic success. We suggest you review these items and add others, and make the choices that you believe are essential for

FIGURE 6-5

Workforce Strategy: Developing a Strategically Successful Workforce

What is your workforce philosophy?
Which choices must your firm make to deliver its competitive advantage?

Listed below are examples of principles that could be the basis of your firm's workforce philosophy. They are intended to stimulate your thinking as you consider how to design and build the best workforce to deliver your firm's strategy. Please check (✓) those that represent your firm now and those you believe are necessary to deliver your firm's strategy and to build the most successful workforce in your industry. These are but a sample of workforce philosophy statements taken from various firms. You may wish to add others.

Now	Future	
☐	☐	1. All employees deserve "lifetime job security."
☐	☐	2. All employees are entitled to an annual increase.
☐	☐	3. Equality is more important than equity.
☐	☐	4. Leadership competencies for top positions should be based on our leaders today.
☐	☐	5. Replacement planning for all top positions is critical.
☐	☐	6. Employee advocacy by the HR function is critical.
☐	☐	7. Staffing strategic capabilities is an imperative.
☐	☐	8. Each employee's performance must improve annually.
☐	☐	9. Every employee must contribute more value to the firm than he or she receives from it.
☐	☐	10. Successful staffing of "A" positions is critical.
☐	☐	11. Having effective leaders at all levels is critical to strategic success.
☐	☐	12. Corporate "owns" and manages the careers of most "A" positions.
☐	☐	13. Developmental investment should be made in "A" players in "A" positions.
☐	☐	14. Developmental investment in "B" players with "A" potential is critical.
☐	☐	15. Performance management is a tool to execute strategy.
☐	☐	16. "C" players must be developed or exited.
☐	☐	17. All employees must contribute to customer/consumer success.
☐	☐	18. No employee "owns" a position.
☐	☐	19. Line managers have workforce responsibilities: mind-set, competency growth, and employee behavior.
☐	☐	20. Line management is to execute workforce strategy.
☐	☐	21. We must topgrade in all "A" positions.
☐	☐	22. "A" players must be in "A" positions.
☐	☐	23. Competency growth is required in all positions.
☐	☐	24. All employees are either strategic resources, operational resources, or surplus.
☐	☐	25. Generating ideas and high levels of performance are the criteria for employee advancement.
☐	☐	26. Differential investment in employees is necessary.
☐	☐	27. "B" players are expected in "B" positions.
☐	☐	28. "C" positions (and "C" work) must be eliminated.
☐	☐	29. Managers must be accountable for their workforces.
☐	☐	30. Knowledge sharing is indispensable to strategic success.
☐	☐	31. Retention of "A" players in "A" positions is vital.

(continued)

FIGURE 6-5

Workforce Strategy: Developing a Strategically Successful Workforce *(continued)*

Now	Future	
☐	☐	32. Our workforce is HR's major deliverable.
☐	☐	33. Management of the workforce should represent at least 25% of a line manager's or executive's performance evaluation.
☐	☐	34. Active learners in all "A" positions are needed.
☐	☐	35. "A" positions are not hierarchical, but are based on strategic value to the firm.
☐	☐	36. All employees must be given timely, candid feedback on their performance.
☐	☐	37. Managers should be the advocate of their employees, based on their performance.
☐	☐	38. Employees should be their own advocates.
☐	☐	39. Replacement planning for all strategic positions is critical.
☐	☐	40. Building a deep, broad succession pool is critical.
☐	☐	41. "A" positions should have a midpoint at the 75th percentile, "B" positions at the 50th, and "C" positions (if we must have a few) no higher than the 25th percentile.
☐	☐	42. Outsourcing is a tool we must use to provide us focus and reduce our costs.
☐	☐	43. Offshoring is a competitive tool we must use to strengthen our competitive advantage.
☐	☐	44. The primary focus/customer of HR's work is line management.
☐	☐	45. The focus/customer of HR's work is the firm's external customers.
☐	☐	46. HR and the CHRO must serve as the firm's corporate conscience.
☐	☐	47. Accountability must become a capability within our firm.
☐	☐	48. The CHRO must become responsible for corporate governance standards.
☐	☐	49. All leaders are expected to communicate the firm's (or business unit's) strategy to the workforce.
☐	☐	50. All leaders will be assessed in part on how well their workforce understands the firm's strategy and its status.

your firm's relationship with its workforce for the effective execution of your firm's strategy. Once you have selected from these, you should draft a workforce philosophy to be used in communicating workforce decision guidelines to your firm's executives and line managers.

Participate in Discussions Determining Desired Firm Culture, Strategic Capabilities, and Leader Behavior Metrics

Executive team members are also expected to participate in workforce strategy discussions, provide input for the cultural requirements of the firm and the identification of strategic capabilities, and help specify behaviors expected of leaders. Because we believe leaders individually need to be held accountable for the mind-set, capabilities, and performance of their workforce, agreement is necessary on these issues and how these would be measured. Strategy execution requires effective workforce management, and thus the executive team must develop workforce metrics to assess leader success in workforce management. Otherwise, insufficient time and attention will be devoted to the role of the workforce in strategy execution.

Beyond assessing a leader's workforce effectiveness, the executive team should also explore identifying examples of behaviors expected of leaders in executing the firm's strategy. Such a tool would provide metrics to inspect what is expected of leaders in managing their workforces. We do not assume that such measures are easy to develop. We have provided in figure 6-6 an example of a firm's attempt to assess a leader's effort to execute a firm's strategy. This instrument is used to collect data from executive team members and lower-level managers' subordinates about the effectiveness of the leader on several dimensions agreed to by the executive team as indicative of leadership success in strategy execution. Although this was designed for a major financial services firm, note that there are several items that would be applicable for most firms attempting to develop such a metric. This form may not perfectly fit your firm's needs to assess leader performance in executing strategy, but should give you some idea of how leadership accountability in strategy execution might be assessed.

Identify the Firm's "A" Positions

As previously noted, the CEO and executive team members are asked to identify the firm's strategic capabilities, those bundles of information, technology, and people that create a competitive advantage and differentiate a firm.

The CEO and business leaders should then be asked to identify not only strategic capabilities, but also "A" positions, those positions that have that profound impact on the firm's competitive advantage. To help them identify "A" positions, the executive team may require definitions, as we outlined in chapter 2.

Big Pharma's CEO and executive team identified six strategic capabilities (R&D, licensing/acquisitions, sales/marketing, government relations, quality, and leadership). Then they assessed how effective

FIGURE 6-6

Assessing Leader Behavior in Strategy Execution (Example)

LEADING STRATEGY EXECUTION: THE CRITICAL BEHAVIORS OF LEADERS TO SUCCESSFULLY EXECUTE STRATEGY

Please use the scale below in answering questions:

One of my major leadership shortcomings	Not as effective as I (or others) would like	Effective	Clearly one of my stronger competencies	Honestly, this is a real strength as seen by myself and others
1	2	3	4	5

How effective is this manager at . . .	Short-coming 1	2	Effective 3	4	Very effective 5
1. providing compelling and credible messages about the need to realize our firm's strategy?					
2. communicating the need for strategy execution in person, one-on-one, *and* in small groups?					
3. using symbols, metaphors, and stories effectively?					
4. setting specific challenging (order-of-magnitude improvement) strategic growth targets?					
5. staying involved, personally and visibly?					
6. discussing our growth strategy at every key meeting, in every resource allocation decision, business review, performance review, and even in informal discussions?					
7. recognizing successes frequently, especially in public forums?					
8. providing persistent, consistent, and eternally optimistic in support and advocacy ("failure is not an option")?					
9. influencing and persuading others to become advocates and contributors to our firm's growth strategy?					
10. altering the metrics that define strategic success?					
11. holding our team members accountable for strategy execution, not just designing solutions?					
12. impatiently reiterating the need for decisive action?					
13. making speed a top priority?					
14. focusing on resistance sources and accurately assessing the degree of resistance?					
15. building the necessary coalitions to overcome resistance?					
16. seeing strategy execution as a personal passion, a change in the firm's strategic agenda, an alteration in the organization's outcomes?					

they are and how effective they must be in each capability in order to become inordinately successful in their markets. In each capability area, the firm must determine "A" positions (using the criteria mentioned earlier or other criteria the firm chooses to identify the positions most critical to the firm's strategic success). In R&D, it could be a biochemist; in joint ventures, a manager of new business development; in marketing, a field sales representative; in government relations, the chief lobbyist; and so on.

Identify "A" Players, and "B" Players with "A" Potential in "A" Positions

A key workforce deliverable is to ensure that we have "A" players in "A" positions. As we described in detail in chapter 2, it is crucial to not only specify what "A," "B," and "C" performance entails, but also to communicate these expectation to the workforce.

Create Development Plans for "A" and "B" Players (in "A" Positions)

It is important that development plans for the growth of "A" players, and especially for "B" players with "A" potential, be discussed and documented. Certainly all employees in "B" positions also deserve developmental efforts, but these may be more self-directed as opposed to those of "A" players and "B" players in "A" positions. Executive time must be devoted to this difficult but critical issue. This is different from the typical performance appraisal process. Here the major elements of the performance appraisal process—performance planning, managing performance (i.e., day to day), and reviewing performance—are included, but the development component is taken out of the traditional process. That is, development, especially for "A" players, is too important to be sublimated in the performance review discussion. In fact, including developmental discussions in the performance appraisal discussion may have unintended consequences. For example, when an employee is not performing, a manager who is reluctant to discuss the performance issue may spend significant time exploring a "safe" discussion of the developmental plans for this employee without addressing the historic performance problems. These problems must be immediately addressed to meet current performance requirements. The developmental or career growth that might enhance the individual's prospects in the future is less important. This development discussion is simply an "out" for many managers and creates the wrong impression with the employee.

Detail Performance Expectations for Direct Reports

Once the "A" positions and "A" players are identified and development plans agreed upon, this information becomes part of the leader's performance plan, as can be seen in figure 6-7. This is an abbreviation of the plan used by a roofing company to document performance agreements and as a tool to execute the firm's strategy. Other data on "B" positions and "C" players could also be added to this, but our focus here remains on those positions and players that leverage the firm's strategic success. In many respects it is similar to other firms' performance planning efforts, with the exception of the detail that is requested concerning each leader's workforce success efforts. In this instance, the CEO recognized that strategy execution required changes in the workforce and that strategy could not be realized unless leaders were held accountable for their workforce, which required the appropriate workforce metrics. This example is a major first step in effective performance planning to execute the firm's strategy. But what should be emphasized is that all performance management efforts should be used as a tool to execute strategy. Far too often, performance planning is done cursorily or based on criteria taken from a job description. Performance planning must be prospective, focusing on financial, customer, business process, *and* workforce metrics necessary to execute the strategy of the firm.

Workforce success metrics for the executive team are the same in the categories to be assessed—leadership and workforce behaviors, workforce competencies, and mind-set and culture. What would differ is the unit of analysis (i.e., for a business unit leader the data should be provided by the business unit—from its employees and customers—to assess how well the leader is performing in the leadership role and how well the workforce is serving the unit's customers). Again, in collecting behavioral information, an important rule is to only rate behavior that has been observed, and thus to assess leaders and customer-facing behavior; the best source of this information is those

FIGURE 6-7

Business Leader Performance Planning Worksheet

Business: _____

Business Leader: _____ Time in Position: _____

Strategy ⊞ : _____

Performance on Scorecard ⟳ :

	Weight	Plan	Metric	Score
• Financial	%			
• Nonfinancial	%			
– Customer	%			
– Business Process	%			
– Workforce	%			

Strategy/Performance Execution Plans:

Strategic Capabilities:

1 2 3 4

"A" Positions	"A" Players	/	Development Plans
•	•		•
•	•		•
•	•		•

Players with "A" Potential:

"A" Positions	"B" Players with "A" Potential	/	Development Plans
•	•		•
•	•		•
•	•		•

Leader Behaviors/180° Feedback:

Acknowledged Strengths	Needs Development	Development Plans
•		
•		
•		
•		
•		

who actually observe this behavior. It sounds simple, but we are frequently surprised at how often this basic guideline is violated. The capability metrics for executive team members should also be determined by the business unit, and the metrics should be the same or similar in the categories used (e.g., percent of viable successors and key talent turnover), but focused on different strategic positions based on the unique strategic capabilities of the business unit (see figure 6-3). The mind-set measures would most likely be identical to the CEO/ overall workforce mind-set metrics (i.e., the use of common questions), but have the opportunity to use unique questions that pertain directly to the explicit focus of the business unit (e.g., operational excellence versus product leadership strategies might have a few different questions).

CHANGING ROLES

This chapter has explored the process of developing three strategies essential for strategy execution: business, workforce, and HR function. It focused on the roles of key players to achieve the best use of the firm's workforce. We have not attempted to offer a uniform way of addressing these issues, but merely to explore workforce philosophy and workforce metrics as tools for strategic workforce decision making that can significantly impact strategy execution efforts. We have tried to not only raise the issue of the importance of the workforce in strategy execution, but also provide a few examples that may be helpful in your strategy execution efforts. In the next chapter, we examine the changing roles of line managers and human resource managers.

7

STRATEGY EXECUTION II

The Roles of Line Managers,
the HR Function,
and Workforce Metrics

B Y NOW WE HOPE you have a sense of what it takes to develop a workforce strategy, philosophy, and metrics, and understand how critical they are for the effective (and efficient) execution of a firm's strategy. As the first step in responding to the *execution challenge,* chapter 6 focused on the roles of the CEO and senior executive team in the strategy execution process. This chapter applies these concepts to line managers and the HR function. As you might expect, there are similarities to the issues discussed in chapter 6. But here we concentrate on the unique challenges line managers (the messengers of strategy execution for most employees) face in implementing workforce strategy and philosophy. The same challenges are also faced by the HR function because it plays a critical role in designing unique systems to realize the workforce strategy and philosophy (i.e., differentiate the workforce) and devise metrics by which line managers and the rest of the organization can be held accountable.

THE ROLE OF LINE MANAGERS

The primary role of line managers is to execute strategy. They are the frontline leaders whose job it is to make the firm's strategy a reality using the workforce assigned to them. This requires line managers to understand the firm's strategy as well as the culture and capability requirements to deliver the performance expected. It also requires an understanding of the firm's workforce philosophy and the data needed for effective workforce decision making. In chapter 6 we articulated sample responsibilities and workforce measures that might be used by line managers to execute strategy (figure 6-3). This figure may be useful to keep in mind for the discussion that follows.

Acknowledge Responsibility for Work Unit Culture, Capabilities, and Performance

Line managers must recognize that they are responsible for the culture, capabilities, and performance of their workforce, and for creating a culture focused on executing the firm's strategy. This responsibility should be a significant part of a line manager's performance evaluation and the major focus of his or her behavior as a leader. Thus, an approach to performance measurement similar to that shown in figure 7-1 should be used with line managers, with similar workforce metrics, but with higher weight given to successfully managing the workforce relative to financial success, and so on. This should be the critical component of a line manager's performance negotiations—explicit and measurable accountabilities for workforce culture, capabilities, and performance, for their job is to elicit the behavior necessary for strategy execution. Notice that the evaluation of line managers includes the same strategic success metrics used for executive team members, including workforce metrics. What differs is that lower-level managers are held accountable for "mission critical" positions, those positions critical to the success of any business unit, including staff positions. Like the CEO and the executive team, line managers are responsible for retaining talent in critical positions, which is captured in the performance planning worksheet. Like senior executives, line managers are also responsible for workforce mind-set and culture, including business acumen, as well as

FIGURE 7-1

Manager/Supervisor Performance Planning Worksheet

Business Unit: _____

Manager/Supervisor: _____ Time in Position: _____

Success Metrics:

	Weight	Plan	Metric	Score
• Financial	%			
• Nonfinancial	%			
– Customer	%			
– Business Process	%			
– Workforce	%			

Strategy/Performance Execution Plans:

Mission-Critical Capabilities:
- •
- •
- •
- •

Key Positions	Key Players	/	Development Plans
•	•		•
•	•		•
•	•		•

High-Potential Employees in Mission-Critical Positions:

Positions	High-Potential Employees	Development Plans
•	•	•
•	•	•
•	•	•

Mission-Critical Incumbents:

Positions	Metric	Target	Status
•			
•			
•			

Leadership Behaviors/180° Survey Results:

	Metric	Target	Status
• Workshop Culture • Leader Behaviors			

their leader behavior (based on 180-degree feedback or similar surveys). Line managers must engage in leader behaviors that provide focus to their workforce and build its capabilities to complete their unit's mission.

Figure 7-2 is an example of a survey instrument used by a large paper company to assess leader behavior in strategy execution. Leader behavior is assessed in the pursuit of strategic success metrics (e.g., customer success) as well as basic workforce leadership responsibilities (e.g., growing competencies, performance management, and leading change). Such instruments provide data to improve leader behavior or highlight the necessity to change leadership.

Acknowledge Responsibility for Their Own Leadership Behavior

Becoming a leader is a significant step for any employee. It means getting work done through others and using (or developing) leadership skills to deliver results. Strategy execution requires leadership to varying degrees. Leaders with willing followers can influence work groups to increasingly higher levels of performance, not simply manage to keep things from getting out of control. Thus, line managers must recognize that they are leaders—leaders who communicate the strategic agenda, mobilize and allocate resources, mold the desired workforce behaviors, and create a strategically focused high-performance culture. They must continually increase their work unit's performance and be responsible for their own behavior as leaders.

Why is this an issue? Because the single difference between managerial and nonmanagerial jobs is the accountability for human resources. In almost any position, employees are accountable for a variety of resources (e.g., financial, material, information, time), but only managerial jobs have resources that "talk back," and the line manager position is the entry position to the decision-making responsibility for the most expensive of the firm's resources: people. One consequence of poor workforce decision making (and inadequate workforce metrics) is promoting employees to managerial/supervisory positions because they are good at their current position. Employees who are very good "doers" are not necessarily good managers or leaders. Mastery of welding does not necessarily mean a good welder should be promoted to welding supervisor. Such positions require leaders with

FIGURE 7-2

Strategy Execution: Line Manager Effectiveness Survey

ABC Paper Company / Multisource Managerial Questionnaire
Workforce Success

	Not Effective			Very Effective		
Creating Strategic Mind-set						
1. Communicating business strategy	1	2	3	4	5	NA
2. Communicating how we will realize our strategy	1	2	3	4	5	NA
3. Informing employees about status of strategic progress	1	2	3	4	5	NA
Growing Employee Competencies						
4. Coaching performance improvement	1	2	3	4	5	NA
5. Counseling employees on career opportunities within ABC	1	2	3	4	5	NA
6. Teaching job-related skills	1	2	3	4	5	NA
7. Mentoring high potentials	1	2	3	4	5	NA
8. Monitoring employee development	1	2	3	4	5	NA
Leading Change						
9. Setting strategic direction	1	2	3	4	5	NA
10. Setting stretch targets	1	2	3	4	5	NA
11. Creating a culture that fits strategic direction	1	2	3	4	5	NA
12. Making quick, accurate decisions	1	2	3	4	5	NA
13. Building teamwork among direct reports	1	2	3	4	5	NA
14. Living the vision	1	2	3	4	5	NA
15. Inspiring the achievement of business results	1	2	3	4	5	NA
16. Sharing information openly and honestly	1	2	3	4	5	NA
Performance Management						
17. Setting business targets (financial, customer, operational)	1	2	3	4	5	NA
18. Clarifying behavioral expectations of employees	1	2	3	4	5	NA
19. Establishing business performance priorities	1	2	3	4	5	NA
20. Providing frequent feedback	1	2	3	4	5	NA
21. Providing candid feedback	1	2	3	4	5	NA
22. Accurately assessing employee performance	1	2	3	4	5	NA
23. Allocating rewards based on performance	1	2	3	4	5	NA
24. Conducting performance reviews	1	2	3	4	5	NA
25. Taking corrective action with employees when necessary	1	2	3	4	5	NA
Environmental Health and Safety						
26. Mandating that EH&S policies are in place	1	2	3	4	5	NA
27. Demanding that EH&S standards are practiced	1	2	3	4	5	NA
28. Working to ensure that all EH&S goals are met	1	2	3	4	5	NA
Customer Focus/Success/Results						
29. Strengthening customer/client relationships	1	2	3	4	5	NA
30. Ensuring that customer/client requirements (e.g., quality, speed, cost) are met	1	2	3	4	5	NA
31. Creating new products and services to offer to existing customers	1	2	3	4	5	NA
32. Designing strategies to enter new markets	1	2	3	4	5	NA

Summary

List three things that this supervisor does very well:
1.
2.
3.

List three things that this supervisor should improve on:
1.
2.
3.

General Comments:

_____

_____

_____

the backbone to set high standards and communicate challenging messages (even to friends), and the willingness to confront performance not contributing to the execution of the firm's strategy. Managing is a difficult job with serious challenges to effective strategy execution.

Detail Performance Expectations of Direct Reports

A major psychic leap for leaders is to recognize that their major responsibility is to get work done through others, the classic definition of any managerial position. Strategy execution requires clarifying performance expectations for each direct report, including the expectation that each employee is to contribute more to the organization more than they take away. Each employee is entitled to know what is expected of them and how well they are performing. There should be no surprises for employees during performance reviews. Thus, firms must ask managers not only to communicate performance expectations but also inspect employee performance to ensure results are delivered.

Execute Workforce Differentiation Decisions

To execute a firm's strategy, line managers must exercise differentiation decisions relative to their workforce. Workforce differentiation and strategy execution are parallel concepts, for both require specifying what is to be accomplished, developing metrics to assess progress, and providing consequences commensurate with performance. Managers are responsible for making workforce differentiation decisions (e.g., selection, development, promotion, and rewards) consistent with the firm's needs to execute its strategy. For this to occur, managers must be evaluated on how well they lead their workforce in executing the firm's strategy using workforce philosophy and metrics similar to those we presented earlier (i.e., those that hold the top of the organization accountable). Thus, all line managers are expected to implement the firm's workforce philosophy, provide workforce metrics and targets, and execute workforce decisions that deliver the firm's strategy. This is a huge responsibility for line managers, who influence the largest segment of the firm's workforce.

Workforce metrics for line managers should focus on supervisory and workforce behaviors, capabilities, and mind-set. In this case, data gathering would target a much smaller work unit, those reporting to the line manager or those for whom the line manager has responsibility. Upward feedback about the line manager would come from the manager's direct reports and workforce behavior data, especially from segments of the workforce in customer-facing positions, where input would come from customers. Workforce capability data could be indexes of "ready now," turnover of key talent, growth of new leader skills, and so on from within the supervisor's work group. Finally, the work group's strategic focus or mind-set could also be assessed with the firm's workforce survey, supplemented with questions pertaining to unique situations faced by the work group. In short, what is being assessed is the workforce's understanding, its ability to do, and its behavior in delivering the strategy of the business.

THE ROLE OF THE WORKFORCE

The CEO and the executive team (including the senior HR leader) are primarily responsible for deciding the firm's strategy, while line management and the workforce are primarily responsible for strategy execution. However, communicating some basic workforcewide expectations can be extremely helpful in strategy execution. These are concepts that can become a part of a firm's workforce philosophy and, if effectively communicated, can have a powerful impact on the firm's strategic success. These include expecting the workforce to understand the firm in its markets (learning from the outside in), to understand that employees must continually grow their capabilities, and to be responsible for their own behavior and strategic performance contributions. These may seem obvious concepts, but our experience is that these are not well communicated, measured, or embraced by the workforce. But this is changing. At Biogen Idec, a $2 billion biotechnology firm, employees are to be their own advocates, or, better yet, managers are to be the advocates for extraordinary employees. HR is not the advocate for the workforce. Thus, employees must be concerned about their own growth and career management and make their needs known. However, for qualified candidates, executives and HR are more than willing to make the developmental/rotational investment in an employee's career growth.[1]

Seek to Understand the Business from the Outside In

Understanding how successful their firm is in the market can help employees recognize what they could do to better execute the firm's strategy *and* enhance their own job security. There are far too many examples of employees failing to understand the marketing status of their firm, including the now-famous example of Sears that we described in chapter 3.[2] The senior leadership team at Sears was astonished to learn that employees thought their most important mission was "to protect the assets of the company," (i.e., prevent shoplifting) not to satisfy customers or investors. Similarly, when asked the company's profit on a dollar of sales, the employees responded forty-three cents; the actual profit was slightly more than one cent. This is evidence of a workforce's lack of understanding of the firm's strategy, markets, stakeholders, and its success with respect to each.

At American Century, mentioned earlier, the workforce scored only 62 percent on the Core Business Knowledge Test (a workforce metric). Such a lack of strategic understanding can occur even at higher levels in a firm. At Electronic Data Systems Corporation (EDS) middle management strategy review meetings revealed that middle managers could not describe the firm's current or future "economic engine." Springfield Remanufacturing represents the most interesting example of what a workforce needs to know to execute strategy. There, all employees must become financially competent by attending classes and passing an examination on the firm's accounting system in order to retain their jobs.[3] In essence, they must learn to think like a banker assessing a business. Ideally, employees should be reminded that certain understandings are critical for effective strategy execution and that leaders are to keep them informed, but it is also their responsibility to learn from any source about their firm's strategy and customers and what must be done to make their firm successful.

This expectation of the workforce is often referred to as business acumen and is an important aspect of the strategic focus necessary for strategy execution. How the "strategic" mind-set can be achieved is the responsibility of leaders at every level, including the CEO, executive team members, line managers, and HR. But the workforce must be expected to understand not only what is communicated, but also that they must seek market/customer data that could help their firm as well as improve their own performance.

How to get the workforce thinking about the business can be illustrated with several examples. One is from General Electric. The importance of safety in aircraft engines was vividly communicated to the workforce by broadcasting the flight recording of a navy pilot as his engine failed and the plane went into Lake Michigan. His animosity toward the plane's engine was unmistakable. Playing this tape for the workforce brought home to GE's Aircraft Engine division the importance of each employee in exercising care in manufacturing.

Medtronic, Inc., a maker of heart valves and other electronic medical devices, holds an annual Christmas party at which patients with Medtronic devices installed thank the workforce for "saving their lives." It is a dramatic demonstration of the role that Medtronic's employees play in saving lives and enhancing the quality of functioning.[4]

Bringing customers in to the business to meet with the workforce is a very powerful tool, and can help employees understand the business from the customer's perspective. At the end of the day, all employees need to understand that their only job security is obtaining and retaining customers. Devoting effort to customer retention is in each employee's self-interest. Effective strategy execution requires that line managers help bring the reality of the competitive marketplace to the shop floor.

Acknowledge That They Must Constantly Grow Their Capabilities and Add New Capabilities

It is important that the workforce acknowledge that they must not only perform well but also consistently improve their own competencies. Most employees want more in annual compensation and will always argue to their own best advantage about how much more experience they have, thus deserving a salary increase. But as they need to be reminded, surviving another year with a firm does not necessarily mean enhanced competencies. Therefore, part of the firm's workforce philosophy might be to communicate to employees that they are, in large part, responsible for their own career growth and must seek ways, inside and outside the firm, to not only enhance their current skills, but also add new skills. Competency growth is the only guarantee of creating a personal competitive advantage and thereby long-term employment security. Obviously, leaders and HR can aid in competency acquisition, but employees ultimately make the decision and take the risk with their own behavior that enables them to grow their competencies.

Acknowledge That They Must Own/Be Held Accountable for Their Own Performance/Behavior

Finally, the workforce must understand that they also must be accountable for their own behavior and that performance has consequences. They should seek—in fact, demand—feedback such that there are never any consequences that surprise them. Outstanding performance should be recognized and rewarded, and unacceptable performance addressed and appropriate consequences provided. Thus, by making a firm's workforce philosophy operational, leaders clarify expectations and differentiate based on performance. In fact, in a few organizations we have observed that when a differentiation approach was equitably implemented or effective HR management systems (e.g., gain sharing) implemented, members of the workforce monitored one another's performance. Otherwise, firms create circumstances where the workforce does not witness the upside of outstanding performance (individually or collectively) and observes few consequences for poor performance. The unintended consequences of not providing feedback enable people to remain based on the presumption that their employer will always survive and so will they. But the reality is that the life span of firms is shorter than our life span as individuals, and the strategy life span of firms is even shorter. An understanding of the importance of each employee's work in executing firm strategy and its consequences can have a powerful effect on strategy execution.

THE ROLE OF THE HR FUNCTION

For all four constituencies—the CEO, executive team members, line managers, and the workforce—there is HR work to be done. Here it is hoped that the senior HR leader can become the "CEO" of the HR function and deliver the strategic workforce needed by the firm. This may also require the senior HR leader to create greater capability within the function by engaging in "HR for the HR function." We will now attempt to discuss what might be done to enable the HR function to become inordinately effective with each of these constituents.

HR and the CEO

As was shown previously in figure 6-3, the major efforts of HR with respect to strategy execution include influencing the firm's workforce strategy and philosophy, determining performance objectives for the senior HR leader, and determining what to communicate to leaders concerning the firm's workforce philosophy (e.g., approach to differentiation), given each leader's joint responsibility with HR to deliver the firm's workforce. These are discussed next.

Work With HR and the Executive Team to Shape the Firm's Business Strategy and Workforce Philosophy

The senior HR leader needs to be a participant in the strategy review meetings with the executive team to represent workforce implications (i.e., behavior, competencies, mind-set, and culture) and contribute to the strategic choices explored. Once the strategy and the brand message of the firm are understood, HR must work with the CEO and the executive team to clarify the cultural expectations and the strategic capabilities necessary. In fact, the senior HR leader may engage the firm in identifying the strategic capabilities using the simple model described in chapter 6), in which the executive team identifies those strategic capabilities (e.g., logistics, distribution, marketing, sales, R&D, and mergers and acquisitions) that enable a firm to achieve its strategic growth expectations.

Once the firm's needed culture and strategic capabilities are identified, the CEO and senior HR leader should negotiate the performance expectations of the HR function. Again, the same categories of strategic success used for other senior executives would apply—that is, financial success, customer success, business process success, and workforce success. Certainly, the HR function can be successful in each of these areas, but as with line executives, the weights may differ. In fact, it may be appropriate that because the workforce is *the* deliverable of HR, 60 to 80 percent of the overall evaluation of the senior HR leader depends on an assessment of the firm's workforce and its contribution to the firm's success. That is, a major determinant of the evaluation of the senior HR leader would depend on metrics indicative of the workforce's mind-set and culture and the extent to which strategic capabilities are populated with "A" players in "A" positions, as well as the performance and behavior of certain positions critical to the organization's success. In addition, the senior HR leader could be evaluated on financial contributions, such as cost-saving initiatives within HR and perhaps customer success with specific programs that HR initiates that impact the customer marketplace (i.e., workforce success), as well as improvements in business processes that led to greater HR efficiency and accuracy. In the past, HR has been primarily evaluated on activities (e.g., transaction accuracy, time to fill openings, and cost reductions) without measuring the major output of HR—the workforce that can deliver the strategy of the firm. An overview of senior HR leader metrics, including examples, is provided in figure 7-3.

Finalize Workforce Philosophy and Strategy and Communicate Them to Management

Leaders and the workforce need to know from HR, line management, and the CEO the firm's philosophy about employee performance and workforce differentiation, and communicate it. Obviously, HR must do this with the executive team, as well as use the executive team to communicate the workforce philosophy and insist that workforce success become a measured accountability of each line manager. Of course, as in any metrics-driven organization, all managers would be evaluated on "workforce success"—how well the workforce impacts the success of the business model—just as they would on any other aspect of the firm's business model.

Statements of workforce strategy (or philosophy) have not been common. In fact, understanding the role of HR and its responsibility for the workforce is a relatively new concept, and yet a few organizations are now clarifying workforce expectations and demanding that HR become accountable for metrics indicative of workforce success, not merely HR activities.

HR and the Executive Team

There are many aspects of the relationship between the HR function and the executive team, but to better enable executive team members to execute the firm's strategy, there are three HR efforts that can significantly impact strategy execution by executive team members. The first is performance management and reward tools. If effective strategy execution requires strategy, metrics, and consequences, then HR

FIGURE 7-3

SHRVP Scorecard: Sample Metrics

Leadership Success

- **Leader Behaviors**
  180° Assessment
  - % understanding HR strategy
  - % understanding how HR strategy is tied to business strategy
  - % understanding improve-ment on:
    - Performance management
    - Credibility
    - Feedback to employees
    - Bonus allocation to HR workforce
    - Coaching effectiveness
- **HR Workforce Success**
  - % passing HR competency "checkout" in HR competency model
- **HR Function Goals**
  - Better HR systems integration
  - Better strategic capability differentiation

  20%

Workforce Metrics

Workforce Mind-set

- **Employee Survey Scores**
  - % understanding we are to be the low-cost provider
  - % believing they know their role in the organization
  - % believing they have the skills to do their job
  - % understanding that teamwork means not letting others fail
  - % understanding that customers are the only source of job security
  - % understanding that customer success is more important than customer satisfaction
  - % understanding that speed is the only way to succeed in our industry

  30%

Workforce Competencies

Strategic Resources
- **Executive Resources**
  - 180° leadership scores of new entrants to executive pipeline
  - Exit rate of "C"-level executives
- **Technical/Professional**
  - Customer Service
    - Ppassing product information examination
  - Logistics/Distribution
    - % acceptance of "first choice" offers
  - Retention % of HiPo technical talent
  - Exit rate of "C"-level technicians

Other Resources

  30%

Contribution to Firm Performance

- ☐ Financial Success
- ☐ Customer Success
- ☐ Business Process Success
- ☐ Workforce Success

- **Financial Success**
  - Productivity contribution of HR function costs relative to revenue
  - Total labor cost/total operating revenue
- **Customer Success**
  - % improvement in secret-shopper scores
- **HR Process Success**
  - Productivity % improvement for benefits cost/employee
  - % improvement in recruiting cost/hire quality
  - % improvement in time to fill vacancies
  - % increase in bonus between top performance versus average performers

  20%

must provide some means of assessing individual performance as well as a method of rewarding contributors. Second, HR also needs to provide a means of tracking "A," "B," and "C" players and provide the tools to assess "A," "B," and "C" players and positions. Finally, HR needs to develop a means by which a leader's behavior in strategy execution can be assessed.

Design Performance Measurement and Reward Tools

For the executive team, the HR function must provide strategy execution tools to ensure greater leader and employee accountability. Performance management *is* a strategy execution tool to detail performance expectations for line managers and for line managers to cascade performance expectations to subordinates. Effective performance management also requires workforce metrics on the extent to which their workforce consists of "A," "B," and "C" players, and which "A" players are to be recognized and rewarded. HR must also develop processes for the exiting of "C" players. Clearly, if performance management is to be used as a strategy execution tool, the use of historical job descriptions, including MBOs, which are not strategically aligned (i.e., not cascaded from the top), will not lead to effective strategy execution.

Worse yet, in many organizations, performance appraisals are not conducted at all or not conducted on time, provide little employee coaching, and often surprise employees. Further, individuals who are terminated for fair, legitimate reasons often sue (and collect!) because performance expectations were not clarified at the beginning of a performance period, nor had a process similar to that described earlier been made operational. It is critical that a process be provided and managers held accountable for the management of their direct reports. Thus, workforce metrics to assess leaders on the management of their most expensive resource are critical.

It should be obvious that in order to execute strategy, every manager must be not only assessed on his or her workforce accountabilities, but also rewarded based on: (1) how well the workforce understands the strategy of the business, (2) the extent that the manager has "A" players in "A" positions and has developmental plans for those "A" players and for "B" players who have "A" potential, and (3) the extent to which the leader is culling the organization's workforce to ensure that noncontributors become contributors or do not remain with the firm.

These issues are intuitively obvious. In fact, an argument can be made that unless these decisions are exercised by executives and line managers, a firm's strategy will not be well executed. However, when organizations have employees who do not perform, they often move them aside (often given an ambiguous assignment—"window watchers" in Japan), and HR receives a requisition to refill the position. In many respects, what may have been an entrepreneurial firm with a flat hierarchy begins to resemble two bloated boxes of equal size (representing high and low performers), with a small pyramid on top representing the office of the CEO. When difficulties emerge, the organization may decide that it must reduce its workforce and cut entry-level workers. If difficulty continues, then professionals and managers must be slashed. Essentially, excess capacity is finally cleared from the firm. Organizations often have euphemisms to label these workers, such as "surplus." This is almost an overt acknowledgment that workers have been kept even though they are not making valued contributions. When managers are asked how easy would it be to identify the top 10 percent or bottom 10 percent of their workforce, most respond by saying they could do it in a heartbeat. And in fact, if the next cutback came, they had already identified who would go based on performance. This is an overt acknowledgment that the accountability for the performance of the workforce is often in short supply and must be addressed if a firm is to effectively execute its strategy and avoid underperformance. Only with effective performance management tools and management accountability for employee performance can strategy be effectively executed.

Design "A," "B," and "C" Tracking Systems

Another role of HR is to ensure that there is a dialogue about the importance of talent in a firm's strategic agenda and to design tools and tracking systems that are useful in strategy execution. Historically, there have been no workforce metrics—no overt way to identify "A" positions, "A" players, "B" players, "C" players, and so on. Without workforce tracking systems, it would be difficult to hold managers accountable. Thus, merely having a metric, even though it may be imprecise and imperfect, creates a mind-set of accountability that hopefully will result in effective workforce decision making. We advocate a data system for workforce decision making that will mandate that executives and line managers make prudent decisions in the best long-term interests of the firm. By using HR tools that can detail performance expectations and by designing metrics to identify "A," "B," and "C" players, leaders can be better held accountable for how well they lead their workforces and differentiate performance.

Build a 180-Degree Strategy Execution Leadership Feedback System

Managers can be held accountable for the exercise of "A," "B," and "C" decisions, but they also can be held accountable for their leadership behavior through feedback from their bosses and direct reports using what is frequently referred to as the 180-degree component of "360-degree" leadership surveys. Thus, feedback can not only identify leaders effective in strategy execution (refer back to figure 6-6), but also provide insight into leaders' effectiveness in exercising their workforce accountabilities. An example of recent survey questions used by a large paper company to get at this issue was shown in figure 7-2.

HR and Line Managers

In working with line managers, HR often has a special challenge. As we noted, lower-level managers, especially supervisors, may never have wanted to be managers; but once they accepted the position, they are often reluctant to give it up, although they may not have grown into top-level supervisory talent. Obviously, this poses selection and development challenges for the HR function. But often firms attempt to execute strategy without making difficult leadership decisions, especially about leaders who have been with the firm for some time. In any case, we recognize that any leadership role is difficult because it involves managing those people at a time when more firms are demanding that leaders make difficult differentiation decisions that may involve their friends. These circumstances are serious obstacles to effective strategy execution.

Despite these issues, HR must find ways of helping leaders, especially managers, make the difficult workforce decisions necessary to execute the firm's strategy. This requires that HR provide line managers with workforce differentiation guidelines for those "A" positions that may report to them (e.g., customer service representatives at

Lands' End, Inc., Dell Computer Corporation's online product experts, or a research scientist at GlaxoSmithKline); provide exit processes such that "C" players are identified and are handled efficiently and with dignity; and give line managers tools to assess their effectiveness in creating the workforce mind-set necessary to execute the firm's strategy.

Provide Workforce Differentiation Guidelines

HR should develop workforce differentiation guidelines for line managers (as well as for executives), as was shown in the previous examples, to help line managers make difficult "A," "B," and "C" decisions. With large populations of employees in strategic positions, HR should make these guidelines position-specific. As managers become familiar with differentiation decisions, HR can play a role in moving from generic guidelines to guidelines for strategic positions (e.g., engineers and customer insight) to guidelines for specific positions. The more specificity, the easier it is to exercise the decisions.

Provide Processes to Exit "C" Players

HR should attempt to help line managers recognize that making decisions about "C" players (especially those who are not contributing to the firm) is a critical part of their job by ensuring the line managers that employees will be treated with dignity and respect as well as helped in the transition process. Thus, once an employee has been declared a "C" (after all coaching and other options have been exhausted), HR must have an efficient process whereby the employee can be notified of severance, unemployment, and so on, and exit can occur smoothly. In today's environment, firms are fairly familiar with how to effectuate this process.

Provide Mind-set and Culture Survey Process

Line managers should also be provided with feedback, with a major focus on their leadership behaviors, from their direct reports in executing the firm's strategy. Such surveys should provide feedback about line managers' leadership effectiveness in creating the culture and managing workforce performance. These data may initially be for developmental purposes only, but over time should become a part of the evaluation and review process for all line managers.

HR and the Workforce

What can HR do to directly influence the contribution to a firm's strategy execution efforts? There are many ways, but two stand out. These concern metrics necessary to assess employee growth, especially in "A" positions, and to assess the strategic focus of the workforce in its efforts at strategy execution. A few examples of metrics tools have been previously provided, but here we explore how HR might make direct contributions to a firm's success in strategy execution through better use of workforce metrics.

Provide Competency Growth Guidelines

HR's responsibilities to the broader-based workforce are to design means of enhancing careers, building competency growth models, posting systems, and doing whatever is necessary to grow workforce competencies. Generally, employees grow mostly by real work experiences. This means that individuals need to rotate through jobs, and such rotations are in the best interest not only of the firm, but also of the employee. As competencies grow, employees become more valuable to the organization, and career opportunities as well as compensation opportunities are enhanced. Growth through rotational assignments may also mean that part of the firm's workforce philosophy should state that no employee owns a job, that the firm owns all positions and employees are expected to grow their competencies and become eligible for other positions.

Competency growth models for strategic positions gauge employee growth and contribute to the firm's competitive advantage. HR time and effort should be devoted to the development of competency growth models. Employee growth and development is often random, as in promotion decision making, including the earlier examples of movement from nonmanagerial to managerial jobs. Career development efforts are often not well managed and must be much more specifically focused than they have been to date. HR can play a significant role in making this occur.

The issue is how to ensure that employees are growing strategic competencies that impact a firm's competitive advantage and are measured on their progress. The use of competency growth models and development discussions with supervisors can certainly help, as can a workforce philosophy that states that, in addition to the employee performance contribution, every employee must grow their competencies.

An example of a competency growth model is that for the technical workforce at DuPont, which is used for the engineering series, from Engineer I through Distinguished Fellow.[5] This series was initiated to accelerate the growth of critical capabilities within DuPont. It is a part of a manual called "Your Career Pathways," which has won several internal and external awards because it attempts to provide assurance that technical talent will continue to grow.[6] In the late 1990s, many junior scientists had capabilities that were more in demand at DuPont than those of senior scientists. DuPont questioned whether it should hire more junior scientists or retrain senior scientists. The issue was, How should a firm grow the strategic talent necessary to win its future in some programmed way? The competency growth grid was a part of DuPont's response. It is tied to pay by using compensation factors associated with the Hay system: know-how, accountability, and problem solving. It is also a progression system, not a promotion system. Thus, when employees are measured against the next level of competence, or workforce metric, and "pass" the criteria, they move to the next level and are compensated for the "worth" of the next-level position.

Another example comes from Nissan R&D in Farmington Hills, Michigan, where cars are designed for the North American market.[7] When foreign firms take residence in another country, often they do not have an advantage with respect to the workforce and therefore must find other means to upgrade their talent to ensure that they can meet or exceed that of any competitor. This was Nissan's dilemma. Thus, besides bringing quality engineering talent from Japan and getting the best talent that they could attract from the United States, Nissan decided that the best way to have highly competitive talent was to engage in a systemic effort to grow talent. Thus, they developed several competency grids that were designed to continually enhance and upgrade the workforce. This effort took more than two years to design using the Japanese practice of *nemawashi,* which involves a series of meetings to discuss in detail the competencies and expectations for each position (in this case, engineering, CAD/CAM, and so on) until all managers reach agreement. Thus, when the design process is complete, there is no "big event" rollout or fanfare necessary. However, once agreement was reached, the system was relatively easy to execute, because many engineers had had a significant opportunity to provide input to the final criteria. These grids, all six of them, are posted outside the design areas of Nissan and upgraded annually by a nine-member team. Each year three members of the team rotate off and new ones rotate on, and engineers self-nominate for promotion and have their portfolio assessed by members of the team responsible for certifying promotion to the next level, which carries a substantial financial reward.

STRATEGY EXECUTION: AN OVERVIEW

Chapters 6 and 7 have attempted to address the roles of executives, line managers, the HR function, and the workforce in strategy execution. To accomplish this, we stated that a firm needs three strategies: business, workforce, and HR. And that there are significant decisions (strategic choice, workforce philosophy, etc.) that must be exercised as well as much work to be done for strategy execution to occur. Much of this is represented in figure 7-4, where we observe the three strategies and some of the efforts and decisions that must be made within each strategy. Since our focus has been on workforce and HR strategy, let us remind ourselves of some of the critical components. To begin, look at the workforce strategy section and notice the primary decisions necessary culture, capabilities, positions, players, and—the most difficult—the workforce philosophy and the possible "new rules" for workforce engagement.

Some examples of these new rules are shown in figure 7-4, such as " 'A' players in 'A' positions," line manager's workforce accountabilities, exiting "C" work (and "C" players), etc. Thus, a workforce strategy congruent with the business strategy requires the most effective and efficient allocation and alignment of the firm's resources to assure the delivery of the intended market differentiation.

The HR function must also have an HR strategy that encourages it to disproportionately invest in the strategy execution and cultural change. These critical HR roles in delivering workforce capabilities and culture are explored in Dave Ulrich's best-selling HR book, *Human Resource Champions*.[8]

HR's deliverable is a workforce that impacts the firm's strategy execution efforts. Workforce metrics thus are measures of mind-set,

FIGURE 7-4

The Strategies Necessary for Effective Strategy Execution

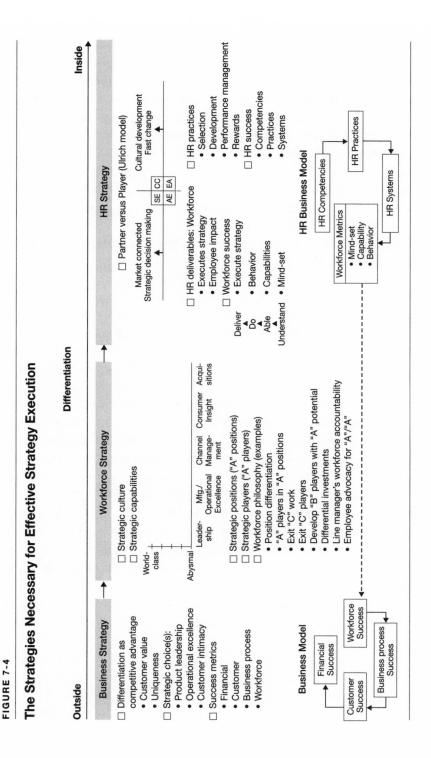

competencies, and behaviors that impact strategic components of the balanced scorecard, and help create workforce success. All HR practices (e.g., selection, development, etc.) should therefore be aligned with delivering workforce success and measured on metrics indicative of workforce success. Finally, delivering the workforce strategy must be an accountability of all leaders and the HR function using the same workforce metrics targets (mind-set, capabilities, and behavior), again as these are shown by the connecting arrows in figure 7-4. Thus, the deliverable of HR must contribute to the success of the firm's business model, and leadership must also be accountable for the success of the workforce because leaders, like HR, influence the workforce's execution of strategy. Without joint accountability effective strategy execution cannot occur.

A NEW PARTNERSHIP

This chapter has explored the roles of line managers and HR in strategy execution. Our intent has been to clarify these roles and provide examples of how these efforts can be significantly enhanced. The major point readers should take away from this is that line managers and HR must have a new partnership in strategy execution with respect to the workforce, and that the efforts of both groups should be devoted to the same metrics. It is also a reminder that strategy execution cannot be achieved only at the top of the organization. Line managers and the HR function substantially influence workforce mind-set and capabilities, both positively and negatively. Effective workforce metrics enable strategic workforce decisions to occur, which can impact the successful execution of any firm's strategy significantly. The challenge is to use all resources to the maximum to effectively execute strategy—line managers and HR are critical components of this effort. In the next chapter, we examine how managers and HR can work together to communicate scorecard data.

8

COMMUNICATION AND
LEARNING PROGRAMS FOR THE
WORKFORCE SCORECARD

I N CHAPTERS 6 AND 7 we described the processes through
which senior executives, line managers, and HR leaders can
work together to develop strategic plans and set accountabilities for the workforce, based on metrics taken from the Workforce
Scorecard. In this chapter we continue our emphasis on responding
to the execution challenge by focusing on communicating Workforce
Scorecard data to managers and encouraging them to use those data
to improve the speed and quality of strategy execution in their own
firms.

What makes communication such an important part of the process
of executing workforce strategy? The essence of the execution challenge is to understand how to use workforce measures after the issue
of what to measure has been resolved. No one is born with expertise
in knowing how to use workforce data as a tool to drive strategy execution. These are skills that have to be learned and, once mastered,
taught to others throughout the organization. But managers should not
underestimate the difficulties associated with making this happen.

Randy MacDonald, formerly SVPHR at GTE and Verizon and now in that same role at IBM, states:

> *My biggest problem is communicating and reinforcing the linkage between HR actions and business results. The business has a clear strategy and targeted business results. The HR strategy is directly linked to the needs of the business and expressed in terms of HR strategic thrusts. What I need now is to effectively communicate and execute on strategic intent, motivate and track performance against organization and business goals, and align HR actions with business results.[1]*

We've seen a number of firms spend considerable amounts of time and money on Workforce Scorecard development, only to seemingly run out of energy when it comes to communicating these measures to the workforce and helping managers to use them effectively. In many firms this situation is exacerbated by the presence of too many (sometimes conflicting) measures, each of which is competing for the attention of managers. This can be confusing and can result in "metrics fatigue" among the firm's most important intended audience. Effective communication strategies, based on the Workforce Scorecard framework, can help the audience by providing a mechanism through which managers can learn about and use metrics to drive strategy execution.

The experience of one large multinational firm in implementing its Workforce Scorecard is typical. The firm's scorecard team initially believed that its work was largely done after it developed and populated the scorecard with the right measures. But what the team found was that most managers throughout the firm—both line and HR—were unprepared to make data-driven decisions about people. The management team had created a world-class workforce measurement system, but it wasn't being used. Managers would look at the data and claim that they understood the implications, but subsequent analyses showed that they weren't using the data effectively to make better decisions about the workforce. They simply didn't know how to do it. The challenge was to show them the relevance of the workforce data for achieving their own goals, and then to teach them how to use those data to drive strategy.

Implementing the Workforce Scorecard effectively means that we need to teach managers how to use it as a decision support tool, and provide incentives for their doing so. Since not all employees learn in the same way, multiple tools and techniques will be required. Communication efforts such as this can seem mundane, but it is in fact a strategic process that requires continual attention from executives. In this chapter we describe a process for effective workforce metrics communication through the use of *Learning Map*®, case studies, and games and simulations.[2]

GOALS OF WORKFORCE METRICS COMMUNICATION PROGRAMS

We've shown that in many firms employees don't have a clear understanding of strategy or their own role in executing it, but that when they do, shareholder value is enhanced. The simple fact is that the more we can get employees to pay attention to performance feedback, the more effective that feedback is likely to be. Communication scholars have found that some of the key attributes or outcomes of workforce communication can be broken down into recognition, understanding, acceptance, and use.

Recognition. The first and primary goal of the firm's communication efforts should be that all employees are aware of the existence of HR and Workforce Scorecards. Before these metrics can drive the intended behaviors, all employees need to understand that they exist and that the firm's senior leadership team endorses and supports them.

Understanding. Just because employees are aware of the scorecard, however, doesn't mean that they understand it. Thus the second goal of the firm's communications efforts should be that each employee understand the firm's strategy, know what his or her role is in executing it, and see a linkage between these behaviors and the firm's measurement processes.

Acceptance. Just as recognition is a necessary condition for understanding, understanding is required for acceptance. Metrics can be useful not only to help managers set expectations about what is important, but also to help create a sense of urgency in the workforce when important gaps can be identified and prioritized.

However, without specific goals, employees won't be motivated to improve their performance.[3] Indeed, the conclusion that employees who set specific, challenging goals outperform their peers who set either no goals or impossibly difficult goals is a central finding of the literature on goal-setting theory.[4] When there is *goal alignment*—that is, when the measure taps the same elements or behaviors that senior executives say are important—employees will really begin to pay attention to these elements.

In addition, research has found that the more important a goal is, the more frequently you should provide feedback on it. This suggests that it is important to put the most effort into measuring your most important strategic objectives. This will encourage employees to pay attention to the goals and to perceive them to be more important. The opposite is also true: If a particular element is not a strategic priority, don't continue to provide feedback on it—you'll be sending the wrong message. In addition, if you really want the workforce to pay attention to a set of measures, make sure they are distributed to the workforce under the signature of the CEO and the senior executive team.

Use. The ultimate measure of success is that workforce metrics help managers to make better decisions about the workforce. While it is important to ensure that managers are considering the workforce issues as a regular part of their decision-making processes, you can't assume that they have the skills or understanding to be able to do so. We now turn to the communication and learning elements required to be sure that they gain these skills and competencies.

DEVELOPING A COMMUNICATION STRATEGY FOR THE WORKFORCE SCORECARD

Since you can't manage what you don't measure, and you can't measure what you don't clearly understand, executing strategy through the workforce requires a clear communication strategy to ensure that the right data reach the workforce. Workforce metrics won't help unless you can get the data into the hands of the people who need them and encourage them to use those data to make better decisions about the workforce. As we've described, employees can't act on measures that they don't see, comprehend, and embrace. All managers—and indeed all employees—have a "theory of the firm" in their heads that helps guide their behavior. Measurement can help ensure that they are all using the same theory of the firm—and also that this is the theory that helps drive strategy execution!

The importance of using metrics to help create a shared mind-set around the processes through which the firm creates value raises the question, Who are the customers for workforce data? Just as we segment marketing strategies for external customers, so too must we develop different internal messages by each segment of the workforce. Effective workforce measurement means that the right people have the right access to the right data at the right time. Overwhelming managers with data that they don't need is a mistake, just as is making managers go looking for strategically relevant data. Moreover, it is probably not realistic to expect all employees in the business to "get it," at least initially. Complete support and acceptance might not even be a realistic or necessary goal, at least in the short run. Tony Rucci, chief administrative officer at Cardinal Health, made this case very clearly:

> *Certainly, it would always be nice to have the proactive support of your CEO. But I think that having the support of your firm's CFO is equally important. The CFO needs to be convinced that nonfinancial metrics are important because they are leading indicators of the firm's financial performance. So, if I didn't have the support of the CEO, I'd begin to work on the CFO. I have often heard CEOs say, "If I could only get the support and buy-in of middle management, we could move forward." But I don't really think that this is the issue. I think that organizations sort themselves vertically, not horizontally, on any number of factors. I believe that only one-third of the employees at any given level in the firm really "get it" and want to change and move the organization forward; one-third of the workforce will comply because they think they have to; and one-third of the workforce will actively resist change efforts of any kind. At Sears, we had twelve members on the executive committee. One-third of them "got it" and were actively involved in the change process; one-third of them*

simply complied; and one-third of them wouldn't change if their life depended on it.

In my career I have spent too much time and energy on the bottom third that doesn't want to change. I have found that you need to focus on the top third, and devote your time, effort, and money to identifying and supporting those people. So, I would say that if you don't have the support of the CEO, too bad, that's life. You need to get on with it. Find those employees in the top third, and give them all your support.[5]

TOOLS FOR COMMUNICATION

Ensuring that we communicate effectively with the top third described by Tony Rucci begins with some very basic questions about the workforce. Do they know what the strategy is? Do they have a clear sense of what their role is in the process? Many senior management teams don't discuss strategy and goals nearly enough with employees—either because they assume that employees already understand it, or because they just aren't sure themselves what the strategy is, and more discussion on this point will make it painfully evident to everyone. Either way, managers have a problem.

Both accessibility and transparency are crucial for the Workforce Scorecard metrics to become useful tools for strategy execution. Not all workforce metrics are of equal importance—managers need to learn which ones deserve their greater attention. An effective communication system will help managers make these distinctions. A wide variety of communication tools can be used to get the message out; for example, an intranet with "briefing books" that describe the metrics that have been developed, their history, how they were calculated, and whom to contact for information is a highly effective communication tool.

The Role of Information Systems

The rapid increases in computing speed and associated improvements in software quality have created significant new opportunities for collecting and reporting workforce data. Companies such as Lawson,

Oracle Corporation, PeopleSoft, Inc., and SAP AG all offer comprehensive enterprise resource planning (ERP) and data warehousing products. Niche players such as CorVu Corporation, Hyperion Solutions Corporation, and PBViews also sell specialized software that can be used to graphically present scorecard data, typically drawing information from the firm's data warehouse.

When implemented correctly, ERP and workforce information systems are important tools that can enable managers to access to their own data to track the progress of strategy execution. They can include a host of important features, including drill-downs and report-outs by area and the ability to e-mail the results to users. When firms are designing and implementing such systems, however, it is important to ensure that strategy drives what metrics that are collected and reported—and not the defaults that the vendor has hardwired into the software. As we've seen, it is likely that many, if not most, of the most important measures associated with strategy execution won't currently be available and will have to be collected. It is also important to keep a record of the decision processes that led to the selection of a particular set of metrics. Why these and not others? Which measures were tried and rejected, and why? An effective workforce measurement system will document the decision processes that led to the selection of the metrics, and make the rationale available to the users.

An example of a firm that does an excellent job at the communication of workforce metrics can be seen at IBM. At IBM, executives communicate "Pay and Performance" ratings to their respective workforces in conjunction with quarterly and annual earnings announcements via an intranet-based application. Each business unit and geographically based organization within IBM reports its standing against targets: ahead of target, on track, or below target. The ratings provide employees with a directional indicator of potential Performance Bonus payout levels for year-end. Accompanying each performance rating are executive communications that typically cover the state of the business, reinforcement of strategic priorities and identification of areas for performance improvement, including customer focus and teaming to further leverage the IBM brand and strategic capabilities—all intended to rally the workforce to higher levels of performance.

Another example of one firm that has done an excellent job of communicating its metrics with the workforce is Verizon Communications. Based on a clearly defined strategy map, the firm developed an HR Scorecard. With the help of the corporate communications staff, Verizon next developed an integrated approach to communicating these metrics with the workforce. They developed a "briefing book" that helped managers understand the metrics, the history of their development, and whom to contact with questions or comments.

In addition to briefing books, Verizon has developed a number of related tools to help the workforce understand the measures as well as their implications for their jobs. Indeed, one of the key lessons from Verizon's experience is the importance of taking a comprehensive approach to the communication of workforce measures. Executives began with a "road show," partnering senior executives with senior HR executives in a series of public presentations. They described the program and the specifics of the measures, and made a very important show of public support for the project. They developed a short video that described the HR Scorecard and how it could be used to improve business results. This video was available on the corporate intranet and could also be e-mailed to interested employees. A board game was introduced to show and teach the needed skills, along with Learning Map that helped all employees understand Verizon's strategy, their own role in executing it, and what the specific measures meant for them. "All-hands" meetings, videotapes, CD-ROMs, and colorful reports were issued each quarter to help the workforce understand the extent to which Verizon was meeting its goals. An extensive corporate intranet was developed, which included detailed case examples and a database of articles on the use and interpretation of workforce metrics. The intranet described the metrics, the process owner for each metric, how the metrics should be used, and where to go for more information. Finally, a competency checkout for all managers on the basics of metrics and causal inference was developed.

The Verizon experience highlights the importance of providing a way for everyone to ask questions and give feedback. Communication needs to be a two-way process. In addition, goals are much more effective if the workforce has a part in setting them and really accepts them. Effective workforce measurement systems provide a mechanism to help make this happen.

The IBM and Verizon examples also point to the potential impact of workforce metrics on managerial actions and strategy execution. An example of the impact of workforce measures on key managerial behaviors can be seen at Bristol-Myers Squibb. BMS has created a retention scorecard, which is intended to: (1) significantly reduce voluntary turnover across the organization, (2) focus managers on the primary means of retaining talent, (3) place emphasis on the reasonable actions that managers can take to broaden the talent mix, and (4) communicate and emphasize organizational priorities. After implementing the scorecard, BMS managers wanted to know: Is the scorecard effective in increasing talent retention in "A" positions?; is information about the workforce all that is necessary to increase retention of key talent, or are monetary incentives necessary as well?

To begin to answer these questions, BMS designed a field study based on three different groups of their field sales force representatives. The primary focus of the study was on the first line supervisors, who manage the field sales force representatives—a critical ("A") position at BMS. The first group of supervisors was provided with a workforce scorecard and a monetary reward ($5,000 each) for reaching retention goals. The second group received the workforce scorecard without any monetary reward. The third group was a control group which received neither the scorecard of monetary reward.

Over a one-year time period, BMS found no difference in the monetary and scorecard-only groups, but they did find that both groups were significantly better at development, management capability, and retention than the control (no scorecard) group. The supervisors were using the data provided to them effectively to reduce high potential turnover, but financial incentives are not the only incentives available to drive increased performance. Retention of "A" players is more about relationships with managers than just money.

COMMUNICATING WORKFORCE STRATEGY AND METRICS AT CARDINAL HEALTH

Another highly successful example of an effective communication program occurred at Cardinal Health. Cardinal Health is a leading supplier of products and services that support the health care industry.

A *Fortune* 20 company with more than $50 billion in revenues, Cardinal Health has nearly sixty thousand employees on six continents. It is also a highly data-driven and results-oriented corporation. Tony Rucci, chief administrative officer, and his team have identified empirical people-customer profitability at Cardinal Health. In Cardinal Health's many different businesses, customer evaluations of Cardinal Health's workforce (covering honesty, timeliness of delivery, professionalism, fairness and clarity in billing, and accuracy) were found to be key drivers of both the intent to purchase from Cardinal Health and actual purchases. A summary of these relationships can be seen in figure 8-1.

Cardinal Health further refined this model in figure 8-2. Cardinal Health partnered with specialists in psychometrics and econometrics to both develop the measures and evaluate the strength of the linkages between the categories. Cardinal Health's executives found that employee attitudes (which they call "the twelve questions") were key drivers of customer satisfaction, which in turn drove both revenues and total shareholder return.

FIGURE 8-1

Customer Perceptions

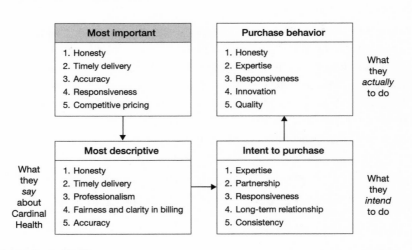

Source: Cardinal Health.

FIGURE 8-2

Building a Model . . . Around Culture

Source: Cardinal Health.

Educating the Workforce at Cardinal Health

Based in large part on the strength of these findings, Cardinal Health's leadership team determined that it needed a way to convey the company's strategy clearly and completely to every employee. The team believed that to drive strategy execution effectively, the workforce needed a high degree of business literacy as well as a very clear understanding of Cardinal Health's businesses and its business priorities. This included educating employees about the health care industry and providing a "line of sight" so employees could see how their work supports and contributes to the success of Cardinal Health customers and the company. This was not an easy goal: At the time, Cardinal Health had forty thousand employees working in hundreds of businesses segmented into several operating units. In fact, more than two-thirds of its employee population came to Cardinal Health via some forty companies Cardinal Health had acquired between 1995 and 2000.

Each of Cardinal Health's businesses lacked information about the other businesses, so it was nearly impossible to provide a single face to the customer. Employees did not share the same base knowledge about the industry, the company, and the customers, so coordinating integrated solutions using all of Cardinal Health's capabilities was a much more difficult task. Cardinal Health's leadership wanted a simple, creative way to bring its strategy, the marketplace challenges, and economics to every employee in a quick, common format that was easily implemented and easily transferable across functions, businesses, and geographic locations.

To begin to directly address these issues, Cardinal Health worked with Root Learning to develop a series of Learning Map modules and electronic Root-vMap platforms. Learning Map modules are large, illustrated drawings that are accompanied by discussion questions and learning exercises. The idea is that small groups of ten to twelve employees gather around a visual and, with the help of a facilitator, follow the discussion guide. Within forty-five minutes or so, the group has a unique but common learning experience. Some of the elements that Cardinal Health covered in these applications were the following:

- The health care marketplace and all the dynamics influencing cost, quality, and efficiency

- The key challenges and opportunities that these market dynamics create for customers of Cardinal Health

- The role individual employees can play in creating customer solutions.

- The changes in the health care industry that are being driven by shifting demographics, increased cost of R&D, government regulations, insurance practices, and commercialization

- The massive consolidation in the health care provider community and among the pharmaceutical companies, resulting in an increase in competition

- The key customer groups and the impact of technology and consumerism

- The current state and future state of Cardinal Health, including strategy, values, and growth initiatives

All modules are built around a metaphor that serves as a visual representation of a concept or an idea—in this case, a water metaphor. Cardinal Health has developed four Learning Map modules designed to help its employees from all businesses, all levels, and all geographies understand the same basic concepts about the company:

Map 1: "A Rapidly Changing Marketplace" (shown in figure 8-3) is about Cardinal Health's marketplace (who its customers are,

FIGURE 8-3

Learning Map for Cardinal Health

Source: Reprinted with permission of Cardinal Health and Root Learning, Inc.

what the dynamics of the marketplace are, and how they influence the company's products and services, trends that may affect the marketplace, how the competition is competing, etc.).

Map 2: "Bringing It All Together" is about Cardinal Health's response to the marketplace (how its products and services fulfill a need, how its strategic drivers are the foundation of everything it does, and how it can mix and match products and services to fulfill customer needs).

Map 3: "Creating Shareholder Value" is about how Cardinal Health attracts investors and creates a return on shareholders' investment (a review of its revenue stream).

Map 4: "Building a Bridge to Inclusion" is about diversity and inclusion and the actions Cardinal Health is taking to achieve its vision.

Demand for the modules was high in the first six months of the maps' availability and remains strong now, over a year later. Over five hundred copies of each of the initial three maps were printed and distributed. The company estimates that about half of its employees worldwide have participated in at least one module. The company has translated the tools into Spanish and hopes to translate them into eleven more languages to cover the full population.

In the first three or four weeks of Cardinal Health's implementing the online versions of the Learning Map modules on the company's intranet, over eight hundred employees downloaded them, making the Learning Map modules among the most popular content the company ever posted.

COMMUNICATING WORKFORCE STRATEGY AND METRICS AT DELL

The success of any strategy hinges on how quickly and effectively it can be implemented through the workforce. Over the past several years, Dell's strategic priorities have helped Dell employees focus on driving and executing the company's strategy. Dell's rapid growth in the early years demanded focus on the business and keeping up with growth momentum. As Dell's market began to mature, the company recognized the need to focus on its employees in new ways that linked people to the business strategy.

Extending Dell's Model to Storage

Dell made its name in the personal computer business before deciding to extend its direct business model into other areas, like storage, software, and services. When Dell initially decided to enter the storage market, it formed a partnership with EMC Corporation as part of that strategy. Dell recognized that one of the biggest challenges was to engage its sales team in this significant shift. Dell's "sales makers" were well versed and adept in selling the concept of Dell's direct model for PCs and hardware. As the sales makers moved to selling even more complex solutions, Dell recognized the importance of having their fully aligned support, understanding, and capability. Dell's leadership team saw the opportunity to engage its sales makers in driving the implementation of this new strategy, attempting to position Dell as a product leader in storage, and enhancing the customers' experience in new ways. In order to maintain its traditional speed of execution as it grew, it needed to engage its employees "at the speed of Dell." To do this, with the help of Root Learning, Dell developed a series of Learning Map modules to help everyone get on board, and fast. The Learning Map modules focused on the following:

- Creating understanding about the realities of Dell's business and establishing context for shifting the company's focus and strategy—particularly the need to manage the increasing amount and complexity of information

- Examining the storage marketplace, including its evolution, the costs, and current trends

- Exploring the structure of customer segments and their changing business needs

- Understanding the relationship between Dell and EMC, and the value proposition the partnership creates for customers

- Discussing the concept of business solutions in the context of storage, and identifying individual actions to support Dell's goal to be a business solutions provider

Financial Acumen for Sales Makers

With the success of its Learning Map programs for storage, Dell looked to apply this learning methodology to other topics, such as increasing the financial acumen of its sales makers. It was critical that Dell's employees not only understand the basics of how Dell makes its money, but also understand how its unique financial structure actually gives it a competitive advantage—a daunting topic for many. Dell and Root Learning developed a series of activities based on a rock climbing metaphor to help employees understand the intricacies of Dell's financial realities. These activities included the following:

- Reviewing Dell's financial growth goals

- Understanding how executing and extending the Dell business model will help Dell reach its goals

- Exploring key financial metrics and the levers that drive them

- Reviewing Dell's money flow, including revenue, gross margin, operating income, NOPAT (net operating income after tax), and ROIC

- Showing how Dell compares its performance with that of its competitors, using some key financial performance indicators

- Highlighting how Dell's financial success benefits Dell's customers and Dell

Because the Learning Map approach is based on visual learning, it has proven engaging in cultures worldwide. The modules were translated into eight languages, with the metaphor holding strong no matter where the discussions were conducted. The company also intends to apply this approach to another strategic priority, focusing on the development of its talented teams around the world. The approach taken by Dell's learning and development teams directly reflects and promotes its strategic initiatives and helps promote an informed and committed community of Dell team members worldwide.

COMMUNICATING WORKFORCE STRATEGY AND METRICS AT PRUDENTIAL FINANCIAL

Still another example of a highly successful and integrated workforce communication effort occurred at Prudential Financial, one of the oldest insurance companies in the United States. In preparation for its transition from a mutual insurance company to a publicly held one, Prudential trained nearly fifty-five thousand employees on the changing environment in the insurance industry, the steps needed to become a publicly held company, general business literacy, and how the company would measure its success after the transition.[6] This process was named One Prudential Exchange, or OPX, and consisted of a series of meetings of the top 150 executives, one-and-a-half-day meetings with the next level of managers to prepare them to act as coaches and facilitators in OPX, and finally more than thirty-five hundred work unit meetings to carry the message to the workforce.

Like Cardinal Health and Dell, Prudential also used Learning Map as a central part of its communication efforts. Prudential evaluated the effectiveness of the OPX process through a series of written evaluations collected from participants, through telephone interviews and surveys, and finally by linking the OPX survey results with subsequent employee opinion survey data. What Prudential found was that positive evaluations of the OPX process were related to subsequent positive employee opinion survey data. Gains of more than 20 percentage points were found on some of Prudential's survey items. In addition, many managers reported that through the process of learning to facilitate the thirty-five hundred OPX meetings, managers' skills at facilitating large group meetings increased significantly.

COMMUNICATING WORKFORCE STRATEGY AND METRICS AT LEGO

The LEGO Company also has an extremely well developed system for communicating workforce metrics and developing the competencies needed to use them.[7] The process is intended to leverage LEGO's investments in its global "Pulse" survey of employee opinions, and the entire process is Web-enabled. LEGO employees can access these tools from anywhere in the world. The program, which has been very highly rated by LEGO employees, consists of a mix of video and text-based elements, with a self-assessment module at the end of the program. To date, managers have scored approximately 90 percent accuracy on the post-test. A summary of LEGO's approach can be seen in table 8-1.

DEVELOPING METRICS COMPETENCIES IN MANAGERS

By now it should be clear that we are advocating new measures of workforce success that are directly linked with the firm's strategy, and new behaviors from managers to use them effectively. New measures and new behaviors may require managers to develop new competencies and capabilities as well. Workforce metrics won't effectively drive strategy execution unless you provide the administrative and technical support—as well as examples—to help managers make it work.

For example, at one large corporation, the leadership team felt that metrics were so crucial to the firm's ability to implement strategy quickly that they created the position of VP of Workforce Measurement. This role was filled by someone with a Ph.D. in HR and considerable consulting and research experience. This person also had a small staff to help with the training and data collection processes. Additional resources were drawn from the firm's marketing and R&D functions (which housed a number of statistics "gurus") as needed. A position description for this role is shown in table 8-2.

Training the Workforce to Use Workforce Metrics

The main message of this chapter has been that the best metrics system in the world won't create much value unless you can get the data into the hands of the people who need them and encourage them to use those data. This raises for us an important question: What can we realistically expect line and HR managers to know about workforce measurement? This is a big problem, especially among HR professionals, because many in the profession are uncomfortable dealing with metrics. New requirements and expectations of the workforce will require the provision of new tools and examples needed to do the work.

Development of competencies in the use of workforce metrics is not unlike most other forms of workforce development. It requires

TABLE 8-1

LEGO's E-Learning Program for Workforce Metrics

Module 1: Introduction (4 pages)	***PowerPoint Presentation*** • Training program overview and explanation of exercises (self-tests) • Explanation of video elements
Module 2: Background and Survey Approach (10 pages)	***PowerPoint Presentation*** • The LEGO Company's mission and strategic priorities • People implications of the LEGO Company's strategy • Purpose of the employee survey; outline of different survey categories ***Video: CEO Presentation*** • CEO outlines the importance of the LEGO Pulse survey as well as the role of managers in changing employee attitudes and how that supports the corporate change initiative
Module 3: Understanding Survey Results (10 pages)	***PowerPoint Presentation*** • Outline of a sample survey page; explanation of survey categories and color coding • Guidance on interpreting results • Template for a post-survey manager "Action Sheet"
Module 4: Acting on Survey Results (10 pages)	***PowerPoint Presentation*** • Global timeline for acting on survey results • Tips for preparing team meetings and sharing results • Action guidelines, options, and strategies ***Video: CEO Presentation*** • CEO outlines the mind-set that he advocates for local management follow-up efforts and highlights that employees must be involved in identifying agendas for improvement
Module 5: Understanding the Wider Organizational Development Initiative (29 pages)	***PowerPoint Presentation*** • Introduction of the organizational development tool "Dream-Out," the vehicle used for generating ideas among the workforce on how to improve survey results and drive organizational development • Discussion of key participants and stages in the Dream-Out process ***Video: CEO Presentation*** • Role and activities of the manager in the Dream-Out process
Validation Test	***Self-Test*** • To what extent are managers able to apply their learning? Exercise presents a series of questions about specific details of the LEGO Pulse reports and about the suggested practice for manager action plans.

Source: The LEGO Group.

TABLE 8-2

Position Description for VP of Workforce Measurement

Key Responsibilities
- Create measurement/metrics infrastructure.
- Conduct applied, targeted internal HR research to address internal customer needs—help create action plans that are driven by research results.
- Participate in the creation of tailored training workshops to address gaps identified through analysis.
- Assist in leadership reviews and bench-strength analyses.
- Participate in the design and implementation of key leadership and organizational effectiveness initiatives (e.g., 180° feedback, balanced scorecard, performance management, competency modeling).
- Participate in the creation and implementation of assessment and measurement solutions (e.g., assessment centers, role-play assessments, pulse-check surveys).

Expected Areas of Concern
- Collaborate with business leaders to develop metrics around the strategic priorities and organization goals.

- Lead the design of data collection tools like surveys and focus groups.
- Conduct analysis with data using SPSS, Excel, and so on to find out relationships and to interpret the data.
- Provide leaders with periodic scorecards on the strategic metrics. Work closely with leaders/HR generalists to identify interventions needed to move the needles on the metrics.
- Partner in the development of the right performance measurement systems and their implementation.
- Interface with various groups in the organization to ensure relevant analyses are brought into forums, town halls, and so on.

Major Skills Required
- Statistical expertise (SPSSx for Windows)
- Research design and analysis
- Project management skills
- Written communication skills
- Presentation skills
- Practical problem-solving skills

---

a mix of approaches and techniques that are directly relevant to the needs of those being taught. The experience at one multinational was probably typical for a well-developed learning system. This firm developed a series of simulations—showing how managers can increase the efficacy of their decisions though the effective use of HR metrics. In addition, the firm encouraged senior HR managers to take up to 3 percent of their budgets to experiment and innovate with HR metrics (beyond the line item for metrics). They had their own budget, prepared internal RFPs, and publicly recognized the best and most innovative use of HR data within the firm.

IBM is another example of a company that takes these new HR competencies seriously. Randy MacDonald, the SVPHR, commissioned specific learning programs around core HR competencies required to support the firm's strategy and drive value at IBM. IBM's "Worldwide Human Resources Professional Development Program" is a learning program that focuses on strengthening the capabilities of its HR professionals. The program consists of three modules: Understanding the Business, Improving Organizational Climate, and Managing Client Relationships. Through the integration of e-learning and traditional classroom instruction, HR professionals engage in a range of activities to help them understand key concepts in these areas, and apply models/tools to identify potential workforce issues and come up with solutions to address them. All of the learning programs have mastery exams and *all* HR professionals (including executives) must pass those exams. MacDonald regularly receives the grades from these exams, reviews the HR professionals' progress, and provides feedback directly to the individuals, when appropriate.

In addition to the online tools, a number of firms have developed one-day seminars that are aimed at HR and line managers. These seminars, which are delivered by one of the senior workforce metrics team staff, focus on practical applications of understanding and using workforce data to drive business results. Participants are encouraged to identify and submit potential projects in advance to the workforce metrics team. A follow-up is scheduled for each team member thirty days after the seminar to identify and resolve any additional issues that might arise. Finally, specialized consultation is made available for those who need it.

USING WORKFORCE METRICS

In this chapter, we have made the point that managing the strategy execution process with workforce metrics requires careful consideration of a series of communication and learning objectives. We've shown examples of how these processes can create value in organizations as dissimilar as Cardinal Health, Dell, IBM, LEGO, Prudential, and Verizon. Finally, we have argued that effective use of workforce metrics to drive strategy will require a new set of competencies and capabilities from the workforce, and that targeted training opportunities will be necessary to make the most of these new metrics. In chapter 9 we synthesize some of the key learnings for HR executives and managers hoping to drive strategy execution with workforce metrics.

9

THE END PRODUCT

I N CHAPTER 1 we offered a very simple premise for this
book: Of all the factors affecting firm performance that
CEOs and senior executives can directly influence, workforce success—or the extent to which a firm can generate a workforce
with the culture, mind-set, competencies, and strategic behaviors
needed to execute its strategy—is the both the most important and
most underutilized asset in many businesses. As a consequence, most
firms have the potential to considerably improve the effectiveness of
their strategy execution and subsequently firm performance, and the
management lever offering the greatest return is improved workforce
success. This is the good news. The bad news is that there is very little
low-hanging fruit. If it were easy to diagnose and implement these
changes, they would have already happened in most organizations. In
the subsequent chapters, we developed a solution to this challenge
based on a new perspective on the role of the workforce in strategy
execution, a new approach to measuring workforce success, and a new
process for implementing workforce strategies.

This chapter closes the loop. It provides an integrative perspective
on these challenges by highlighting the defining characteristics of
organizations that have successfully met them. Earlier chapters have
provided the rationale and explanation for our approach to managing
workforce success. This chapter highlights the key features of the

"end product." In addition to providing a summary statement of the managerial implications of the previous chapters, we encourage readers to use this chapter as a diagnostic tool. For managers who are in the process of implementing all or part of the approach we describe, this chapter will provide a checklist to gauge their progress. Alternatively, there are many managers who are just starting to reassess how their workforce strategy (or the lack of one) can be a more effective contributor to strategy execution. For them it's not just a question of "how to get from here to there," but more simply, Where do we stand at the moment and what does "there" look like? For those managers, this chapter can be used as a quick diagnostic of how far they have to go and where the areas of emphasis need to be.

THE RIGHT PERSPECTIVE

A key premise of this book has been that senior managers need to adopt a new perspective on the strategic potential of their workforce strategies. This includes the CEO, senior executives, line managers, and the HR professionals in a position to drive strategy execution. This new perspective means new behaviors, new performance expectations, and new ways of managing strategy execution and the workforce. Organizations that have successfully adopted this new perspective on workforce strategy will have six distinguishing characteristics.

1. The CEO expects senior executives, line managers, and the HR leadership team to be able to explain the influence of workforce success on successful strategy execution.

There are several important implications for organizations that score highly on this attribute. First, it means that the CEO "gets it." While there will always be an emphasis on bottom-line financials in for-profit firms, in these organizations the CEO understands the role of workforce success as a leading indicator of financial performance and expects others to have the same understanding. The CEO understands that the workforce is more than a cost to be minimized and how, if managed correctly, workforce success can be a source of competitive advantage.

Second, this is more than a "hobby horse" for the CEO, and workforce success is a routine component of any discussions of strategy execution. The CEO expects senior executives, line managers, and the HR leadership team to be able to explain how workforce success is or is not contributing to effective strategy execution in their respective areas of the business. This discussion does not focus exclusively on labor costs, head-count, and budget variance. For some firms, adopting this new perspective may be a prerequisite for the development of a fully operational workforce measurement system. Nevertheless, line managers and business leaders can explain how workforce success is influencing strategy execution, even in the absence of measures that fully support that analysis.

This new perspective is also built on a solid analytical foundation. The CEO, senior executives, and senior HR professionals have engaged in a systematic process that articulates the system of strategy drivers that define successful strategy execution. Whether this process is a more formal strategy map, as described by Kaplan and Norton, or a more informal process, there is a common understanding about what drives successful strategy execution and where workforce success fits and doesn't fit in the process of executing strategy.[1] As a result, there is a clear line of sight between all dimensions of workforce success and strategic business outcomes. Conversations between the CEO and senior executives, as well as conversations between senior HR professionals and senior executives, reflect that common perspective.

2. The CEO expects to see measures of workforce success and holds senior executives accountable for these performance measures.

Even where measures are not available, the right perspective should mean that conversations among the CEO, senior executives, line managers, and the HR leadership team reflect a strategic perspective on workforce success. However, at some point, performance measures will be introduced into those conversations, and sooner rather than later. Specifically, the CEO should expect to see measures of workforce success provided as part of routine discussions about progress in strategy execution. As importantly, the CEO will hold senior line managers accountable for the management of workforce success and expect to see measures that reflect that dimension of their performance.

While having the CEO hold senior executives accountable for workforce success is perhaps the threshold indicator of success, this same perspective should cascade down to how line managers run their businesses. When line managers understand this new perspective on workforce strategies, the Workforce Scorecard will be used as a primary business tool for executing their piece of the firm's overall strategy. Line managers will routinely look to the execution of their workforce strategy as an explanation and solution to their business problems. For example, line managers will know which of their subordinates are in "A" positions and which of these are "A" players or have "A" potential. Both line managers and HR professionals will expect to spend a disproportionate amount of time and resources developing and rewarding "A" players in "A" positions. Likewise, the culture will legitimize as appropriate the exiting of "C" players, and in many cases the "C" players will see the writing on the wall and leave on their own. Line managers will be held accountable on both of these dimensions.

3. The CEO and senior executives understand why a differentiated *workforce strategy is essential for effective strategy execution, how it is implemented, and how it is measured.*

When the CEO and senior executives have the right perspective on workforce success, they will understand the importance of a differentiated workforce strategy. This doesn't mean that every firm will differentiate its strategy in the same way, but it does mean that the extent of differentiation will be systematically considered as a strategic decision. Firms with this perspective will not tend to rely heavily on employee "feel-good" platitudes or employer-of-choice strategies that have only the most tenuous relationship to the execution of the firm's business strategy. They understand that *strategic* is not synonymous with corporatewide and lowest-common-denominator initiatives that affect all employees equally.

CEOs and senior executives with the right perspective understand that workforce strategy has both a core and a customized dimension. The core dimension is that part of the workforce strategy that has a significant influence on most or all of the strategy drivers in the organization. An example might be leadership development with a strong rotational dimension. The focus is on a broad experience, not just on the unique business demands of the particular assignment. You might also find more emphasis on the core dimension of the workforce strategies in organizations that rely on acquisitions and are attempting to integrate those different businesses under one brand.

Again, the key attribute of firms with the right perspective on firm success is not what is in the core and what is customized; it's that this decision was informed by the larger strategy execution requirements of the organization. What you won't find in firms with the right perspective is an undifferentiated workforce strategy. These undifferentiated strategies will tend to reflect a popular people strategy or best practice in the industry, but have little direct relevance to the successful execution of the firm's strategy. In contrast, the organization with a carefully developed workforce strategy will have customized those elements, as necessary, to meet the unique demands of particular strategy drivers. This takes a lot more effort than a one-size-fits-all strategy, but the results are well worth it.

Finally, a differentiated workforce strategy will be reflected in a clear recognition that some jobs are more strategically relevant than others and that a disproportionate investment will be made in the workforce in those positions. The disproportionate investment will come not only in the form of financial resources, but in the time and energy of line managers and HR professionals. The result is a high-performance culture where low performance isn't tolerated, and those who don't perform know who they are and often simply leave on their own.

4. Senior executives and line managers understand the difference between workforce success that drives strategic performance and HR services.

In organizations where senior executives and line managers understand the strategic role of workforce success, they take a different perspective on the activities of the HR function. Line managers in these firms do not subscribe to just the traditional client/service support role for the HR function. They see the opportunities, and want more of a partnership with HR leaders. There is a clear demarcation between what HR does to support workforce success and what HR does in the way of traditional operational support services. While a part of the HR function may continue in the "service" business model, these support services will have no clear line of sight to strategy execution and will be evaluated largely as a cost center. In this new perspective, line managers not only expect something more, they demand something different.

Senior executives and line managers who have adopted this new perspective will first and foremost expect that the HR management systems that attract, hire, develop, and reward talent will be consistent with, rather than in conflict, the firm's workforce strategy. The various elements of this HR management system will reinforce one another based on clearly identified strategy drivers that define effective strategy execution. Most of the energy and resources devoted to the line manager–HR professional relationship will focus on the strategic impact of this HR management system.

5. Senior executives, line managers and senior HR professionals have shared (though not necessarily equal) accountability for workforce success and strategic performance drivers.

Companies that have genuinely integrated workforce strategy as a key driver of strategy execution do more than simply offer slogans such as "People are our most important asset" while leaving traditional reporting relationships and performance management practices intact. This new perspective reflects an understanding that workforce success, properly managed, is an intangible asset. This asset value has to be managed with the same attention as other valuable assets in the organization. Because this asset value is directly proportional to the relationship between workforce success and the performance of strategy drivers, both line managers and HR professionals need to be held accountable for developing and maintaining the value of that relationship. That is, managers place relatively greater emphasis on the value-creating component of workforce success that on cost control.

Traditionally, line managers have been held accountable for business outcomes, but not workforce success. HR professionals have been held accountable for HR efficiency or activities, but not business outcomes. Exploiting the full asset value of a workforce strategy requires a new relationship between HR professionals and line managers, much as in a joint venture. This shared responsibility in turn requires a commensurate change in accountability. In effect, line manager accountability moves down the value chain, while HR professional accountability needs to move up.

The relative distribution of that accountability is negotiable and could vary within the firm. But it needs to be explicitly acknowledged and not treated as a work-around under traditional reporting relationships. One tendency to be avoided is to limit HR's accountability to HR activities. As described in chapter 7, we recommend that HR professionals have some "skin in the game" around business outcomes that are "workforce" intensive. In other words, for those strategy drivers where success is heavily dependent on workforce performance, the HR professional should have some "bottom line" accountability. This matters because performance contracts, whether explicit or implicit, are necessarily incomplete. This new perspective requires that HR professionals always be looking farther up the value chain—beyond the bounds of the HR function—toward successful strategy execution. Executing the workforce strategy should be their immediate priority; HR professionals should be motivated to make the changes and improvements that will lead to more effective execution of the larger strategy.

6. The role of HR professionals reflects their understanding of how workforce success drives strategic business outcomes.

This new perspective has a dramatic effect on the role of *some* HR professionals. We don't expect that all HR administrative functions will disappear, but there will be a new and recognized role for the HR professional whose primary task is to drive the workforce dimension of the firm's strategy. This new role is premised on a clear line of sight between workforce success and successful business performance. These new HR professionals are not employee relations specialists, they are strategy managers. This new bridge role requires more business acumen and analytical skills than the traditional HR professional would need, but also more skill at diagnosing the workforce dimensions of business problems than would be expected of line managers.

This new role also reflects the kinds of problems that HR professionals and line managers discuss and how they go about analyzing those problems. In organizations where line managers and HR professionals understand this new perspective, you will find much more systematic workforce analysis as the basis for solving business problems. Much more effort and attention are given to identifying root causes of workforce problems, and discussions between HR professionals and line managers enable them to analyze these problems in terms of leading and lagging indicators. Recognizing the leading quality of the workforce strategy means that business problems are anticipated on the basis of workforce issues that ultimately drive those business problems. IBM's workforce strategy and metrics "czar," Garrett Walker, states:

> *At IBM both line and HR managers often tend to focus on the short-term and monthly business metrics and performance. This makes us very good at tactics, but also limits our strategic focus on what actions we should be considering that build employee capability for future growth. Balancing the short-term performance requirements for revenue/profit/productivity/cost with the required longer term workforce investments in support of future growth opportunities is critical. The right workforce metrics reinforce the need for both, and help to highlight the value of workforce investments which will provide bottom-line impacts in future periods. It is imperative that line executives understand the workforce implications of investment decisions and the Workforce Scorecard provides that insight.* [2]

THE RIGHT MEASURES

A second premise of this book is that a new perspective on workforce strategy is not enough. Measures matter, both as a guide to management and as a basis of performance management. The Workforce Scorecard outlines not only a new kind of workforce measure but also a new role for these measures in the strategy execution process. Organizations that have successfully adopted this new approach to workforce measurement will be distinguished by eight key attributes.

1. Senior managers focus on a small number of workforce measures, and everyone understands why they are important.

One of the most important characteristics of organizations that have elevated workforce success to a strategic consideration is that when the CEO and senior executive team are presented with "strategic" workforce measures, they understand what they are looking at and why they are looking at them. The organization has a "vital few" measures that are the focus of strategic workforce decision making. Managers in these firms realize that data are not information. You won't see HR professionals and line managers poring over six inches of printouts every quarter trying to figure out which of the results are important and which aren't. Line managers and HR professionals already know which measures are important. Instead, time and energy are productively focused on what management changes are required given those measurement results.

Having a shared understanding of why those few measures are strategically relevant is equally important. It's not uncommon to find organizations that have a single "people" measure that is held up as equally important as measures of customer satisfaction and financial results. Perhaps the people measure is the result of an attitude survey or other measure of employee satisfaction. The organization has the "few" right, but they forgot the "vital" part. The problem is that no one can describe the clear business logic that links that measure to customer satisfaction or financial success. In other organizations, turnover and HR efficiency might be the focal measures. But all too often these are the same firms where you find senior HR professionals making presentations to the CEO and the senior executive team, describing the many variations and trends in workforce turnover, and getting questions like "What does this mean?" or "Why is this important?" In short, doing it right means limiting the number of workforce measures *and* having measures that both line managers and HR professionals agree are strategically relevant. Again, IBM's Garrett Walker states:

I believe that we have raised the level of visibility for workforce metrics and are in the process of fully integrating them into the business and management systems. In 2004, we identified a set of top tier metrics that reflect and integrated view of business strategic objectives, aligned with supporting workforce priorities and programs. This has resulted in a streamlined limited set metrics organized into a workforce scorecard: Randy MacDonald [the SVPHR] is able to communicate to the top set of business leaders a view of our workforce metrics with both a long-term view of the desired state of our workforce and also a view of the short-term performance in terms of progress towards the longer term targets.[3]

*2. There is no gap between what is measured and what
is managed.*

We've said that in the context of strategic performance measurement, measures are answers to questions. This is especially true in the case of workforce measures because the line of sight between workforce success and business success is usually indirect. In firms that do not take this perspective on measurement, managers will either ignore workforce measures because they are irrelevant, or make misguided workforce decisions because they are under the impression that these measures are relevant to questions of strategy execution, when in fact they aren't. In the latter case, the observation that what gets measured, gets managed is a cautionary one.

There is usually one important indication that managers believe that workforce measures closely map the important business decisions involved in the strategy execution process. In firms that have narrowed the gaps between measures and management decision making, these measures will play an important role in the performance reviews of line managers and HR professionals, as we described in chapter 6 and 7. The firms believe in the strategic importance of the underlying business processes captured by those measures, and as a result hold managers accountable for their performance in those areas. Similarly, because these measures are leading indicators of financial performance, managers are rewarded for strong performance on these dimensions, even in those years when financial performance may be below target.

*3. The firm's strategic workforce measures are based on
its unique strategic requirements rather than available
external benchmarks.*

In firms with the right perspective on workforce strategy, the key workforce measures have been developed in-house. They are not taken from a list of Ten Best Measures or copied from an industry competitor. HR professionals do not have to "sell" line managers on the value of a measure by demonstrating that other firms in the industry use this measure. This is not a case of myopic decision making and "not invented here." Line managers understand that the strategic role of a workforce strategy is largely dependent on the firm-specific practices used to execute the firm's larger strategy.

In these firms there is an understanding of what constitutes a best practice in the area of workforce measurement. Too many managers think that the best practice is the measure, when in fact the best practice is the *process* that develops the measure. This misunderstanding is one of the biggest barriers to developing effective workforce measures. Firms with the right perspective on measurement will have developed their own measures because they realize that these measures are the result of an analytical process that is necessarily firm specific. The analytical process could be the same in two different firms, but unless those two firms execute the same strategies in exactly the same way, we wouldn't expect them to develop the same strategic workforce measures. By contrast, managers and particularly HR professionals who rely on external benchmarks to evaluate HR or workforce performance are inherently focusing on lowest-common-denominator efficiency and cost-based measures, which bear little or no relation to the *strategic* imperatives of most firms.

4. The workforce measures managers focus on today are much different from the ones they focused on five years ago.

One of the most telling indicators of whether an organization has developed appropriate workforce measures is the extent to which it relies on legacy measures. The new perspective we describe implies an entirely new role for and valuation of workforce success and consequently new performance metrics for line managers and HR professionals. This measurement revolution, while gaining momentum, is still in its early stages. There is often more smoke than fire. One of the surest ways to determine whether a firm really understands this new perspective and "gets it" is to ask what percentage of its key workforce measures were being used five years ago. The answer should be very few.

This is a subtle point because in HR one of the first steps down the road toward better workforce measurement is often a step backward. Rather than develop genuinely new measures that answer important strategic questions, HR managers make the mistake of reformulating legacy measures as "strategic" measures. We call this "HR alchemy." Traditional accounting, cost, and efficiency measures are combined into new measures, given labels like "human capital value added," and this is considered progress. It is old wine in new bottles.

Legacy measures are hard to abandon because they often reflect a historical record with implicit benchmarks indicating change over time. But this misses the point. Those measures rarely capture anything of strategic significance in terms of workforce success, so these historical changes—whether they look like progress or failure—really matter very little. To repeat, these legacy measures aren't an answer to an important question, so there is no need to keep giving the answer.

5. The measurement process recognizes that the relationship *between workforce success and business outcomes is the key factor in determining the value of a workforce measure.*

Managers routinely think in terms of cause and effect, but when it comes to workforce measures, there is traditionally an emphasis on measurement levels. For example, the rate of turnover increased from 6 percent in a particular job category to 8 percent. At that point there is usually speculation about what this change means for certain business outcomes. In firms with the right perspective on workforce measurement, the process is reversed. In these firms the measures are selected *based on* the expected *relationship* between those workforce drivers (turnover perhaps) and specific business outcomes. The value of the workforce measure, and in fact the use of the measure, is premised on an initial diagnosis that workforce success reflects a narrow set of valued business outcomes. For example, in firms with the right perspective on workforce measurement, there may be three dimensions of workforce success that are thought to influence performance on a particular strategy driver or business outcome. When those three dimensions of workforce success are measured, there is no speculation about what might be the business significance of those measurement levels. That discussion, which focuses on relationships, has already taken place. IBM's Garrett Walker comments:

> *Our measurement process and the Workforce Scorecard serves as a forward thinking tool that has the metrics that provide management with actionable insight to drive greater workforce performance. For example, if an emerging high-growth business opportunity is not receiving the right number of skilled resources to capitalize on the opportunity, management will see that reflected in the metrics and take action to rebalance resources to that critical business need.*[4]

What might be a matter of some discussion, and speculation, is the *magnitude* of the relationship. The second way in which relationships are integrated into the measurement process is to move beyond hypothetical relationships to empirical relationships. This is where you find firms that are at the leading edge of workforce measurement. For some or all key workforce measures, managers can make statements like "A 10 percent decrease in 'employee strategic focus' is a problem because it will reduce customer wallet share by 2 percent within the next year." Or, "The 2 percent increase in voluntary turnover in the sales force needs to be monitored, but it takes at least a 5 percent increase to create a meaningful change in repeat sales." In some respects this is the most difficult challenge in developing a comprehensive workforce measurement system, but it can also yield the greatest rewards. Once an organization begins to establish these kinds of relationships between measures of workforce performance and valued business outcomes, line managers in particular bring new enthusiasm and focus to workforce strategy issues.

One of earliest and comprehensive examples of estimating quantitative relationships between workforce measures and business outcomes was the experience at Sears in the1990s.[5] Under the leadership of Tony Rucci and Steve Kirn, Sears first developed the hypothesis that in order to grow revenues, Sears had to be a "compelling" place to shop, which would only happen if Sears was a "compelling" place to work. This business model implied a set of relationships through which employee attitudes about work drive the quality of the shopping experience, which in turn drives revenues. That hypothetical model was borne out by a series of quantitative estimates that linked workforce measures to customer attitudes and ultimately revenue changes.

A more recent example is the experience at Allstate Insurance Company. For years HR at Allstate had collected traditional workforce measures on turnover, hiring, and so on, but there was no clear line of sight between these measures and important business outcomes. Like many other companies, Allstate has recently devoted more attention to leadership competencies and developed a Leadership Index based on those attributes. Most firms would stop there. Led by Joan Crockett, Senior Vice President, Human Resources, and Karleen Zuzich, Assistant Vice President, Human Resources, Allstate took the next important step. The company was able to establish a quantitative relationship between ratings on the Leadership Index and various customer claim measures, like claim satisfaction and policy renewals. Now the Leadership Index took on a much more important role, and the relationship between HR and claims leadership reflected that new perspective.

6. The organization collects measures that capture differential investments in "A" positions and "A" players.

A key indicator of a differentiated workforce strategy is whether an organization makes differential investments in its strategic or "A" positions, and similarly in its "A" players in those positions. Firms that do this well track those investments. Workforce success measures are categorized by "A" positions and "A" players, in addition to more traditional demographic categories. Exit rates for "C" players are calculated. Recruiting channels and hiring procedures are analyzed for their yield of "A" players. Compensation systems and bonus-pool allocations are evaluated for the distributions to "A," "B," and "C" players. HR professionals and line managers are held accountable for implementing this strategy of differential investment, and performance reviews include a discussion of these issues.

While we agree with the observation that what gets measured, gets managed, some firms have been very successful at implementing a policy of disproportionate investments without elaborate measurement systems. The perspective is embedded in the culture from the CEO on down, and it is not a question of using the measurement system to drive change. For example, we know of a *Fortune* 500 company where the CEO spends a disproportionate amount of time on hiring and leadership development decisions for senior managers in "A" positions. In the last two years, a quarter of this group has left the firm, more than half of these at the invitation of the company. We consider this type of experience the exception rather than the rule, but it's worth remembering if you are fortunate enough to work in such an organization.

7. HR routinely focuses on and measures the alignment or fit between the HR management system and strategic business outcomes of importance to line managers.

Increasing differentiation in the workforce strategy means that the fit and alignment between the HR management system and the firm's strategy drivers will be more important. Industrywide best practices are not enough. In some cases, good fit can be an enterprisewide initiative, such as executive development. High-potential leaders are rotated through various assignments that focus on different aspects of the firm's overall strategy execution process. Other aspects of HR fit, however, may be more narrowly focused on a specific strategy driver. An example would be the selection, development, and compensation practices for the sales workforce in a pharmaceutical company.

Firms that have the right perspective will routinely be asking questions about how the whole HR management system fits together to reinforce the firm's strategy. Unfortunately, strategic alignment is not just a one-time event. Practices can evolve, or there is pressure to commoditize them for efficiency reasons, and alignment can suffer. While a measure of fit or alignment is necessarily a subjective assessment, it should be monitored on a regular basis. One simple way to do this is to include questions on alignment in employee surveys (on a quarterly or annual basis) and then compare those results with how the HR professionals, and perhaps line managers, answer those same questions.

8. The organization has HR professionals with the technical expertise necessary to develop appropriate measures and explain the analysis to business leaders.

HR professionals have not traditionally been required to have an in-depth knowledge of measurement. The practice of measurement was typically limited to the development or approval of items on an employee survey or translating accounting-based measures into HR efficiency metrics. Sometimes it simply meant choosing among measurement "vendors." Strategic performance measurement requires a new set of competencies. The emphasis on relationships rather than levels means not only that HR professionals need to think in terms of causal effects and business outcomes outside of the HR function, but also that they must have some understanding of the how, the why, and the limitations of estimating those relationships.

This is a critical new competency for the organization. Either the organization is going to hire in-house talent (like Allstate or Bristol-Meyers Squibb) with these skills, or it is going to bring in a consultant (like Cardinal Health) with strong econometric and psychometric skills. But in either case, senior HR professionals have the analytical literacy to make use of this new competency. HR professionals will understand why these measurement techniques are important and where they have limitations, so they can have an informed conversation with line managers.

An example of a firm that excels in this domain is Bristol-Myers Squibb (BMS). Perhaps because of the nature of their business (science-based discovery), managers at BMS are encouraged to collect data and test the "theory of the case" for important workforce management initiatives. However, data are not the only answer to solving the challenges associated with designing and implementing a workforce scorecard. Peter Fasolo, VP of Leadership Development and Organizational Effectiveness at BMS, says:

> *Analytics and research methodology move the profession toward having a fact-based discussion about the workforce and away from discussions based on "I think" and "I feel." Whatever you measure inside the organization needs to be directly linked to the strategy of the enterprise. If you don't have a target you shouldn't measure it. And if you measure it, you also need to put resources against the goal to help improve it. For example, at BMS a team of I/O psychologists trained in statistics and validation work assist in the design, collection, and interpretation of workforce data. Finally, HR can't be the sole agent or owner of the workforce metrics—there needs to be an equal partnership with line leaders. The trap is that the profession becomes the exclusive owner of the metrics—the line executive team must drive the changes in partnership with the human resources function. Metrics proficiencies can be outsourced as well, if they are not truly strategic.*[6]

There is an important lesson here that is often lost on HR professionals when they first confront the measurement challenge. To repeat what we said earlier, the best practice in measurement is the process, not the measure itself. Don't ask others, What measures do you use? Instead ask, How did you develop your measures? A simple example is the experience at Cardinal Health. Tony Rucci, the chief administrative officer, understands workforce measurement. He knew that leadership was an important driver of workforce success, but needed a measure. Cardinal Health didn't look for a list of top-ten leadership measures. Instead, it developed its own measure, following sound measurement principles, based on the specific business demands at Cardinal Health. More importantly, the firm then validated it against subsequent ratings of leadership potential. The result was a workforce measure that had a demonstrated relationship to the specific strategic demands of Cardinal Health. Moreover, the senior executive team knew that this measure was developed for its special circumstances, and focused more on managing with the measure instead of questioning its validity.

THE RIGHT EXECUTION

Finally, firms not only have the right perspective and the right measures, they also execute the measurement process differently. In these firms, you expect to see different measures, but you should also expect to see a much different organization around those measures. Measurement is not treated as an independent activity. It actually changes the way line managers and HR professionals approach the execution of the overall workforce strategy. Firms that do it right will have six characteristics:

1. HR professionals spend less time on employee performance problems than they did five years ago.

Ideally, this is both a proportional and an absolute change in the time spent on employee performance problems. First, there should simply be fewer performance problems. Both HR and line managers devote more time and energy to separating "A" and "C" players at the point of hire. Alternatively, if the firm prefers to make the decision based on actual performance, there is a systematic culling process, an up-or-out decision, within a reasonable period. Line managers, who must make this decision, understand it. HR professionals understand it. And most importantly, the new hires understand it. Applicants who prefer a less rigorous evaluation system will withdraw and look for work elsewhere.

This example highlights two other reasons why HR professionals will spend less time on performance problems. First, line managers will spend more time on them, or at least more time making sure they don't have to be handled by HR. Line managers will be held accountable for developing the "A" players and exiting the "C" players. Employees become performance problems primarily when "C" players are allowed to stay with an organization beyond the point that is justified by their performance. Line managers must make those performance evaluations and remove those employees before they become a problem. In fact, they won't even apply.

Second, this emphasis on performance differentiation will ultimately develop a high-performance culture that will improve the workforce self-selection. As performance differentiations become a more salient and central feature of the workforce strategy, not only will the pool of *potential* employees begin to change, but the composition of voluntary turnover will also begin to change. "C" players will increasingly see the writing on the wall and choose to leave before they become a problem.

As a result, HR professionals will have more time for the strategic dimension of their job. We realize that as organizations become leaner, few managers feel they have room for additional responsibilities. Indeed, one of the greatest challenges to implementing a more strategic perspective in many HR functions is that HR professionals have been expected to continue to be administrative experts and put out the same employee relations fires while at the same time adding these new strategic activities. It can't be done. When the firm is managing the workforce strategy more appropriately, however, it means a reallocation of effort, not an increase in effort for HR professionals.

2. The relationship between workforce success and strategy implementation defines the ROI of new HR initiatives.

Just as line managers tend to manage what gets measured, the same is true for HR professionals. Traditionally, HR professionals were HR-function focused. The emphasis was first on the initiative and secondarily on the business implications of those initiatives. It's not that HR professionals didn't think these initiatives were good for the company; it's just that the business case was a very general one and not carefully based on the strategy drivers in their own organization.

In organizations with the right perspective on workforce strategy, that workforce strategy is executed in part by HR initiatives that are strategically focused. Not all HR initiatives will rise to this level of importance. Some will simply improve HR operational efficiency. There should, however, be a disproportionate investment in strategic rather than operational initiatives, simply because the strategic initiatives have a greater payoff. HR initiatives can be evaluated like any other investment, based on their rate of return, rather than just their cost. The key point here is not that a hard-and-fast prospective ROI number is easily calculated for every potential initiative, but rather that the potential "return" is defined more broadly than is traditionally the case in HR. For efficiency-based HR functions and initiatives, the return is limited to some form of cost savings (denominator management). The return improves because costs fall. For strategically focused HR functions, the focus is on improved business outcomes, based on a clear line of sight to the firm's strategy drivers. The return improves because the numerator increases. Conversations within HR focus on causal relations between HR initiatives and business solutions (numerator management), not HR solutions.

IBM is a good example where line managers and HR are focusing on opportunities to improve workforce productivity through better numerator management (value creation rather than cost reduction). They realize they can't "shrink to greatness . . . can't cut your way to success" by simply controlling labor costs, but instead are aggressively pursuing several initiatives that will increase workforce value creation. For example, one unit may have several hundred million dollars in sales revenue turn on whether another unit has a properly trained sales force. Providing strategically targeted and timely skill development to support this new growth is a strategic workforce initiative.

More broadly IBM is considering several "game-changing" actions with respect to how they manage and value the workforce. In particularly they are looking at new ways to measure workforce value and how to optimize that value. This approach will attempt to link workforce value design much more closely to the offerings and solutions they support, allowing IBM to further differentiate itself in the marketplace. For example, IBM has completely reshaped the workforce in its PC division, primarily in response to competitive pressure and rapid commoditization in this particular industry. In doing so, IBM has been able to move non-core functions such as production and testing to suppliers. The result is a streamlined, highly focused team of research, design, and marketing professionals.

3. Creating a shared mind-set is not taken for granted.

Organizations that have successfully leveraged workforce strategy as a key driver in the execution of their enterprise strategy will have successfully created a shared mind-set. There is a clear understanding of what needs to be done to execute the firm's strategy, the role of the workforce strategy, and the role of measurement in this process. This understanding extends beyond the senior executive team and includes the larger workforce as well. Employee survey questions that tap "employee strategic focus" show that employees understand how their job fits in the larger execution of the firm's strategy.

These organizations have taken concrete initiatives to build this shared mind-set and strategic literacy. This is more than the CEO giving a videoconference and explaining the big picture. Employee understanding is not taken for granted. It is monitored and measured. Special attention is given not only to explaining the larger strategy, but more importantly to explaining how individual roles and responsibilities drive strategy execution. Learning Map and small group sessions are commonly used to facilitate this learning process.

4. The HR function has a staffing structure that effectively balances the tension between being a strategic partner and delivering efficient and effective HR services.

Using the workforce strategy as a strategic lever requires changes from the CEO, senior executives, line managers, and the HR function. This means the HR function will necessarily rethink its own organizational structure. Taking on a shared responsibility for workforce success creates an inherent structural tension if the HR function is organized primarily as a client/service organization. The strategic role requires different performance measures, different perspectives on the alignment of the HR management system, and a different relationship with line managers.

Restructuring HR would typically be one of the last pieces of the puzzle. Initially, organizations will simply attempt to expand certain individual roles within the existing structure. The magnitude of the challenge relative to the available time and resources available in such a part-time role quickly make this initial phase untenable. A common approach to expanding the measurement capability of the firm is the development of niche specialties within Centers of Excellence. Organizations that have moved well along the measurement learning curve often create a group of measurement specialists (e.g., Sun Microsystems' HR Lab) who understand the more technical aspects of the measurement challenge, yet can translate those technical issues into clear implications for decision makers. Ultimately, the organization will find that the strategic relationship between line managers and HR professionals has to be staffed by HR professionals whose responsibility is largely independent of the service delivery role. IBM's Garrett Walker notes:

HR at IBM has always been good at communicating the workforce contributions to the business, that is not new. However the communication has been more subjective/qualitative or anecdotal and was not the basis for setting priorities for major business investments or asset allocation. In our current highly competitive resource- and expense-constrained environment where excellence in innovation, growth, revenue, cost, and productivity is a competitive advantage, the Workforce Scorecard clarifies the anecdotal conversations, it tells us if we have the right HR priorities and if the programs/initiatives are delivering to the business.[7]

5. Strategic workforce measures are "owned" and coordinated by a single individual or task force.

Organizations that recognize the increasing importance of intangibles also realize that managing those intangibles is inherently more difficult because the measurement of those intangibles is inherently more difficult. What sets these firms apart is that their response to the *difficulty* of the challenge is commensurate with the *importance* of the challenge. One of the most important decisions a firm will make with respect to strategic workforce measurement is giving ownership of these measures to an individual or a task force that has the knowledge, energy, and resources to exploit the full value of these new measurement systems.

Who owns these measures and the resources they have to fully implement this new perspective on measurement is an important signal that workforce measurement is a strategic imperative. Unlike many traditional measures of financial success, workforce measures are overwhelmingly leading indicators. They are not end results, and only have value to the extent that they drive other intermediate outcomes, which in turn drive financial success. This implies that the most effective measurement organization for exploiting the value of workforce measures is one that includes all of the dimensions of the strategic value chain. This means that those responsible for financial, marketing, operations, and workforce measures should spend as much, or more, time communicating among themselves as they do communicating with their respective functional managers. Measurement is managed as a strategic capability instead of an operational responsibility.

6. Senior executives, line managers, and HR professionals consider the results of the measurement system worth the implementation effort.

Implementing a new workforce measurement system is not easy. It challenges the traditional thinking about the role of the workforce, and calls for new responsibilities and accountabilities for line managers and HR professionals. But at the end of the day, line managers and HR professionals will say that the return was worth the effort. Not because the organization adopted a superficial add-on that required little time and energy, but rather that in spite of the additional effort and resources, the benefits are apparent and they wouldn't want to go back to the "old way." Line managers in particular don't consider the new measurement system another bit of organizational "overhead" that distracts them from their real job. Instead, line managers understand how their "real" job has been redefined and that these measures help them perform more effectively. This in turn changes the dynamics of the relationship between line managers and HR professionals and dramatically reallocates their conversations toward strategic rather than operational and service issues.

A COMPREHENSIVE DIAGNOSTIC

We introduced this chapter as an integrative diagnostic device designed to help you see the big picture in your organization. Based largely on our own professional observation of companies that have moved along this learning curve, it provides a developmental checklist to keep in mind as you attempt to implement these ideas. Any single organization might not have all of these attributes, yet it can successfully develop an effective workforce strategy. Nevertheless, in our judgment it's a case of "the more the better." Each of these attributes reflects a building block in the foundation of a successful workforce strategy. It is less important how that foundation is created and more important that it be solid and designed to do what is required to execute your firm's strategy.

Table 9-1 summarizes these attributes in a comprehensive diagnostic metric that you can use to rate your own organization.

TABLE 9-1

The Capability to Manage and Measure the Human Capital Dimension of Strategy Execution: A Diagnostic Tool

Instructions: Provide an evaluation for each question using the following format: 1 = not at all, 3 = to a modest extent, 5 = to a great extent.

The Right Perspective

_____ 1. The CEO expects senior executives, line managers, and the HR leadership team to be able to explain the influence of workforce success on successful strategy execution.

_____ 2. The CEO expects to see measures of workforce success and holds senior executives accountable for these performance measures.

_____ 3. The CEO and senior executives understand why a *differentiated* workforce strategy is essential for effective strategy execution, and how it is implemented and measured.

_____ 4. Senior executives and line managers understand the difference between workforce success that drives strategic performance and HR services.

_____ 5. Senior executives, line managers, and senior HR professionals have shared (though not necessarily equal) accountability for workforce success and strategic performance drivers.

_____ 6. The role of HR professionals reflects their understanding of how workforce success drives strategic business outcomes.

The Right Measures

_____ 7. Senior executives focus on a small number of workforce measures, and everyone understands why they are important.

_____ 8. There is no gap between what is measured and what is managed.

_____ 9. The firm's strategic workforce measures are based on its unique strategic requirements rather than available external benchmarks.

_____ 10. The workforce measures managers focus on today are much different from the ones they focused on five years ago.

_____ 11. The measurement process recognizes that the *relationship* between workforce success and business outcomes is the key factor in determining the value of a workforce measure.

_____ 12. The organization collects measures that capture differential investments in "A" positions and "A" players.

_____ 13. HR routinely focuses on and measures the alignment or fit between the HR management system and strategic business outcomes of importance to line managers.

_____ 14. The organization has HR professionals with the technical expertise necessary to develop appropriate measures and explain the analysis to business leaders.

The Right Execution

_____ 15. HR professionals spend less time on employee performance problems than they did five years ago.

_____ 16. The relationship between workforce success and strategy implementation defines the ROI of new HR initiatives.

_____ 17. Creating a shared mind-set is not taken for granted.

_____ 18. The HR function has a staffing structure that effectively balances the tension between being a strategic partner and delivering efficient and effective HR services.

_____ 19. Strategic workforce measures are "owned" and coordinated by a single individual or task force.

_____ 20. Senior executives, line managers, and HR professionals consider the results of the measurement system worth the implementation effort.

In closing, we hope that this book has helped to provide you with both the tools and the motivation to advance the strategy execution and workforce metrics agendas in your own organization. If your score on the diagnostic survey in table 9-1 is disappointing, we hope that this result will provide additional incentive to begin the measurement journey in earnest. If you are one of the few firms to receive a high score on this test, we hope that you will use this knowledge to help leverage and improve what you have already done. In either case, we hope that you will continue to improve the quality of strategy execution in your firm through developing the right perspective on the contribution of the workforce to firm success, the right metrics to track your progress, and the right execution strategy to ensure that managers are ready, willing, and able to use workforce metrics to drive business success.

Notes

FOREWORD

1. Larry Bossidy, Ram Charan, and Charles Burck, *Execution: The Discipline of Getting Things Done* (New York: Crown Business, 2002).

2. Dave Ulrich, "Organizational Capability as a Competitive Advantage: Human Resource Professionals as Strategic Partners," *Human Resource Planning* 10, no. 4 (1987): 169–184; Dave Ulrich and Dale Lake, *Organizational Capability: Competing from the Inside Out* (New York: Wiley, 1990); Dave Ulrich, "The Leader of the Future: Credibility × Capability," in *The Leader of the Future,* ed. Frances Hesselbein, Marshall Goldsmith, and Dick Beckhard (San Francisco: Jossey-Bass, 1996); Dave Ulrich and Norm Smallwood, "Capitalizing Your Capabilities," *Harvard Business Review* (June 2004).

3. Dave Ulrich and Norm Smallwood, *Why the Bottom Line Isn't* (New York: Wiley, 2003).

4. This formula is derived from work by Steve Kerr: effectiveness = quality * acceptance. Personal conversation with Steve Kerr.

5. Dave Ulrich and Wayne Brockbank, *The HR Value Proposition* (Boston: Harvard Business School Press, 2005).

PREFACE

1. Brian E. Becker, Mark A. Huselid, and Dave Ulrich, *The HR Scorecard: Linking People, Strategy, and Performance* (Boston: Harvard Business School Press, 2001).

CHAPTER 1

1. Here we make the distinction between benchmarking studies that focus on determining the *levels* associated with a particular variable across firms (e.g., What is the average cost per hire in three hundred firms?) and benchmarking studies that focus on the *process* associated with a single outcome in a single firm

(e.g., How does FedEx handle its distribution and supply chain logistics?). We believe that benchmarking processes may well lead to strategically valuable information and understanding, while benchmarking levels is unlikely to do so, as we describe in greater detail later in the text.

2. Robert S. Kaplan and David P. Norton, *The Strategy-Focused Organization: How Balanced Scorecard Companies Thrive in the New Business Environment* (Boston: Harvard Business School Press, 1996).

3. Brian E. Becker, Mark A. Huselid, and Dave Ulrich, *The HR Scorecard: Linking People, Strategy, and Performance* (Boston: Harvard Business School Press, 2001).

4. We use the terms *measures* and *metrics* as synonyms throughout the text.

5. Becker, Huselid, and Ulrich, *The HR Scorecard.*

6. Wayne F. Cascio, *Responsible Restructuring: Creative and Profitable Alternatives to Layoffs* (New York: Berrett-Koehler, 2002).

7. Baruch Lev, *Intangibles* (Washington, DC: Brookings Institution, 2001), 5.

8. Ibid., 9.

9. Thomas Stewart, "Real Assets, Unreal Reporting," *Fortune,* July 6, 1998, 207.

10. Clayton Christensen and Michael Raynor, *The Innovator's Solution* (Boston: Harvard Business School Press, 2003).

11. Baruch Lev and Suresh Radhakrishnan, "The Measurement of Firm Specific Human Capital," NBER working paper no. 9581.

12. Lev, *Intangibles,* 1.

13. Christopher D. Ittner and David F. Larker, "Coming Up Short on Nonfinancial Performance Measurement," *Harvard Business Review* (November 2003): 91.

14. Ibid., 90.

15. Larry Bossidy, Ram Charan, and Charles Burck, *Execution: The Discipline of Getting Things Done* (New York: Crown Business, 2002).

16. Becker and Huselid, "High Performance Work Systems and Firm Performance." See also William Joyce, Nitin Nohria, and Bruce Roberson, *What Really Works: The 4+2 Formula for Sustained Business Success* (New York: HarperBusiness, 2003).

17. B. E. Becker and M. A. Huselid, "Measuring HR's Performance? Benchmarking Is Not the Answer!" *HR Magazine* (December 2003).

18. For reviews of this literature, see James G. Combs, Angela T. Hall, and Yongmei Liu, "High Performance Work Practices and Organization Performance: A Meta-Analysis," working paper, 2004; Becker, Huselid, and Ulrich, *The HR Scorecard;* and Becker and Huselid, "High Performance Work Systems and Firm Performance."

19. See Dave Ulrich and Norm Smallwood, "Capitalizing on Capabilities," *Harvard Business Review* (June 2004), 1–8.

20. Jeffrey Pfeffer and Robert I. Sutton, *The Knowing-Doing Gap: How Smart Companies Turn Knowledge into Action* (Boston: Harvard Business School Press, 2000).

CHAPTER 2

1. Bradford D. Smart, Ph.D., *Topgrading: How Leading Companies Win by Hiring, Coaching, and Keeping the Best People* (New York: Prentice Hall Press, 1999).

2. Larry Bossidy, Ram Charan, and Charles Burck, *Execution: The Discipline of Getting Things Done* (New York: Crown Business, 2002), 95.

3. See Steve Kerr, "On the Folly of Rewarding A While Hoping for B," *Academy of Management Journal* 18 (1975): 765.

4. For a discussion of the distinctions between HR philosophy, HR policies, HR programs, HR practices, and HR processes, see R. S. Schuler, "Strategic Human Resource Management: Linking the People with the Strategic Needs of the Business," *Organizational Dynamics* (summer 1992): 18–32.

5. R. E. Miles and C. C. Snow, *Fit, Failure, and the Hall of Fame* (New York: The Free Press, 1994); Michael Porter, *Competitive Advantage: Creating and Sustaining Superior Performance* (New York: The Free Press, 1985).

6. Dave Ulrich and Dick Beatty, "From Partners to Players: Extending the HR Playing Field," *Human Resource Management* 40, no. 4 (2001): 293–307. In addition to Ulrich and Beatty's focus on aligning core strategy with workforce mind-set, other authors have explored how employee role behaviors and HR management systems will differ across core strategies. The seminal contributions in this area include Randall S. Schuler and Susan E. Jackson, "Linking Competitive Strategies with Human Resource Practices," *Academy of Management Executive* 1, no. 3 (1987): 207–220; R. S. Schuler and S. E. Jackson, "Organizational strategy and organization level as determinants of human resource management practices," *Human Resource Planning* 10, no. 3, 125–141; R. S. Schuler and S. E. Jackson, "Determinants of human resource management priorities and implications for industrial relations," *Journal of Management* 15, no. 1, (1989): 89–99; R. S. Schuler, S. E. Jackson, and J. C. Rivero, "Organizational characteristics as predictors of personnel practices," *Personnel Psychology* 42, no. 4, (1989): 727–786; and S. E. Jackson and R. S. Schuler, "Understanding human resource management in the context of organizations and their environments," *Annual Review of Psychology* 46 (1995): 237–264.

7. Michael Treacy and Fred Wiersema, *The Discipline of Market Leaders: Choose Your Customers, Narrow Your Focus, Dominate Your Market* (Boulder, CO: Perseus Publishing, 1997).

8. Robert S. Kaplan and David P. Norton, *The Strategy-Focused Organization: How Balanced Scorecard Companies Thrive in the New Business Environment* (Boston: Harvard Business School Press, 1996).

9. B. E. Becker and B. Gerhart, "Human Resources and Organizational Performance: Progress and Prospects," *Academy of Management Journal* (Special Issue: Human Resources and Organizational Performance) 39, no. 4 (1996): 779–801; B. E. Becker and M. A. Huselid, "High Performance Work Systems and Firm Performance: A Synthesis of Research and Managerial Implications," ed.

G. Ferris, *Research in Personnel and Human Resource Management* 16 (1998): 53–101; J. E. Delery and D. H. Doty, "Modes of Theorizing in Strategic Human Resource Management: Tests of Universalistic, Contingent and Configurational Performance Predictions," *Academy of Management Journal* 39, no. 4 (1996): 802–835; M. A. Huselid, "The Impact of Human Resource Management Practices on Turnover, Productivity and Corporate Financial Performance," *Academy of Management Journal* 38, no. 3 (1995): 635–672.

10. For an additional theoretical description of these differences, see B. E. Becker and M. A. Huselid, working paper, "Value Creation Through Strategy Execution: The Role of SHRM Theory and Practice" (available from the authors).

There is also a developing academic literature that explores the composition and firm-level impact of various HR management systems and subsystems. For example, in B. E. Becker and M. A. Huselid, "Human Resource Management Systems, Complementarities, and Firm Performance," (working paper, 1995, available at www.markhuselid.com), and M. A. Huselid and B. E. Becker, "The Impact of High Performance Work Systems, Implementation Effectiveness, and Alignment with Strategy on Shareholder Wealth," Academy of Management *Best Papers Proceedings* (1997): 144–148; we demonstrated the impact of several different *HR Architectures* (underlying themes or philosophies that guide the development and implementation of an HR management system) on corporate profitability and shareholder value. M. A. Huselid, "The Impact of Human Resource Management Practices on Turnover, Productivity and Corporate Financial Performance," *Academy of Management Journal* 38, no. 3 (1995): 635–672) compared how the alignment of these systems with corporate strategy versus a "best practices" approach affected firm performance in 968 firms. In B. E. Becker, and M. A. Huselid, "High Performance Work Systems and Firm Performance: A Synthesis of Research and Managerial Implications," in *Research in Personnel and Human Resource Management,* ed. G. Ferris, vol. 16 (1998): 53–101 we showed that the returns from investments in these systems were nonlinear (with the greatest returns at the lowest and highest levels of the distribution). We also showed that the returns differed for what we described as bureaucratic and non-bureaucratic work systems, across industries, across levels of capital intensity, and for managerial compensation subsystems. See also M. A. Huselid and B. E. Becker, "The Strategic Impact of High Performance Work Systems," working paper, available at <www.markhuselid.com>.

More recently, Lepak and Snell (1999) have made an important contribution to the literature by developing a model that shows how the degree of value and uniqueness of human capital interact to create four different "modes" of employment (knowledge-based, job-based, contract work, and alliances), which in turn suggest four different configurations of HR management practices (commitment-based, productivity-based, compliance-based, and collaborative-based). Lepak and Snell (2002) and Lepak, Takeuchi, and Snell (2003) have subsequently provide validity data for their model. See David P. Lepak and Scott A. Snell, "The Human Resource Architecture: Toward a Theory of Human Capital Allocation and Development," *Academy of Management Review* 24, no. 1 (1999): 31–48; David P. Lepak and Scott A. Snell, "Examining the Human Resource Architecture: The Relationships Among Human Capital, Employment, and Human Resource Configurations." *Journal of Management* 28, no. 4 (2002): 517–543.; and David P. Lepak, Riki Takeuchi, and Scott A. Snell, "Employment Flexibility and Firm Performance: Examining the Interaction Effects of Employment Mode, Environmental Dynamism, and Technological Intensity," *Journal of Management* 29, no. 5 (2003): 681–703.

11. Michael E. Porter, "What Is Strategy?" *Harvard Business Review* (November–December 1996): 61–78.

12. Ibid., 62.

13. Robert S. Kaplan and David P. Norton, *Strategy Maps: Converting Intangible Assets into Intangible Outcomes* (Boston: Harvard Business School Press, 2004).

14. For an additional theoretical description of these differences see B. E. Becker and M. A. Huselid, working paper, "Value Creation Through Strategy Execution: The Role of SHRM Theory and Practice" (available from the authors).

15. Robert Kaplan, "Using Strategic Themes to Achieve Organizational Alignment," *Balanced Scorecard Report,* reprint no. B0111A, 2001; Robert Kaplan, "Wells Fargo Online Financial Services (A)," Case 9-198-146 (Boston: Harvard Business School, 2001); Robert Kaplan, "Wells Fargo Online Financial Services (B)," Case 9-199-019 (Boston: Harvard Business School, 1998). Harvard Business School cases provide useful illustrations because they make additional contextual detail available that is beyond the scope of this book.

16. Source: Garret Walker, Director of Global Resourcing and HR Strategy at IBM. Interview with Mark Huselid, summer 2004.

17. Bradford D. Smart and Geoffrey H. Smart, "Topgrading the Organization," *Directors and Boards* 21, no. 3 (Spring 1997): 28.

18. Robert Simons and Antonio Davila, "Siebel Systems: Organizing for the Customer," Case 9-103-014 (Boston: Harvard Business School, 2002).

19. Smart, *Topgrading: How Leading Companies Win,* 34.

20. Becker, Huselid, and Ulrich, *The HR Scorecard.*

CHAPTER 3

1. Michael E. Porter, *Competitive Advantage: Creating and Sustaining Superior Performance* (New York: The Free Press, 1985).

2. C. K. Prahalad and Gary Hamel, "The Core Competence of the Corporation," *Harvard Business Review* (1990); Gary Hamel and C. K. Prahalad, *Competing for the Future* (Boston: Harvard Business School Press, 1994); C. K. Prahalad and Venkatram Ramaswamy, *The Future of Competition: Co-Creating Unique Value with Customers* (Boston: Harvard Business School Press, 2003).

3. Robert S. Kaplan and David P. Norton, *Strategy Maps: Converting Intangible Assets into Intangible Outcomes* (Boston: Harvard Business School Press,

2004); Robert S. Kaplan and David P. Norton, *The Strategy-Focused Organization: How Balanced Scorecard Companies Thrive in the New Business Environment* (Boston: Harvard Business School Press, 1996).

4. Some of the items in tables 3-1, 3-2, 3-3, and 3-4 were adapted from Brian E. Becker, Mark A. Huselid, and Dave Ulrich, *The HR Scorecard: Linking People, Strategy, and Performance* (Boston: Harvard Business School Press, 2001).

5. Peter Fasolo, interview with Mark Huselid, summer 2004.

6. Denise M. Rousseau, "Assessing organizational culture: The case for multiple methods," in *Organizational Climate and Culture,* ed. B. Schneider (San Francisco: Jossey-Bass, 1990).

7. William Joyce, Nitin Nohria, and Bruce Roberson, *What Really Works: The 4+2 Formula for Sustained Business Success* (New York: HarperBusiness, 2003).

8. Louis V. Gerstner Jr., *Who Says Elephants Can't Dance? Inside IBM's Historic Turnaround* (New York: HarperBusiness, 2002).

9. Larry Bossidy, Ram Charan, and Charles Burck, *Execution: The Discipline of Getting Things Done* (New York: Crown Business, 2002).

10. See Anthony J. Rucci, Steven P. Kirn, and Richard T. Quinn, "The Employee-Customer-Profit Chain at Sears," *Harvard Business Review* (January–February 1997): 83–97; and Steven P. Kirn, Anthony J. Rucci, Mark A. Huselid, and Brian E. Becker, "Strategic Human Resource Management at Sears," *Human Resource Management* 38, no. 4 (1999): 329–336.

11. B. E. Becker and M. A. Huselid, "High Performance Work Systems and Firm Performance: A Synthesis of Research and Managerial Implications," ed. G. Ferris, *Research in Personnel and Human Resource Management* 16 (1998): 53–101.

CHAPTER 4

1. See Brian E. Becker, Mark A. Huselid, and Dave Ulrich, *The HR Scorecard: Linking People, Strategy, and Performance* (Boston: Harvard Business School Press, 2001).

2. Ibid., 48.

3. Wayne F. Cascio, *Responsible Restructuring: Creative and Profitable Alternatives to Layoffs* (New York: Berrett-Koehler, 2002).

4. Some of the items in tables 4-2, 4-3, 4-4, and 4-7 were adapted from Brian E. Becker, Mark A. Huselid, and Dave Ulrich, *The HR Scorecard: Linking People, Strategy, and Performance* (Boston: Harvard Business School Press, 2001).

5. Interested readers should consult Peter Senge's work on systems dynamics for more information. See Peter M. Senge, *The Fifth Discipline: The Art and Science of the Learning Organization* (New York: Bantam Doubleday Dell Publishing Group, 1990), and also Peter M. Senge, Art Kleiner, Charlotte Roberts, Richard B. Ross, and Bryan J. Smith, *The Fifth Discipline Fieldbook* (New York: Currency Doubleday, 1994).

6. Deborah Barber, Mark A. Huselid, and Brian E. Becker, "Strategic Human Resource Management at Quantum," *Human Resource Management* 38 (1999): 321–328.

7. For summaries of this body of work see M. A. Huselid, "The Impact of Human Resource Management Practices on Turnover Productivity and Corporate Financial Performance," *Academy of Management Journal* 38, no. 3 (1995): 635–672; B. E. Becker and M. A. Huselid, "High Performance Work Systems and Firm Performance: A Synthesis of Research and Managerial Implications," ed. G. Ferris, *Research in Personnel and Human Resource Management* 16 (1998): 53–101; and James G. Combs, Angela T. Hall, and Yongmei Liu, "High Performance Work Practices and Organization Performance: A Meta-Analysis," working paper, 2004. Available from James G. Combs, Department of Management, College of Business, Florida State University.

8. Mark A. Huselid., S. E. Jackson, and R. S. Schuler, "Technical and Strategic Human Resource Management Effectiveness As Determinants of Firm Performance." *Academy of Management Journal* 1, no. 40 (1997): 171–188.

9. Sara Rynes, Amy Colbert, and Kenneth Brown, "HR Professionals' Beliefs About Effective Human Resource Management Practices: Correspondence Between Research and Practice," *Human Resource Management* 41 (2002): 149–174; Sara Rynes, Amy Colbert, and Kenneth Brown, "Seven Common Misconceptions About Human Resource Practices: Research Findings versus Practitioner Beliefs," *Academy of Management Executive* 16 (2002): 92–102.

10. Additional examples of the use of these metrics can be found in Becker, Huselid, and Ulrich, *The HR Scorecard,* chapter 6.

11. Rynes, Colbert, and Brown, "HR Professionals' Beliefs About Effective Human Resource Management Practices."

12. The column headings in figure 4-6 (Objective, Measure, Target, and Initiative) were adapted from the framework used in Robert S. Kaplan and David P. Norton, *The Strategy-Focused Organization: How Balanced Scorecard Companies Thrive in the New Business Environment* (Boston: Harvard Business School Press, 1996).

13. S. E. Jackson and R. S. Schuler, "Human Resource Management in the Context of Organizations and Their Environments," *Annual Review of Psychology* 46 (1995): 237–264; R. S. Schuler and S. E. Jackson, "Linking Competitive Strategies with Human Resource Practices," *Academy of Management Executive* 1, no. 3 (1987): 207–220.

CHAPTER 5

1. B. E. Becker and M. A. Huselid, "Measuring HR's Performance? Benchmarking Is Not the Answer!" *HR Magazine* (December 2003).

2. See B. E. Becker and M. A. Huselid, "High Performance Work Systems and Firm Performance: A Synthesis of Research and Managerial Implications," ed. G. Ferris, *Research in Personnel and Human Resource Management* 16 (1998): 53–101.

CHAPTER 6

1. Michael E. Porter, "From Competitive Advantage to Corporate Strategy," *Harvard Business Review* (May–June 1987); Michael Treacy and Fred Wiersema, *The Discipline of Market Leaders* (Reading, MA: Addison-Wesley, 1995).

2. Gary Hamel and C. K. Prahalad, *Competing for the Future* (Boston: Harvard Business School Press, 1996).

3. William Joyce, Nitin Nohria, and Bruce Roberson, *What Really Works: The 4+2 Formula for Sustained Business Success* (New York: HarperBusiness, 2003).

4. R. E. Kopelman and L. Reinharth, "Research Results: The Effect of Merit-Pay Practices on White Collar Performance." *Compensation Review* 14, no. 4 (1982); R. L. Heneman, *Merit Pay: Linking Pay Increases to Performance Ratings* (Reading, MA: Addison-Wesley, 1992); R. E. Kopelman, J. L. Rovernpor, and M. Cayer, "Merit Pay and Organizational Performance: Is There an Effect on the Bottom Line?" *National Productivity Review* (1991): 299–307; J. L. Pearce, W. B. Stevenson, and J. L. Perry, "Managerial Compensation Based on Organizational Performance: A Time Series Analysis of the Effects of Merit Pay," *Academy of Management Journal* 28 (1985): 261–278; B. Gerhart and G. T. Milkovich, "Organizational Differences in Managerial Compensation and Firm Performance," *Academy of Management Journal* 33 (1990): 663–691; T. M. Welbourne and A. O. Andrews, "Predicting the Performance of Initial Public Offerings: Should Human Resource Management Be in the Equation?" *Academy of Management Journal* 39 (1996): 891–919.

5. R. F. Felton and M. Watson, "Changeacross the Board," *McKinsey Quarterly,* no. 4 (May 2002): 30–45.

6. John K. Waters, *John Chambers and the Cisco Way: Navigating Through Volatility* (New York: John Wiley & Sons, 2002).

7. Joann Muller, "Global Motors," *Forbes* (January 12, 2004): 62–68.

8. R. S. Schuler and S. E. Jackson, "Linking Competitive Strategies with Human Resource Practices," *Academy of Management Executive* 1, no. 3 (1987): 207–220.

9. Adapted from Bradford D. Smart, Ph.D., *Topgrading: How Leading Companies Win by Hiring, Coaching, and Keeping the Best People* (New York: Prentice Hall Press, 1999), 16–17.

CHAPTER 7

1. Dick Beatty interview with Craig Eric Schneier, Ph.D., Executive Vice President, Human Resources, Biogen Idec, Inc., summer 2004.

2. Anthony J. Rucci, Steven P. Kirn, and Richard T. Quinn, "The Employee-Customer-Profit Chain at Sears," *Harvard Business Review* (January–February 1997): 83–97.

3. Jack Stack, *The Great Game of Business* (New York: Doubleday/Currency, 1992).

4. Bill George, *Authentic Leadership: Rediscovering the Secrets to Creating Lasting Value* (San Francisco: Jossey-Bass, 2003).

5. Further information on DuPont's approach can be found in Richard W. Beatty, B. Nicholas Dimitroff, and Dennis J. O'Neill, "Developmental Pay: Aligning Employee Capabilities with Business Needs," in *The Performance Imperative: Strategies for Enhancing Workforce Effectiveness*, eds. Howard Risher and Charles Fay. (San Francisco: Jossey-Bass, 1995), 323–342.

6. Richard W. Beatty, James R. Beatty, and Dennis J. O'Neill, "HR's Next Challenge: Building and Retaining Intellectual Capital," *Employment Relations Today* (Autumn 1998): 33–48.

7. Dave Ulrich and Dick Beatty, "From Partners to Players: Extending the HR Playing Field," *Human Resource Management* 40, no. 4 (2001): 293–307; Further information on Nissan's approach can be found in Richard W. Beatty, James R. Beatty, and Dennis J. O'Neill "HR's New Challenge: Building and Retaining Intellectual Capital," *Employee Relations Today* (autumn 1998): 33–48.

8. Dave Ulrich, *Human Resource Champions: The Next Agenda for Adding Value and Delivering Results* (Boston: Harvard Business School Press, 1997).

CHAPTER 8

1. Garrett Walker and J. Randall MacDonald, "Designing and Implementing an HR Scorecard," *Human Resource Management* 40 (2001): 365–377.

2. *Learning Map®* is a trademark of Root Learning, Inc., of Maumee, Ohio. Learning Map products are soley owned by Root Learning, Inc. and cannot be reproduced or modified in any form without the company's express written permission.

3. Susan J. Ashford and Gregory Northcraft, "Robbing Peter to Pay Paul: Feedback Environments and Enacted Priorities in Response to Competing Task Demands," *Human Resource Management Review* 13 (2003): 537–559.

4. Edwin A. Locke and Gary P. Latham, *A Theory of Goal Setting and Task Performance* (Englewood Cliffs, NJ: Prentice-Hall, 1990); Ashford and Northcraft, "Robbing Peter to Pay Paul."

5. Mark A. Huselid and Brian E. Becker, "An Interview with Mike Losey, Tony Rucci, and Dave Ulrich: Three Experts Respond to HRMJ's Special Issue on HR Strategy in Five Leading Firms," *Human Resource Management* 38 (1999): 353–365.

6. Richard McKnight, Jody Doele, and Kim Christine, "One Prudential Exchange: The Insurance Giant's Literacy and Alignment Platform," *Human Resource Management* 40 (2001): 241–247.

7. We wish to thank Christian Iversen, VPHR at The LEGO Company, for permission to reprint this table, which also appeared in *A New Measurement Mandate: Leveraging HR and Organizational Resources to Enhance Corporate Performance* (Corporate Leadership Council: Washington, DC, 2001), 75.

CHAPTER 9

1. Robert S. Kaplan and David P. Norton, *Strategy Maps: Converting Intangible Assets into Intangible Outcomes* (Boston: Harvard Business School Press, 2004).

2. Garrett Walker is Director of Global Resourcing and HR Strategy at IBM. Interview with Mark Huselid, summer 2004.

3. Ibid.

4. Ibid.

5. See Anthony J. Rucci, Steven P. Kirn, and Richard T. Quinn, "The Employee-Customer-Profit Chain at Sears," *Harvard Business Review* (January–February 1997): 83–97.

6. Peter Fasolo, interview with Mark Huselid, August 2004.

7. Walker interview.

Index

About the Authors

Mark A. Huselid is professor of human resource management in the School of Management and Labor Relations (SMLR) at Rutgers University. Professor Huselid has published and consulted widely on the linkages between workforce management and measurement systems, strategy execution, and firm performance. Professor Huselid's book *The HR Scorecard: Linking People, Strategy, and Performance* (with Brian Becker and Dave Ulrich) was published in 2001 by the Harvard Business School Press. *The HR Scorecard* has been translated into nine languages and is an international best seller. Professor Huselid was the editor of the *Human Resource Management Journal* from 2000 to 2004 and is a current or former member of numerous editorial boards.

Brian E. Becker is professor of human resources and chairman of the Department of Organization and Human Resources in the School of Management at the State University of New York at Buffalo. Professor Becker has published widely on the financial effects of employment systems in both union and nonunion organizations. His current research and consulting interests focus on the relationship between human resources systems, strategy execution, and firm performance. He is coauthor, along with Mark Huselid and Dave Ulrich, of *The HR Scorecard: Linking People, Strategy, and Performance* (Harvard Business School Press, 2001).

Richard W. (Dick) Beatty is professor of human resource management at Rutgers University and a member of the Core Faculty of the University of Michigan's Executive Education Center. Professor Beatty is an associate editor of *Human Resource Management Journal,* was president of the Society for Human Resource Management Foundation, was a recipient of the society's Book Award, and twice received the Research Award from the Human Resource Planning Society. He is the author of *Performance Appraisal: Managing Human Behavior at Work* (with H. John Bernardin, Kent Publishing Company, 1984) and *Human*

Resource Management: An Experiential Skill-Building Approach (with Craig E. Schneier, Addison-Wesley, 1977). His research interests are in human resource strategy and measuring all aspects of workforce performance.

For more information about the concepts described in this book, please visit http://www.theworkforcescorecard.com.